The Odes of Solomon for Awakening

The Odes of Solomon for Awakening

A Commentary on the Mystical Wisdom of the Earliest Christian Hymns and Poems

Swami Nirmalananda Giri
(Abbot George Burke)

Odes translated from the Syriac by
Brother Simeon Goldstein

Light of the Spirit Press
Cedar Crest, New Mexico

Published by
> Light of the Spirit Press
> lightofthespiritpress.com

> Light of the Spirit Monastery
> P. O. Box 1370
> Cedar Crest, New Mexico 87008
> www.ocoy.org

Copyright © 2021 Light of the Spirit Monastery. All rights reserved.

ISBN-13: 978-1-955046-03-9

Library of Congress Control Number: 2021940274
Light of the Spirit Press, Cedar Crest, New Mexico

The image on the cover is based on an ancient fresco in the Catacombs of Priscilla in Rome

Bisac Categories:
OCC012000   BODY, MIND & SPIRIT / Mysticism
REL047000   RELIGION / Mysticism
REL013000   RELIGION / Christianity / Literature & the Arts
REL015000   RELIGION / Christianity / History

First edition, (June 2021)
06012024

Contents

Preface ix
Ode 1 1
Ode 3 6
Ode 4 12
Ode 5 16
Ode 6 23
Ode 7 29
Ode 8 48
Ode 9 59
Ode 10 65
Ode 11 68
Ode 12 81
Ode 13 88
Ode 14 90
Ode 15 95
Ode 16 99
Ode 17 104
Ode 18 111
Ode 19 120
Ode 20 125
Ode 21 132
Ode 22 137
Ode 23 143
Ode 24 150
Ode 25 156
Ode 26 162
Ode 27 167
Ode 28 169
Ode 29 178
Ode 30 183

Ode 31 185
Ode 32 188
Ode 33 189
Ode 34 192
Ode 35 197
Ode 36 200
Ode 37 203
Ode 38 205
Ode 39 214
Ode 40 219
Ode 41 222
Ode 42 227
Glossary 236
About the Author 244

PREFACE

Notes on the Odes by Hierodeacon Simeon Goldstein, the translator of the Odes

Discovery of the Odes

This great work of mystical depth, divine insight, and spiritual illumination is, like the Dead Sea Scrolls, one of the truly great spiritual and literary discoveries of the Twentieth Century. But unlike the Dead Sea Scrolls which were dramatically discovered by shepherds in a desert cave, the Odes were prosaically found in neglected manuscripts gathering dust on the shelves of London libraries. Before 1785 the Odes were only known by references in lists of apocryphal books, and from a Latin quotation by Lactantius. Then in 1785 a manuscript containing selections from five of the Odes was bought by the British Museum from the heirs of a London physician, Dr. Anthony Askew. This was the Codex Askewianus which contains the only known version of the *Pistis Sophia*, itself a great work of spiritual wisdom. The *Pistis Sophia* contains selections from five of the Odes of Solomon: Ode 1 (in chapter 59), Ode 5: 1-11 (in chapter 58), Ode 6: 8-18 (in chapter 65), Ode 25 (complete, in chapter 69), and 22 (complete, in chapter 71). The *Pistis Sophia* designates these specifically as "Odes of Solomon."

Then, on January 4, 1909, J. Rendel Harris was sorting through some Syriac leaves which had been lying for nearly two years on some bookshelves in his office. Soon his attention was riveted by Syriac passages which were identical with those quoted in the *Pistis Sophia* and the passage quoted by Lactantius. This was indeed the lost book of the

Odes of Solomon. It was published that same year as *The Odes and Psalms of Solomon: Now First Published from the Syriac Version* (Cambridge: University Press, 1909).

Nothing at all was known of the previous history of the manuscript, except that it had been on Harris' shelves for as long as two years, and had come from "the neighborhood of the Tigris." Unfortunately, the opening leaves which contained all of the first and second Odes and the beginning of the third, are missing. As already mentioned, the first Ode is found in the Coptic of the *Pistis Sophia*, but the second and beginning of the third are regrettably still lost to us.

Professor Harris did not know when he discovered the manuscript containing the Odes, that there was a much older manuscript of the Odes which had been in the British Museum for seventy years. It had belonged to the monastic library of the El Surian Monastery which is located in the Nitrian Desert about sixty miles west of Cairo, and had been brought to England by Dr. H. Tattam in 1843. F.C. Burkitt found it in the British Museum Library and published his discovery for the first time in 1912. (F. C. Burkitt, "A New MS of the Odes of Solomon," *Journal of Theological Studies*, XII. 1912. 372-85.) This manuscript is known as the Codex Nitriensis and contains only Odes 17:7b through 42:20 (the end).

In addition to the Coptic and Syriac manuscripts already mentioned, there is a Greek Manuscript–the Bodmer Papyrus XI which is housed in the Bodmer library in Geneva. It contains the eleventh Ode in a version similar to the Syriac, except for a passage of seven lines which follows verse 16 and are not found in the Syriac codex.

The manuscript found by Harris has been dated to the fifteenth century, that discovered by Burkitt to the tenth, the Greek papyrus to the third, and the Coptic *Pistis Sophia* to the fourth.

Original Language and Date of Composition

There are many different opinions concerning the original language in which the Odes were written. One scholar, W. Frankenburg, was so sure that Greek was the original language that he translated them into

Greek. (W. Frankenburg, "Das Verständnis der Oden Salomos" (*Beihefte zur Zeitschrift für die alttenstamentliche Wissenschaft* 21; Giessen, 1911). Another scholar, H. Grimme, on the other hand, was so convinced that Hebrew was the original language that he translated them into Hebrew! (H. Grimme, *Die Oden Salomos: Syrisch-hebräisch-Deutsch.* Heidelberg, 1911).) The most reliable scholars, translators, and editors of the Odes, however–J. R. Harris, A. Mingana, A. Vööbus, J. A. Emerton, and James H. Charlesworth (James H. Charlesworth, "Odes of Solomon: A New Translation and Introduction," in *The Old Testament Pseudepigrapha*, vol. 2. Garden City, New York, 1983. p. 726.)–are convinced that the Odes were composed in Syriac (or Aramaic). The evidence for this is very strong and is based on what has been called "the attractive quality of the extant Syriac." (See R.M. Grant: "The Odes of Solomon and the Church of Antioch," *Journal of Biblical Literature* 63. 1944. 363-97; and V. Corwin, "St. Ignatius and Christianity in Antioch," *Yale Publications in Religion* 1; New Haven, 1960. pp. 71-80.) Most scholars also agree that the Odes were probably composed sometime around A.D. 100. One of the strong arguments for such an early date is the discovery of references and perhaps even quotations from the Odes in the writings of St. Ignatius of Antioch. (J. R. Harris and A. Mingana, *The Odes and Psalms of Solomon*, Vol. 2, London, 1920, p. 385.)

Author

We do not know who wrote the Odes of Solomon. The title Odes or Ode of Solomon which is given in the *Pistis Sophia* and as a heading to the single Ode in the Bodmer Papyrus has led scholars to classify this work among the Pseudepigrapha–that is, among works falsely attributed to biblical characters or times. But as the word Shalom or Sh'lom in Hebrew or Syriac means "peace" or "rest," the title could be translated "The Odes of His Peace (or Rest)." This is especially fitting since the theme of rest is so prevalent in the Odes. As Harris and Mingana point out:

"...The name of Solomon attached to the Odes is something more than an outside, bookmaker's or bookseller's, label; it must be used in the internal interpretation of the Odes as Odes of Rest, for that is one of the root-meanings of Solomon's name, and he is supposed to have this name as being historically the man of peace." (Charlesworth, *Op. Cit.*, p. 727.)

Although the identity of the author of the Odes remains a mystery, the closeness of the tone and content of the Odes to the tone and content of the writings of St. John the Evangelist, together with St. Ignatius' familiarity with and use of the Odes (St. Ignatius was a disciple of St. John) suggest that the Odes could have grown up in the spiritual soil prepared by St. John and his disciples, in or around Antioch. J. H. Charlesworth states that specialists have defended the theory that "…the Odes are from the same community or region in which the Gospel of John was composed, and were familiar to [St.] Ignatius or contained the same Christian tone and ideas as those found in his letters.…" (James H. Charlesworth, *The Odes of Solomon: The Syriac Texts*, Missoula, MT, 1977, p.vii.)

Problems of Interpretation

A critical edition of the Odes of Solomon opens with the following statement: "The Odes of Solomon is… the earliest Christian hymn-book, and therefore one of the most important early Christian documents. Yet theories about the origin and nature of this document have risen and fallen in such rapid succession as to reduce it to an enigma."

Why do the scholars and translators have so much difficulty in understanding the Odes? One difficulty arises from the fact that their interpretations are often based on what they consider to be the external, religious, historical, social, and cultural backgrounds of the Odes. Thus when the Odes (in 10 or 29) speak of "Gentiles," they say that this expresses the author's early Jewish-Christian attitudes towards non-Jews. When Ode Six speaks of the spread of waters over the earth, it is said to "signify the expansion of Christianity." References to the "scum of the sea" (in Ode 18:11) are said to indicate the location in which the Odes were composed, as someone who lived near the sea would have used this metaphor.

Another thing that puzzles scholars about the Odes is their point of view. Who is speaking in the Odes? An Ode that begins from a human point of view suddenly changes to the point of view of Christ. The translators at that point supply a heading–"(Christ Speaks)"–to let the reader know that the point of view has changed. But has it really changed, or has the Odist entered into the very mind of Christ or himself become "Christ" through mystical union with him? This has especially caused problems in the translation and interpretation of Ode 36 in which the writer explicitly describes his own experience of elevation and transformation into Christ.

Thus many of the scholars' difficulties arise from the fact that they do not grasp the levels of mystical experience the Odist is expressing. Their erudition belongs to the external and exoteric spheres, and the author of the Odes is writing out of the depth of a mystical experience which belongs to an entirely different realm.

The Mystical Theology of the Odes

Since the Odes are mystical and esoteric, they teach, or more correctly, express the classical and universal mystical truths of Christianity. In the following paragraphs I will enumerate some of the truths they express. For some, verses are simply quoted from the Odes in which these ideas are found. Others will be discussed a bit more fully.

1. Nothing exists outside of God or in opposition to him.

"For thus it was from the beginning, and will be to the end. That nothing should be contrary, and nothing should rise up against him." (6:3,4)

"And there is nothing that is outside of the Lord, for he was before anything came into being." (16:18)

Thus we see that the idea of creation *ex nihilo* (out of nothing) was not a part of the earliest Christian theology–as it is not a part of any truly mystical theology in any of the world's religions.

2. Physical creation veils the true reality of which it partakes, but this veil must be pierced and transcended for true gnosis or knowledge to be attained.

"The likeness of that which is below is that which is above. For everything is above, and below there is nothing, but it is believed to be by those in whom there is no knowledge." (34:4,5)

3. Christ incarnates as man, so that man can become Christ.

"He became like me in order that I might receive him; in form he was considered like me so that I might put him on." (7:4)

This concept of clothing oneself with God–with God's Love, his Name, his Light, his Grace–is a prominent image used again and again in the Odes as a metaphor for the means and process of *theosis* or divinization of the individual. Note the following verses:

"I am putting on [the love of the Lord]. I have been united to him for the Lover has found the Beloved, And because I love him that is the Son I shall become a son. For he who is joined to him Who is immortal, will also himself become immortal." (3:1,7,8)

"And I put off darkness, and clothed myself with light. And I was lifted up in the light, and I passed before him." (21:3, 6)

Getting back to the idea of man becoming Christ, we find the explicit use of the term anointing (or "Christing") in 36:6: "And he anointed me from his own perfection, and I became one of his near ones."

4. Theosis is attained by unceasing meditation on God through clinging to the repetition of the Holy Name which has been revealed to us for our salvation.

"And my righteousness goes before them, and they shall not be detached from my Name, for it is with them.... And ye shall be found incorrupt in all ages, on account of the Name of your Father." (8:19, 22)

"And all those who are against me were afraid of me; and I became the Lord's by the Name of the Lord." (25:11)

"For the sign in them is the Lord, and the sign is the way of those who cross in the Name of the Lord. Put on therefore the Name of the Most High and know him, and you shall cross without danger, because the rivers shall be subject to you." (39:7-8)

"Let us therefore all of us unite together in the Name of the Lord, and let us honor him with its goodness. And our faces will shine in his light, and our hearts will meditate in his love, by night and by day." (41:5-6)

5. The Saints dwell in God and God in the Saints and through them God is revealed in the world and helps the world.

"…The Most High shall be known in his Saints.…The Seers shall go before him, and they shall be seen before him." (7:16, 18)

"For the dwelling-place of the Word is man, and his truth is love." (12:12)

"And the foundation for everything is Thy rock." (22:12)

The Name of God in the Odes of Solomon

And the Praise of his Name he gave us, our spirits praise his Holy Spirit. (6:6)

And my righteousness goes before them, and they shall not be detached from my Name, for it is with them. (8:19)

And ye shall be found incorrupt in all ages, on account of the Name of your Father. Alleluia. (8:22)

Let me be well-pleasing before Thee because of Thy glory, and because of Thy Name let me be saved from the Evil One. (14:5)

I have put on incorruption by means of his Name, and I have put off corruption by his grace. (15:8)

Glory and Honor to his Name. Alleluia. (16:20)

Praise and great beauty to his Name. Alleluia. (18:16)

Praise and honor to his Name. Alleluia. (20:10)

Thou wert there and helped me, and in every place Thy Name was round about me. (22:6)

And the letter became a large volume, which was entirely written by the finger of God; and the Name of the Father was upon it; and of the Son and of the Holy Spirit, to rule unto the ages of ages. Alleluia. (23:21,22)

And all those who are against me were afraid of me; and I became the Lord's by the Name of the Lord. (25:11)

Fill ye water for yourselves from the living fountain of the Lord, for it has been opened to you. And come all ye thirsty and take a drink, and rest by the fountain of the Lord. For pleasing it is and sparkling, and it gives rest to the soul. For much sweeter is its water than honey, and the honeycomb of bees is not to be compared with it. Because it flowed from the lips of the Lord, and it gave a Name from the heart of the Lord. (30:1-5)

He opened his mouth and spoke grace and joy, and he spoke a new song of praise to his Name. (31:3)

My chosen ones have walked in me, and my ways I will make known to them that seek me, and I will promise them my Name. Alleluia. (33:13)

For the sign in them is the Lord, and the sign is the way of those who cross in the Name of the Lord. Put on therefore the Name of the Most High and know him, and you shall cross without danger, because the rivers shall be subject to you. (39:7,8)

And a way has been appointed for those who cross after him, and for those who adhere to the course of his faith, and worship his Name. Alleluia. (39:13)

Let us therefore all of us unite together in the Name of the Lord, and let us honor him with its goodness. And our faces will shine in his light, and our hearts will meditate in his love, by night and by day. (41:5,6)

The Messiah in truth is one; and he was known before the foundations of the world, that he might enliven souls for ever by the truth of his Name: (41:15)

And I set my Name upon their heads, for they are free men and they are Mine. Alleluia. (42:20)

Ode 1

Arise, shine; for thy light is come, and the glory of the Lord is risen upon thee (Isaiah 60:1).
I will give thee a crown of life (Revelation 2:10).

> The Lord is on my head like a crown, and I shall not be without him.
> They wove for me a crown of truth, and it caused Thy branches to bud in me.
> For it is not like a withered crown which buddeth not.
> But Thou livest upon my head, and Thou hast blossomed upon me.
> Thy fruits are full-grown and perfect; they are full of Thy salvation. Alleluia.

The Lord is on my head like a crown.
"In that day shall the Lord of hosts be for a crown of glory, and for a diadem of beauty, unto the residue of his people" (Isaiah 28:5).

The halo upon the head, which we find in the depictions of holy ones in all religions, is the Glory of the Presence of God which rests upon all holy things and persons. It is the cloud of light that rested upon Mount Sinai and upon the tabernacle when God spoke with Moses, and out of which God spoke on the Mount of Transfiguration. It is the Lord himself, for Saint John tells us: "God is Light" (I John 1:5). Jesus simply called It "the Light of Life" (John 8:12).

It is often shown surrounding the entire body of a saint or angel, but usually it is only around the head. This is because the powers of enlightenment reside or are channeled through the higher psychic centers of awareness that are located in the head on the astral and causal levels, known to the yogis as the sahasrara chakra. In meditation the awareness is usually centered in the head, even if not at a specific point.

The Light of God rests upon the head of the meditator as it rested upon the Ark of the Covenant and surrounded the disciples on the Mount of Transfiguration. It is sometimes seen as a white light around the head of an advanced person, especially when they speak. On such occasions it usually extends only a couple of inches from the head, but I have a photograph of Saint John Maximovitch (whom I met) in which the light is radiating for more than a foot around his body as he speaks in church.

And I shall not be without him.

Separation from God is the root of all our troubles. There is nothing wrong that does not arise from that separation, and there is nothing right that is not produced by the ending of the separation. When I say separation, however, I do not mean it in a literal sense, but rather to denote the estrangement of our awareness from God. For since God is All it is impossible to be separated or even slightly distanced from him. God is perfect Unity, and that unity cannot be disrupted by any separation from him. Our separation from God is a loss of awareness of our oneness with him. It is blindness of heart, an illusion, only. When we seek God we are really seeking the consciousness of our eternal oneness with God, the One. The sense of Divine Presence will steadily grow within us, for "the path of the just is as the shining light, that shineth more and more unto the perfect day" (Proverbs 4:18). Those whose feet are settled firmly on the path and are steadily moving along it will always be aware of their unity with God, even though it will be slight in the beginning. This is why the yogi is the most cheerful and optimistic person in the world. He knows his goal and he knows the way.

They wove for me a crown of truth.

"You set a crown of pure gold upon his head" (Psalms 21:3). The Divine Light is the Truth (Reality) and is the crown upon the head of the advancing yogi. The symbol of a woven crown denotes the subtle energy channels known in Yoga as nadis. In the astral and causal counterparts of the brain the nadis are seen as a tightly-woven network of threads of light within which the psychic centers of higher awareness are set as glowing gems in a crown. In ancient India the crowns of kings were material depictions of this spiritual crown which is seen by the inner sight when the yogi's inner bodies become awakened and empowered through meditation.

Who are "they" who wove the crown of truth? First of all, it is the Elohim, the creator-mothers who said: "Let Us make man in Our image, according to Our likeness" (Genesis 1:26). The Aquarian Gospel says this about them: "When the Triune God breathed forth, lo, seven Spirits stood before the throne. These are Elohim, creative spirits of the universe. And these are they who said, Let us make man; and in their image man was made.... In early ages of the world the dwellers in the farther East said, Tao is the name of Universal Breath.... And Tao Great was One; the One became the Two; the Two became the Three, the Three evolved the Seven, which filled the universe with manifests.... And in the same old book we read of man: he has a spirit knit to Tao Great; a soul which lives within the seven Breaths of Tao Great" (Aquarian Gospel 9:19-21, 25, 27). These seven have woven for us the potential crown which is actualized by our effort and the assistance of those "helpers in the higher realms that may be importuned" (Aquarian Gospel 23:25). This is the Communion of Saints. For Christians, the first to be called upon is the Lord Jesus, for he said: "Lo, I am with you always, even to the end of the age" (Matthew 28:20). We may also call upon his (and their) mother, Mary, whom evil spirits greatly fear though she is their mother, too. The great Archangels Michael, Gabriel and Raphael may also be called upon for help, as well as any saints we may know and feel kinship with. (It is a good and practical thing to become acquainted with the saints through reading and imitating their lives.)

And it caused Thy branches to bud in me.

Trees are used in many religious traditions to symbolize creation. In the Bhagavad Gita (15:1) there is mention of "the eternal ashwattha [fig] tree," and in Nordic religion there was the *weltatem*, the World-Ash tree that formed the axis of the earth. Both are rooted in divinity, and their outermost branches and leaves are the living beings upon the earth. In yoga the tree is the symbol of the individual human being. The roots of the tree are the network of energy channels in the head, and the branches and leaves are the limbs and senses of the body. At the same time it is considered that the roots are in God, so the budding of the branches of God is a symbol of divinity manifesting through our humanity, of the human being transmuted into the divine. The appearance of the crown of truth upon our head is that which in Eastern Christianity is called *theosis*: deification.

For it is not like a withered crown which buddeth not.

The life of the spirit is not barren, but buds forth, making us living branches of him Who said: "I am the rose of Sharon, And the lily of the valleys" (Song of Solomon 2:1). Of those who persevere, the prophet Isaiah said of their presently desert-like and desolate souls: "The wilderness and the solitary place shall be glad for them; and the desert shall rejoice, and blossom as the rose. It shall blossom abundantly, and rejoice even with joy and singing: they shall see the glory of the Lord, and the excellency of our God" (Isaiah 35:1-2) within their own being.

But Thou livest upon my head, and Thou hast blossomed upon me.

God has always lived within and without us, but only the opened eye of the spirit beholds the blossoms of his Presence. Yogananda's favorite song was *In the Garden*, for he thought of it as speaking of the entry of the meditator into the garden of his inmost heart where God walks and speaks with us.

Thy fruits are full-grown and perfect; they are full of Thy salvation.

When a person fully awakens to his divine potential, then the actualization of that potential is not far away. Through his perseverance "the fruits of the spirit" flower, bud, and come to complete fruition in him, "full of salvation," for it is the total and perfect union of our consciousness with God's Eternal Consciousness that is salvation. "For the fruit of the Spirit is in all goodness and righteousness and truth" (Ephesians 5:9).

"There is laid up for me a crown of righteousness,… and not to me only, but also to all the also that love his appearing" (II Timothy 4:8).

Alleluia.

"Alleluia" comes at the end of all the Odes to indicate that the ode is complete. It literally means "Praise ye the Lord" and was a common ending in Hebrew spiritual songs.

ODE 3

[Ode 2 has been lost.]

As many of you as have been baptized into Christ have put on Christ (Galatians 3:27).

I am putting on the love of the Lord.
And his members are with him, and I am dependent on them and he loves me.
For I should not have known how to love the Lord, if he had not loved me.
For who is able to distinguish love, except the one that is loved?
I love the Beloved and my soul loves him, and where his rest is there also am I.
And I shall be no stranger, for with the Lord Most High and Merciful there is no grudging.
I have been united to him for the Lover has found the Beloved,
And because I love him that is the Son I shall become a son.
For he who is joined to him Who is immortal, will also himself become immortal.
And he who has pleasure in the Life, will become living.
This is the Spirit of the Lord which is not false, which teacheth the sons of men to know his ways.
Be wise and understanding and vigilant. Alleluia.

I am putting on the love of the Lord.

At the moment we are clothed in the material body. The Zoroastrian sage, Kaspar, said: "Man was a thought of God, formed in the image of the Septonate, clothed in the substances of soul. And his desires were strong; he sought to manifest on every plane of life, and for himself he made a body of the ethers of the earthly forms, and so descended to the plane of earth. In this descent he lost his birthright; lost his harmony with God, and made discordant all the notes of life. Inharmony and evil are the same; so evil is the handiwork of man" through the body which the Essene teacher Elihu called "the body of desires" (Aquarian Gospel 58:25-28).

"The lower self, the carnal self, the body of desires, is a reflection of the higher self, distorted by the murky ethers of the flesh. The lower self is an illusion, and will pass away; the higher self is God in man, and will not pass away. The lower self is the embodiment of truth reversed, and so is falsehood manifest" (Aquarian Gospel 8:7-9). It is the body of desires that separates us from God by turning us outward away from the inner kingdom of God toward the transient world and creating in us a myriad of desires, none of which can be fulfilled because nothing in the world can ever be possessed, but only grasped and eventually lost.

There is, however, another body, the "body of union" that is the immortal spirit. Regarding this the Essene teacher Salome said: "Now spirit loves the pure, the good, the true; the body of desires extols the selfish self; the soul becomes the battle ground between the two" (Aquarian Gospel 9:28). Those who ensure the victory of the spirit over the flesh are the ones who truly love God, for true love results in the union of the lover and the loved.

And his members are with him, and I am dependent on them and he loves me.

Sri Ramakrishna said: "God cannot be seen with these physical eyes. In the course of spiritual discipline one gets a love body endowed with love eyes, love ears, and so on. One sees God with those love eyes. One hears the voice of God with those love ears. With this love body the soul communes with God." "Devotees acquire a love body, and with its help they see the Spirit-form of the Absolute." In actuality this love body is also the Body of God. The eyes with which the illumined behold God are the divine eyes. The ears with which he hears the divine voice are the ears of God. All the members of his love body are really the limbs, the faculties of God. The love that flows to him from God is immediately turned back toward God as an offering.

This is why alchemy is often used as a symbol for spiritual life. In alchemy a substance is taken and its fluid completely removed. Then the dry and the liquid elements are recombined and once more separated by distillation. This may be done many times, for in alchemical theory each time the separation/union is accomplished the substance is profoundly changed and its natural properties are immeasurably increased and made pure. So it is with God and his devotees as their love moves in a continual cycle like a single breath moving within two bodies. Each time the individual pours the divine love back into the infinity of God, just so much more it increases in potency and is returned by God to him.

Knowing that the ability to reach out for God is a capacity given to the questing soul by God, that in the realm of divine experience only the divine faculties are awake and functioning, the spirit says: "I am dependent on them." This is the secret of real religion, of genuine spiritual life and transformation. Being a purified image-reflection of God, it ascends to divine love and loves God with his own love. It truly does live in and by God.

For I should not have known how to love the Lord, if he had not loved me.

So it is: until we reflect God we do not seek or love him. A person's seeking of God is proof that that God is drawing near to him. We never upstage God. He is always there before us.

Swami Muktananda Giri, the mother of Anandamayi Ma, was the embodiment of perfect humility. Her quiet simplicity was a marvel. From my first meeting with her a singular thing occurred: I never managed to pronam (salute her with joined hands) first. She always saluted me first. The moment she glimpsed me she would put her hands together in salutation. After a few months I decided that I was going to salute her first the next time we met, for it was I that should be showing respect to her, not the other way around. Early one morning I entered the gate of Bhagat House, the home of the Raja of Solan in Hardwar. The gate was forty or fifty feet from the doorway to the hall where Ma often sat with Giriji, as we called her. As I turned right into the gate I was thinking that this time I would pronam to Didima first. But when I looked from the gate toward the door of the hall I saw Didima sitting there looking at me with joined hands! In this way she taught me what I have written in the previous paragraph.

For who is able to distinguish love, except the one that is loved?

In *Night of the Iguana* Tennessee Williams speaks of "man's inhumanity to God." This at first is a shocking, even seemingly absurd, idea, but reflection will prove its validity. Human hardheartedness toward the loving God is a sorrowful wonder. Yet it cannot be otherwise, for until the active love of God is mirrored in the heart there is simply no way a person can realize the love of God for him. Only God can awaken us to his love. "And that not of yourselves; it is the gift of God" (Ephesians 2:8), said Saint Paul.

I love the Beloved and my soul loves him.

The emotions, senses, mind, and intellect can conceive attractions and even addictions for objects: that is their nature, they cannot do otherwise. But they cannot love God. Only the spirit loves, and spirit can only love spirit. Consequently our spirit can love nothing else but God. But our lower self loves everything else, including its fantasy-idols of religiosity and its pathetic distortions that it thinks are valid concepts of God and spiritual aspirations and love of God. Only when such things are expelled from us can there be hope of loving God. Idolatry is the prevalent sin of us all. Without an awakened soul how could there be love of God?

And where his rest is there also am I.

In Hebrew and Aramaic "rest" does not mean something done when a person is tired, but rather it means a place of retreat, with the implication of the point of a person's origin, his native place. Therefore the "rest" of God means his primal, essential being. Since the individual spirit is one in essence with God, its rest is the same: God. That is why

Saint Paul wrote: "There remaineth therefore a rest to the people of God" (Hebrews 4:9).

The lover of God knows this and seeks that rest, that oneness with God, alone. The attitude of a true lover of God was expressed by Jesus when he said: "The Son of man has nowhere to lay his head" (Matthew 8:20). The human being can come to rest nowhere but in God. Relative existence offers no rest or shelter for the wise. But only love of God reveals this truth to the questing spirit.

And I shall be no stranger, for with the Lord Most High and Merciful there is no grudging.

How can we be a stranger to him who is our inmost being? Only through the deluded experience of estrangement from God. We think: "I am one and God is another," but no such illusion taints God. Therefore he does not grudge us being one with him. We, on the other hand, grudge God's unity with us because it interferes with "our" ways and thoughts. We desire separation from God: this is the depth of our perfidy toward him "with whom there is no variation or shadow of turning" (James 1:17). We do not need to "win God's friendship," we need to stop being inimical toward him. "Clinging to egotism, power, haughtiness, desire and anger, these malignant people hate me in their own and in others' bodies" (Bhagavad Gita 16:18).

I have been united to him for the lover has found the beloved.

This works from both sides. God "finds" us and we "find" him. The "findings" are simultaneous, as are the "seekings." As they say in India: "When anyone chooses God, it is because he has already chosen them." ("You did not choose me, but I chose you" John 15:16.)

And because I love him that is the Son I shall become a son.

The concept of a trinity within the Divine Nature is found in all viable religions, expressing the transcendent, immanent, and active aspects of the One. In Christianity this is conveyed by the symbolic terms Father, Son, and Holy Spirit. The "Son" is the Mahat Tattwa, the Presence of God within creation. This is the aspect of God that is communicable and knowable to us. It is the intermediary between the individual spirit lost in the maze of relative existence and the transcendent Reality, the Father.

Those who love God in his approachable aspect become united to him and also become "sons of God" in their journey to perfect identity with the transcendent Father. Love is the uniting force: love arising from the spirit.

For he who is joined to him Who is immortal, will also himself become immortal.

He who is joined to Christ will become a Christ: this is the literal meaning of the word "Christian." How far from this glorious truth have Christians strayed and become Churchians instead. As long as we are separated from God we shall be mortal, bound to the endless cycle of birth and death; but as soon as we are united with him we shall transcend that cycle–as does he.

And he who has pleasure in the Life, will become living.

"No man can serve two masters: for either he will hate the one, and love the other; or else he will hold to the one, and despise the other. Ye cannot serve God and mammon [materiality]" (Matthew 6:24). We cannot love the illusion that is "the world" and love God at the same time. (By "the world" I mean the world of human folly and illusions, not the world of God's creation.) They cancel each other out automatically. We cannot delight in the nothing that is relativity and delight in God as well. However, the lover of God does not renounce the world: he is *freed* from it! It is no longer real enough to him to either dislike it renounce it. It is nothing in his eyes, for he has seen the ALL.

This is the Spirit of the Lord which is not false, which teacheth the sons of men to know his ways.

All that has been said by this ode is, according to the singer, the Spirit of the Lord: that is, the effect of the Spirit of the Lord in the life of the questing spirit. The Spirit of the Lord teaches the sons of men the way to become the sons of God. For "where the Spirit of the Lord is, there is liberty" (II Corinthians 3:17) from all bonds and errors of earth. And: "we all, with open face beholding as in a glass the glory of the Lord, are changed into the same image from glory to glory, even as by the Spirit of the Lord" (II Corinthians 3:18). Therefore:

Be wise and understanding and vigilant.

May it be so!

ODE 4

No man O my God changeth Thy Holy Place, nor can he change it and put it in another place.
Because he hath no power over it, for Thy sanctuary Thou hast designed before Thou didst make other places.
That which is the elder shall not be altered by those that are younger than Itself; Thou hast given Thy heart O Lord to Thy believers.
Never wilt Thou fail, nor be without fruits.
For one hour of Thy faith, is more precious than all days and years.
For who is there that shall put on Thy grace and be rejected?
For Thy seal is known, and Thy creatures are known to it.
And Thy hosts possess it, and the pure archangels are clothed with it.
Thou hast given us Thy fellowship; it was not that Thou wast in need of us, but that we are in need of Thee.
Distill Thy dews upon us, and open Thy rich fountains that pour forth to us milk and honey.
For there is not regret with Thee, that Thou shouldest regret anything which Thou hast promised.
And the end was revealed before Thee.
For what Thou gavest Thou gavest freely, so that no longer wilt Thou draw back and take them again.
For all was revealed before Thee as God, and ordered from the beginning before Thee.
And Thou O Lord hast made all. Alleluia.

In 1962, *He Sent Leanness*, a book of prayers that people really say in their hearts was shown to me by a friend. She particularly liked the very short one that simply said: "O Lord,.... Give up this awful experiment of making men like Christ." These words embody the age-old struggle between God and man: the struggle of God to make man into god and the struggle of man to make God into man, or at least to make him give up and accept man as man and nothing more. Yet, the moment good sense and honesty arises in the questing mind the truth is seen:

No man O my God changeth Thy Holy Place, nor can he change it and put it in another place.

The Holy cannot be made unholy, the True cannot be made false, the Infinite cannot be made finite, the Unchanging cannot be made changeable, the Divine cannot be made human.

Because he hath no power over it, for Thy sanctuary Thou hast designed before Thou didst make other places. That which is the elder shall not be altered by those that are younger than Itself.

Although discouraged by the old saying, it *is* possible to teach your grandmother to suck eggs, but not your God. Do not try.

Thou hast given Thy heart O Lord to Thy believers.

The unholy can be made holy, the ignorant can be made wise, the finite can be elevated to infinity, the changeable can be made unchanging, and the human can be made divine, for all that is done by God. How? By giving his "heart," his Consciousness, to those who seek him. It is not God's grace, love, kindness or mercy we need. We need *God*. We need to merge with divinity and become divine.

Never wilt Thou fail, nor be without fruits.

So if God is really involved in a person's spiritual life, it will not fail or be without positive effect. Only when God has been excluded will there be failure and fruitlessness. That is why Jesus said: "By their fruits you will know them" (Matthew 7:20).

For one hour of Thy faith, is more precious than all days and years. For who is there that shall put on Thy grace and be rejected?

Seeds thousands of years old were found in an Egyptian tomb. When planted they sprouted and grew into healthy plants. The darkness of that tomb which had prevailed for ages was dispelled in a moment at the entry of light. It is the presence of God that gives light and life: not the general all-pervading presence, but the Living Presence that is encountered in the depths of our being by those who turn inward and persevere. When the seed in the ground is moistened by rain and warmed by sunlight, life stirs within it and upward growth out of darkness and into the light begins. In the same way those who continually place themselves in the active presence of God through japa and meditation will be silently and subtly changed. Because of misunderstanding and outright false information most people think that meditation is supposed to be some kind of spectacular display of lights, sounds, and sensations. When this does not take place they find fault with their practice. But actually we are like the seed in the ground. We need only sit in the right conditions and growth will occur spontaneously. Our task is to provide the right conditions, the right inner environment, and then sit and wait. That is all. But that is plenty, as those who do it know full well. "But we all, with unveiled face, beholding as in a mirror the glory of the Lord, are being transformed into the same image from glory to glory, just as by the Spirit of the Lord" (II Corinthians 3:18).

Part of the idea of this ode is that when we put ourselves in the Presence our spiritual unfoldment is inevitable. We need only take thought for how to ever be in the Presence and how to so order our life that nothing can prevent our spontaneous transformation. "Can a man take fire to his bosom, and his clothes not be burned?" asked Solomon regarding this (Proverbs 6:27). God is like King Midas: whatever he touches turns divine. We cannot sit in water without being wetted, we cannot sit in the air without being dried, and we cannot sit in the fire without being burned. In the same way we cannot "sit" in God without being deified.

For Thy seal is known, and Thy creatures are known to it.

A master sculptor takes wax, wood, stone or clay and shapes it into the form that exists within his mind. So God by his acting Presence shapes us into his "form." "Seal" does not mean closing something like an envelope, but seal in the sense of a soft substance being impressed by a seal and made to take on a distinctive shape (or purpose as in legal seals).

The seal of God is that which causes us to recover our original form—and more. And this is accomplished by his being near us, by touching us.

And Thy hosts possess it, and the pure archangels are clothed with it. Thou hast given us Thy fellowship; it was not that Thou wast in need of us, but that we are in need of Thee. Distill Thy dews upon us, and open Thy rich fountains that pour forth to us milk and honey. For there is not regret with Thee, that Thou shouldest regret anything which Thou hast promised. And the end was revealed before Thee.

This last statement tells us why God has so much care for us: he sees the final result, the attainment, the perfect state, that shall in time be ours eternally. And he acts on that, whereas we react only to the brief moment in which we erroneously think we are caught. Ignorant religion attributes the same error to God and proclaims that he shall react to our sins, our weakness and our ignorance rather than to our ultimate divinity, and that we are to fear and try to avoid this reaction. But the truth is otherwise, which is why Saint Paul, a former persecutor and killer of Christians, could say: "Forgetting those things which are behind and reaching forward to those things which are ahead, I press toward the goal for the prize of the upward call of God in Christ Jesus" (Philippians 3:13-14). Hence the odist says in conclusion:

For what Thou gavest Thou gavest freely, so that no longer wilt Thou draw back and take them again. For all was revealed before Thee as God, and ordered from the beginning before Thee. And Thou O Lord hast made all.

"Do not cast away your confidence, which has great reward" (Hebrews 10:35). Therefore we need neither doubt nor fear.

ODE 5

I will give thanks unto Thee O Lord, because I love Thee.
O Most High Thou wilt not forsake me, for Thou art my hope.
Freely I have received Thy grace, I shall live thereby.
My persecutors will come and not see me.
A cloud of darkness shall fall on their eyes, and an air of thick gloom shall darken them.
And they shall have no light to see, so that they may not take hold upon me.
Let their counsel become dull, so that whatever they have cunningly devised may return upon their own heads.
For they have devised a counsel, and it did not succeed.
They prepared themselves wickedly, but they were found to be worthless.
For my hope is upon the Lord, and I will not fear.
And because the Lord is my salvation, I will not fear.
And he is as a garland on my head, and I shall not be moved.
Even if everything should be shaken, I stand firm.
And if all things visible should perish, I shall not die.
Because the Lord is with me, and I am with him. Alleluia.

I will give thanks unto Thee O Lord, because I love Thee.
This entire creation has been spread out for us to make possible our evolution into conscious and perfect sons of God. To truly thank God we must use his creation for the intended purpose: our ascent to Divine Consciousness. That is why David sang: "What shall I render

to the Lord For all His benefits toward me? I will take up the cup of salvation, and call upon the name of the Lord" (Psalms 116:12-13). In other words, seeing the blessing of God David has determined to drink of the cup of immortality and be saved from all limitation and ignorance that attends relative existence. The purpose of a school, however excellent its physical facilities may be, is to learn and leave. We are good students if we avail ourselves of this very birth to liberate ourselves from further birth.

But the odist says love is the motive for his thanks. What, then, is love of God? The most accurate analysis of the nature of love is to be found in Swami Yukteswar Giri's *The Holy Science*, where he demonstrates that love is a positive magnetic attraction which brings that which is separated into union with the attractor. In spiritual life this union is a merging of identities in which the individual Self, the atman, experiences the Divine, the Paramatman, as the infinite Self of his finite Self.

"Among the virtuous, four kinds seek me: the distressed, the seekers of knowledge, the seekers of wealth and the wise. Of them, the wise man, ever united, devoted to the One, is pre-eminent. Exceedingly dear am I to the man of wisdom, and he is dear to me. All these indeed are exalted, but I see the man of wisdom as my very Self. He, with mind steadfast, abides in me, the Supreme Goal. At the end of many births the wise man takes refuge in me. He knows: All is Vasudeva. How very rare is that great soul" (Bhagavad Gita 7:16-19).

Love is not blind, it is perfectly clear in its seeing; therefore Krishna calls a lover of God one who is characterized by *viveka*, by discrimination between the unreal and the Real, between the temporal and the Eternal, between not-God and God. A worthy person seeks to love God for the right reason based on the knowledge of one's Self and God. In the book of Revelation the liberated souls sing unto God: "Thou art worthy" (Revelation 4:11). A true lover of God lives out this statement through his arduous practice of yoga which will bring him to God and make him one with God. To love is to seek, to find, to become one. As Swami Sivananda said: "Bhakti [loving devotion] begins with two and ends with one."

The Sanskrit root of bhakti is *bhaj*, which means to love, to adore, to revere, and–most significantly–to share in. And so the sequence is: we love, reverence, worship and finally share in the Being of God, for in both Greek and Sanskrit the words translated "worship" literally mean "to draw near." Sri Ramakrishna likens the true devotee to a salt doll that enters the ocean and melts, merging with it so it can no longer be separated from the water. Yet it is present in the water, it has not ceased to be or lost its identity, as the salt taste proves.

O Most High Thou wilt not forsake me, for Thou art my hope.

In a recorded talk Yogananda said that looking back on his life there is one thing he has learned above all: God never forsakes the devotee. How could he? It is not in his nature to do so. God, "the Father of lights, with whom is no variableness, neither shadow of turning" (James 1:17), is our hope because "If we believe not, yet he abideth faithful: he cannot deny himself." (II Timothy 2:13). That is why the odist further sings:

Freely I have received Thy grace, I shall live thereby.

In the New Testament, the Greek word translated "grace" is *charis*, which means to be calmly joyful. Interestingly, it has the definite connotation of being impersonal: the grace-filled rejoice, not in their egos, but in God. It also has the implied character of happy optimism. *Charis* also means to live out that divine joy. "For God, who commanded the light to shine out of darkness, hath shined in our hearts," from which that light of grace shines out into the world (II Corinthians 4:6). "Ye are the light of the world" (Matthew 5:14). So to live is to be in divine joy, not drunk on the false inebriation of the ego, but alive and awake in the vision of God that comes about from union with God. "In sacred joy I live, in sacred joy I melt," declared Yogananda. There is really only one "thing" after all: God.

My persecutors will come and not see me. A cloud of darkness shall fall on their eyes, and an air of thick gloom shall darken them. And they shall have no light to see, so that they may not take hold upon me. Let their counsel become dull, so that whatever they have cunningly devised may return upon their own heads. For they have devised a counsel, and it did not succeed. They prepared themselves wickedly, but they were found to be worthless.

Reading this I immediately thought of a song that was written by a member of the little Protestant church I was raised in. The author was one of America's unknown remarkable people. Not only was he a hymn writer and spiritual author, he was a great healer who every day cured through prayer those who came to him. And where did he cure them? In a hospital, for he was completely bedridden for many years! Daily a trickle of people came into his room and left freed from their ills, though he himself was seriously ill. As Nagendranath Bhaduri, the "levitating saint" said to Yogananda: "God plants his saints sometimes in unexpected soil, lest we think we may reduce him to a rule!"

The refrain of the song I recalled was: "He keepeth himself in the love of the Lord, and the wicked one toucheth him not." This is the secret of divine protection. If we keep elevating our vibration, especially through yoga practice, negative people will drop out of our life (sometimes not without a final attempt to drag us back down) and other negative people will just not "see" us at all. Blessed isolation!

As this ode indicates, those who live in higher awareness are either invisible to evil people or so distasteful to them that they avoid them. Exceptions may occur if there is a need to reap some special karma, such as our having bothered good people in a previous life, but not usually.

Literal invisibility also can occur if an aspirant needs protection from people intent on harming or hindering him. I know of several such incidents and have experienced it a few times myself.

When someone's aura is very strong, any negative energies directed at them will bounce back and strike those who sent it. I have witnessed quite a few situations in which the would-be harmer was harmed himself. This is especially true in relation to yogis who are steady in their practice. One time a yogi friend of mine walked into a newly-started business and was instantly insulted and made to leave by the astonishingly hostile owners. The next day the chief of police and the mayor (!) came in and told them they had only twenty-four hours to get out of town–and they did. I met a man from Africa who was being "prayed to death" by a witch doctor. When he contacted an esoteric Christian teacher and learned to strengthen his personal magnetism (for protection, not retaliation), the witch doctor fell dead in two days.

For my hope is upon the Lord, and I will not fear. And because the Lord is my salvation, I will not fear. And he is as a garland on my head, and I shall not be moved. Even if everything should be shaken, I stand firm. And if all things visible should perish, I shall not die. Because the Lord is with me, and I am with him.

There are two ways to look at divinity. One is to see it as absolutely distinct from ourselves and therefore outside us. The other is to see it as absolutely one with us, and therefore within us. The results of these two views are quite different in their effect on us. One produces anxiety, insecurity, and even fear, though there may be occasional patches of "faith" and "hope" to artificially relieve the unease. The other produces confidence, tranquility, and inner strength. Those that subscribe to the outer view of God continually speak of the need for "trusting in" and "surrendering to" God, developing a total and pious dependence on God, firm in a conviction of their nothingness and valuelessness. Those that hold to the inner view are intent on the necessity for self-knowledge and the liberation of their inner potential to manifest the divine. One group sees themselves as sinners, the other sees themselves as embryonic gods. What totally different worlds these two live in! And more: what a totally different world is created or shaped by those who hold such views.

Some friends of mine had a very successful Montessori school. Quite a few of their students were "behavior problems" that were rejected by the public school system. One five-year-old had been expelled from as many schools as his age. In his second or third week of attendance he did something "bad." He looked at one of the teachers and said: "I'm a little 'devil' aren't I?" She smiled and replied: "Not to me. I think you are a little angel." The poor boy was utterly flummoxed. "I am an *angel?*" he asked, his voice expressing total amazement. "Yes; you are to me," she answered. And from that moment on his behavior was ideal. Because he really was an angel, but had not known it.

The real Gospel (Good News) of authentic Christianity is that of "Christ in you, the hope of glory" (Colossians 1:27). Our Christ nature is potential and must be brought forth, and since we have no other nature to manifest it is just a matter of now or later.

Once we realize that the Lord is our inmost being, the words of the Ode become extremely clear. The only comment needed is this poem of Emily Bronte:

> No coward soul is mine,
> No trembler in the world's storm-troubled sphere:
> I see heaven's glories shine,
> And Faith shines equal, arming me from Fear.
>
> O God within my breast,
> Almighty, ever-present Deity!
> Life, that in me has rest,
> As I, undying Life, have power in Thee!
>
> Vain are the thousand creeds
> That move men's hearts: unutterably vain;
> Worthless as withered weeds,
> Or idlest froth amid the boundless main,
>
> To waken doubt in one
> Holding so fast by Thy infinity,
> So surely anchored on
> The steadfast rock of Immortality.
>
> With wide-embracing love
> Thy Spirit animates eternal years,
> Pervades and broods above,
> Changes, sustains, dissolves, creates, and rears.

Though earth and moon were gone,
And suns and universes ceased to be,
And Thou wert left alone,
Every existence would exist in Thee.

There is not room for Death,
Nor atom that his might could render void:
Thou–thou art Being and Breath,
And what thou art may never be destroyed.

ODE 6

Many of the Odes of Solomon are expressions of the illumined soul, as is this sixth ode. It is also an exposition of how the deifying power of God, the Holy Spirit embodied in (and as) the Divine Word, accomplishes its work in the individual.

> As the wind moves over the harp, and the strings speak, so speaks in my members the Spirit of the Lord, and I speak by his love.
> For it destroys whatever is foreign, and everything that is bitter.
> For thus it was from the beginning, and will be to the end.
> That nothing should be contrary, and nothing should rise up against him.
> The Lord has multiplied the knowledge of himself, and is zealous that these things should be known which by his grace have been given to us.
> And the Praise of his Name he gave us, our spirits praise his Holy Spirit.
> And there went forth a stream and became a river great and broad, for it flooded and broke up everything and it shattered and brought it to the Temple.
> And the restraints of men were not able to restrain it, nor the arts of those whose business it is to restrain waters.
> For it spread over the face of the whole earth, and filled everything.
> Then all the thirsty upon the earth drank, and thirst was relieved and quenched.

> For from the Most High the drink was given.
> Blessed then are the ministers of that drink, who are entrusted with that water of his.
> They have refreshed the parched lips, and have aroused the paralyzed will.
> And souls that were near departing, they have held back from death.
> And the limbs which had fallen, they straightened and set up.
> They gave strength for their coming, and light to their eyes.
> For everyone knew them in the Lord, and by the waters they lived an eternal life. Alleluia.

As the wind moves over the harp, and the strings speak, so speaks in my members the Spirit of the Lord, and I speak by his love.

Just as "the Spirit of God moved upon the face of the waters" (Genesis 1:2) in the beginning of creation, so the Holy Spirit, the Holy Breath, moves upon the inner constitution of the progressing individual and "speaks" within him. From that proceeds inner development (evolution), as well as intuitive illumination of his intellect to guide him in the ways of continual unfoldment of his spiritual potential. Eventually he in his turn "speaks" by the power of the Holy Spirit, the Love of God.

This has the implication that what has been automatic in the individual because it is the action of the Holy Spirit alone becomes in time the "doing" of the individual himself. The flame is passed from the Holy Spirit to the aspirant, so that what was heretofore subliminal becomes a matter of full consciousness and intention so that he is competent to evolve himself and "work the works of God" (John 6:28).

"So speaks in my members the Spirit of the Lord" also implies that the body evolves along with the consciousness of the individual. This is why touching the body of a saint can awaken the inner consciousness and heal the outer body as well as the heart and mind. The bones of Elisha raised the dead (II Kings 13:21), the touch of Jesus' clothing healed the sick (Matthew 14:35,36; 9:20-22; Mark 5:25-34), as did the shadow of Saint Peter (Acts 5:15) and cloths touched to the body of Saint Paul. (Acts 19:11-12).

In relation to this I wrote in the fourth chapter of *Soham Yoga*:

There are many Sanskrit words with which the yogi must become conversant. Two are Samskara and Vasana. Samskaras are impressions in the mind, either conscious or subconscious, produced by previous action or experience in this or previous lives. They are propensities of the mental residue of impressions–subliminal activators, prenatal tendencies. A Vasana is a bundle or aggregate of similar samskaras manifesting as subtle desire. It is a tendency created in a person by the doing of an action or by enjoyment which induces the person to repeat the action or to seek a repetition of the enjoyment. A Vasana is a subtle impression in the mind capable of developing itself into action, and is the cause of birth and experience in general–the impression of actions that remains unconsciously in the mind.

One of the most renowned yogis of the twentieth century was Swami ("Papa") Ramdas of Anandashram (Kanhangad, Kerala). In *Gospel of Ramdas* he says the following regarding the body, yoga and vasanas.

"Vasanas may be driven out of the mind. But they persist in the body. One whose mind is free from vasanas is said to have *manosiddhi*; one whose body is free from vasanas is said to have *kayasiddhi*. One who has *kayasiddhi* is said to have completely eradicated all his vasanas both from his mind and body. That is perfection in yoga. Some jnanis stop at eradicating the vasanas from the mind and do not care about their ejection from the body. But there are some siddhas who have perfected the body also. By so doing, they say they are divinizing the body. They make the light of the atman permeate the body to such an extent that every particle of the body is made holy and shines with the divine radiance" (p. 374).

"Jnanis stop with the experience of nirvikalpa samadhi and they consider the body and all the universe as illusion or non-existent. Even after the experience of nirvikalpa samadhi, though the mind is free from vasanas, the body is not. Of course, jnanis do not care about it as the body and everything connected with it is unreal. But the yogis are not satisfied with this realization. Thy make the body also pure and illumined. That is Purna [Full, Complete] Yoga. Then every particle of his body is radiant with spiritual splendor. Now the yogi has attained perfection of the body also, the grandest spiritual experience" (pp. 595, 596).

For it destroys whatever is foreign, and everything that is bitter.

The Holy Spirit is healing and purifying, "for it destroys whatever is foreign, and everything that is bitter." Anything that is alien to our eternal nature, such as ignorance, sin and suffering (both of which are but the results of ignorance) are annihilated by the Spirit consciousness.

For thus it was from the beginning, and will be to the end.

All that is not eternal is dispelled by the action of the Holy Spirit, by the Holy Life within us. It does this so:

That nothing should be contrary, and nothing should rise up against him.

That which opposes good cannot rise up against God or against us *except in our will,* for we are inseparable from God. All that opposes our ascent to Divine Consciousness either within or without is melted away in the "fire" of the Holy Spirit.

The Lord has multiplied the knowledge of himself, and is zealous that these things should be known which by his grace have been given to us.

Jesus habitually referred to the Holy Spirit as "the Spirit of Truth" (John 14:17; 15:26; 16:13). This is because the Holy Spirit reveals that which is true and makes all that She touches "true" (real). She, "the spirit of wisdom and revelation" (Ephesians 1:17), reveals God and makes gods of those who receive that revelation. Furthermore, the Holy Spirit "…is zealous that these things should be known which by his grace have been given to us." That is, the Holy Spirit both shows us what things are channels of deifying power, of divine grace, and teaches us the ways of inner life and development by which we may increase our treasure of spiritual evolution. "For as many as are led by the Spirit of God, they are sons of God" (Romans 8:14). "We all, with open face beholding as in a glass the glory of the Lord, are changed into the same image from glory to glory, even as by the Spirit of the Lord" (II Corinthians 3:18).

And the Praise of his Name he gave us, our spirits praise his Holy Spirit.

We cannot praise that which we do not know, nor can we praise something that is (or does) nothing praiseworthy. But the Divine Name is not unknown to the established seeker for It works the Divine Work within us. This sentence also indicates that the Name of God and the Holy Spirit are the same, as Jesus knew and taught from his life in India. (See *Soham Yoga*.) Our spirits praise the Divine Name because it is freeing us, as the next verse describes.

And there went forth a stream and became a river great and broad, for it flooded and broke up everything and it shattered and brought it to the Temple.

This is also spoken of in the Bible: "There is a river, the streams whereof shall make glad the city of God, the holy place of the tabernacles of the most High" (Psalms 46:4). "And he showed me a pure river of water of life, clear as crystal, proceeding out of the throne of God and of the Lamb." (Revelation 22:1). What a magnificent symbology of the workings of the Holy Spirit-Word.

At first the movings of the Holy Spirit in the form of the Word/Divine Name are a stream, but if it is allowed to continue unimpeded and even helped along by our application of spiritual discipline it soon becomes a river both strong and wide in its effects. Finally, it floods and permeates all of us, loosens its bonds, and brings us into the Temple of Divine Consciousness, into the depths of Divinity Itself.

And the restraints of men were not able to restrain it, nor the arts of those whose business it is to restrain waters. For it spread over the face of the whole earth, and filled everything.

In the beginning stages of our spiritual life it is not sure just how things will go, for within us indeed are "those whose business it is to restrain [the] waters" of the Holy Spirit's working, particularly the workings of Shabda Brahman, the Divine Sound. But once that Force advances and grows, then the outcome is inevitable: we shall be brought into the Temple.

"Him that overcometh will I make a pillar in the temple of my God, and he shall go no more out: and I will write upon him the name of my God" (Revelation 3:12), which he justly praises, for It has "filled everything" "that God may be all in all" (I Corinthians 15:28).

Then all the thirsty upon the earth drank, and thirst was relieved and quenched.

Total fulfillment. And no surprise:

For from the Most High the drink was given.

And that drink was God himself. "In the beginning was the Word, and the Word was with God, and the Word was God" (John 1:1).

In India some people have a most beautiful and meaningful family name: Namacharya–Teacher of the Name. This ode glorifies those who know and teach the meaning and power of the Divine Name, for through that Holy Name:

Blessed then are the ministers of that drink, who are entrusted with that water of his. They have refreshed the parched lips, and have aroused the paralyzed will. And souls that were near departing, they have held back from death. And the limbs which had fallen, they straightened and set up. They gave strength for their coming, and light to their eyes. For everyone knew them in the Lord, and by the waters they lived an eternal life.

Such is the glory and the power of the Divine Word. "So speaks in my members the Spirit of the Lord, and I speak by his love."

ODE 7

As the impulse of anger against evil, so is the impulse of joy over what is loved, and brings in of its fruits without restraint.

My joy is the Lord and my impulse is toward him, this path of mine is beautiful.

For I have a helper–the Lord; he has generously shown himself to me in his simplicity, because his kindness has diminished his dreadfulness.

He became like me in order that I might receive him; in form he was considered like me so that I might put him on.

And I trembled not when I saw him, because he was gracious to me.

Like my nature he became that I might learn him, and like my form that I might not turn back from him.

The Father of knowledge is the Word of knowledge.

He Who created wisdom is wiser than his works.

And he Who created me when yet I was not, knew what I should do when I came into being.

Wherefore he pitied me in his abundant grace, and granted me to ask from him and to receive from his sacrifice.

For he it is Who is incorruptible, the perfection of the worlds and their Father.

He has allowed him to appear to them that are his own, in order that they may recognize him that made them, and not suppose that they came of themselves.

For knowledge he hath appointed as its way; he hath widened it and extended it and brought it to complete perfection.
And has set over it the traces of his light, and I walked therein from the beginning even to the end.
For by him it was wrought, and he rested in the Son.
And for its salvation he will take hold of everything; and the Most High shall be known in his Saints.
To announce to those that have songs of the coming of the Lord, that they may go forth to meet him and may sing to him, with joy and with the harp of many tones.
The Seers shall go before him, and they shall be seen before him.
And they shall praise the Lord for his love, because he is near and seeth.
And hatred shall be taken from the earth, and along with jealousy it shall be drowned.
For ignorance hath been destroyed upon it, because the knowledge of the Lord hath arrived upon it.
Let the singers sing the grace of the Lord Most High, and let them bring their songs.
And their heart shall be like the day, and like the excellent beauty of the Lord their pleasant song.
And let there be nothing without life, nor without knowledge nor dumb.
For (the Lord) hath given a mouth to his creation, to open the voice of the mouth towards him, and to praise him.
Confess ye his power, and show forth his grace. Alleluia.

There was an old vaudeville routine where someone would be telling news to another. At one point, the hearer would say: "That's good," and the narrator would say: "No, that's bad," and continue on to explain. Later the hearer would comment "That's bad," and the narrator would contradict and say, "No, that's good." And so it would go on: "That's good," "No, that's bad," "That's bad," "No, that's good," until the end which was always "bad." In junior high school I heard a joke version that began: "Fortunately, a man was flying in an airplane; unfortunately, the engine quit; fortunately, he had a parachute; unfortunately, the parachute did not open;" and it, too, went on to end most unfortunately. This is really the way of most religion. No matter how positive the initial statements may be, fear and condemnation get injected somewhere along the line, ultimately resulting in a conviction of incapacity and unworthiness.

A few years ago on the internet I found a website that expounded the innate perfection of all sentient beings, affirming that liberation was the natural goal of all humanity. Then it went on to fulminate and fume against anyone who dared to disbelieve their One and Only True Master, describing the eternal darkness and suffering that would be the lot of unbelievers. That was awful, but worse was to come: the horrendous fate of disciples who dared to read anything but the Master's writings or to even walk into a building owned by another spiritual organization. There was a lot of talk about how the Master mystically implanted some kind of enlightenment device (I am not joking or satirizing) in the astral bodies of all disciples, and how these devices would become deformed if the disciple committed the crimes just mentioned, or even began to question the Master's words. As a result they, too, would wander eternally in darkness and pain, but it would be much worse than that of the unbelievers.

I have found this malignant schizophrenia in virtually every spiritual group I have met or made the mistake of joining. Things are all smiles and sunshine at the first, eventually developing into clouds, rain, thunder, lightning, and terror. Bad You! Bad You! Another version of: Bad Dog! Bad Dog!

In *Pilgrim's Regress*, C. S. Lewis satirizes this by having someone tell a tenant how much–oh, how much–the landlord loves his tenants. So much so, that the landlord had prepared a pit of fire for any tenant that insulted his love by breaking the rules. So, the messenger concluded, we must all love the landlord very much and trust in his love so he will not torture us in the fire pit–something he very much did not want to do. Is it any wonder that so many "true believers" are crazy in a part of their mind?

Here is an example. After my first trip to India I stayed for a while in the home of a devoted yogi. One day she answered the doorbell and I heard the following.

Grace: "Hello, how are you?"

Unseen man: "Oh, I'm still thrilled with Christ!"

The Unseen, not permitted to come in the house, then invited Grace to come to some kind of church party at someone's home. Grace managed to graciously decline and get the door closed. Then she turned to me and said: "I won't ever go anywhere with him again! That man is a minister who wanted to convert me. Once I went with him to a party, and while we were there he told me: 'You know, tonight on the way home I could stop the car and poke your eyes out and make you accept Jesus as your Savior.' So I called my daughter to come get me and take me home. But he keeps calling and coming over. He claims he saw Jesus in a vision once–but only his feet." I did not want to ask her how he recognized Jesus by his feet. I knew that something as logical as "by the stigmata" would not be forthcoming.

But it does not have to be that way. In fact, we should refuse to ever let it be that way with us. Moreover it was not so originally with the followers of Jesus, as is revealed in this ode.

As the impulse of anger against evil, so is the impulse of joy over what is loved, and brings in of its fruits without restraint. my joy is the Lord and my impulse is toward him, this path of mine is beautiful. For I have a helper–the Lord; he has generously shown himself to me in his simplicity, because his kindness has diminished his dreadfulness.

In Indian spiritual writings we are told that human response can be divided into two streams: attraction and aversion, raga and dwesha. Raga is attachment/affinity for something, implying a desire for it. Raga may range from simple liking or preference to intense desire and attraction. Dwesha is aversion/avoidance for something, implying a dislike for it. Dwesha may range from simple non-preference to intense repulsion, antipathy and even hatred. Raga-dwesha is the continual cycle of desire/aversion, like/dislike that can be emotional (instinctual) or intellectual.

In the purified mind raga-dwesha is still present, but as a manifestation of viveka: discrimination based on spiritual insight (jnana). Therefore negativity evokes an active aversion as the force known as vikshepa: a pushing away, an ejection of the negativity. "Anger" is not a very good translation, actually. "Rejection" or "elimination" would be better. Even the Greek word in the New Testament translated "anger" is *orge*, which means to have an intense feeling or reaction. It implies a strong rejection, rather like that of a healthy immune system in response to toxicity. So Saint Paul wrote: "Be ye angry [*orgidzo*], and sin not" (Ephesians 4:26). That is, feel strongly about something but do not let it lead to egoic passion. Interestingly, *orge* and *orgidzo* also mean to intensely *desire* something, to reach out for it with strong attraction. As psychology has discovered, desire and aversion are really the same thing moving in opposite directions.

The author of the ode, then, is telling us that there is a deep-rooted impulse-response to objects, that in the purified heart there is repulsion for evil and attraction for good: the Supreme Good being God.

Here the poet is also telling us that joy (delight) arises in the pure heart when it contemplates that which is loved. Joy is the response, not a grudging sense of duty or a feeling of incapacity and incompetence: the common response to externalized religion. This is how we know whether or not we love God. It is not just dedication (loyalty), reverence, awe or admiration that we should and will feel, but joy: ananda.

And this joy is a generous response. It both gives and receives, therefore it "brings in of its fruits without restraint." There is simply no need here for consoling, coaxing and "inspiring" the devotee. Needing no external influence, with joy he embraces that which leads to the Divine Vision. For this reason Jesus said that "the kingdom of heaven is like unto treasure hid in a field; the which when a man hath found, he hideth, and for joy thereof goeth and selleth all that he hath, and buyeth that field" (Matthew 13:44). There is no idea of sacrifice here even though all else is sold in order to buy that field wherein the treasure is hid. This is the perfect picture of a yogi. Regarding Jesus himself, whom we look upon as having sacrificed his life, Saint Paul assures us that Jesus "for the joy that was set before him endured the cross, despising the shame" (Hebrews 12:2). His perspective was joy, for he was the embodiment of love.

If we desire to have the same delight, Krishna further says: "Having come to this impermanent and unhappy world, devote yourself to me. With mind fixed on me, devoted, worshipping, bow down to me. Thus steadfast, with me as your supreme aim, you shall come to me.... the immortal, immutable, abode of everlasting dharma and of absolute bliss" (Bhagavad Gita 9:33-34; 14:27). To exchange unreality, darkness and death for Reality, Light and Immortality! That is truly joy.

To abundantly and "without restraint" gather in "the fruit of the Spirit: love, joy, peace, longsuffering, gentleness, goodness, faith, meekness, temperance" (Galatians 5:22-23): that is joy.

My joy is the Lord and my impulse is toward him.

This is a completely theocentric matter. God is the total focus. As the desert father, Saint Arsenios the Great, said: "Unless you say: 'God and I alone exist,' you will never find God."

Certainly religion is important, even essential, but it is only a instrument. No one admires the piano or the violin, but rather the brilliant pianist and violinist. Religion is a tool to be used by the seeker; the seeker is not to be a tool of religion.

On the other hand we cannot imagine a sane pianist or violinist claiming they have no need of a piano or a violin, so neither should we credit someone who says they need no religion. Nonsense is never sense.

There is within each one of us an elemental impulse toward God. Although our intelligence (buddhi) must cooperate in our return to God, still it is never a merely intellectual or emotional impulse. Rather it is inherent in our essential being itself. It is part of our eternal nature. Therefore to be an awakened person means to be experiencing and acting upon this godward impulse.

This path of mine is beautiful.

How is the path beautiful? "The path of the just is as the shining light, that shineth more and more unto the perfect day" (Proverbs 4:18). It is beautiful because it increasingly brings us nearer the Divine Beauty:

God. Again, God is the measure of the matter, not the seeker or the mechanics or requirements of the search.

For I have a helper–the Lord.

We are not alone on the path. The Lord of Beauty himself is our companion. But he is not a passive companion. Rather:

He has generously shown himself to me in his simplicity, because his kindness has diminished his dreadfulness.

In Eastern religion, including Eastern Christianity, it is a fundamental tenet that God is a Simple Being in the sense of being totally incomplex. God has no parts, but is an Absolute Unity. It is when we start splitting God up and turning him into a pie chart, like we have done to ourselves and the world around us, that we get into trouble because we are trying to turn the Real into an illusion. It is when we see God as a multiplicity, attributing an infinity of forms, attributes, actions, and reactions to him, that confusion results. But the author of the ode has seen God truly, has not only seen but *experienced* the Divine Unity. So it all comes down to what it always does: spiritual experience which results only from spiritual practice. "Now the God of hope fill you with all joy" (Romans 15:13).

He became like me in order that I might receive him; in form he was considered like me so that I might put him on. And I trembled not when I saw him, because he was gracious to me. Like my nature he became that I might learn him, and like my form that I might not turn back from him.

The purpose of creation is the perfect union in consciousness of the individual spirit and the Cosmic Spirit. The entire field of relative existence is a divine ladder which the spirit ascends in order to perfectly perceive and manifest its eternal nature as part of Divinity. The important thing to remember in considering this is that the cosmos is the Cosmic Itself.

These two verses from Ode Seven are remarkable. But the vision of the author of this ode did not end with him, for it was an eternal vision. Nearly two thousand years later, Bishop James Ingall Wedgwood wrote this prayer for the Mass of the Liberal Catholic Church:

"Uniting in this solemn Sacrifice with Thy holy Church throughout all the ages, we lift our hearts in adoration to Thee, O God the Son, consubstantial, co-eternal with the Father, who, abiding unchangeable within Thyself, didst nevertheless in the mystery of Thy boundless love and Thine eternal Sacrifice breathe forth Thine own divine life into Thy universe, and thus didst offer Thyself as the Lamb slain from the foundation of the world, dying in very truth that we might live.

"Omnipotent, all-pervading, by that self-same sacrifice Thou dost continually uphold all creation, resting not by night or day, working evermore through that most august Hierarchy of Thy glorious Saints, who live but to do Thy will as perfect channels of Thy wondrous power, to whom we ever offer heartfelt love and reverence."

He became like me in order that I might receive him; in form he was considered like me so that I might put him on.

The idea here is that God has transmuted himself into the cosmos so it can become the means of our ascent to his perfect Consciousness and our assimilation of that Divinity. That is why Saint Paul speaks in the book of Hebrews of our being partakers of Christ (Hebrews 3:14), of the Holy Spirit (Hebrews 6:4) and of the very holiness of God (Hebrews 12:10). Saint Peter not only tells us that it is possible to be a partaker of the glory of divinity (I Peter 5:1), we can also "be partakers of the divine nature" Itself (II Peter 1:4).

This is real Christianity: the making of human beings into Christs. We think we are encased in matter, but it is only a dream of matter. In reality we live at every moment in Spirit. "For in him we live, and move, and have our being" (Acts 17:28). Yet at the moment it is matter we need to lead us upward to recognition of the real nature both of "things" and of ourselves. For the intention of all of this is that eventually we all "might put him on" and dwell in that consciousness forever.

And I trembled not when I saw him, because he was gracious to me.

In that awareness, fear is banished forever.

Like my nature he became that I might learn him, and like my form that I might not turn back from him.

The purpose of this is that in time the two will become One.

The Father of knowledge is the Word of knowledge.

The Source of Gnosis is the Word of Gnosis. This has a few meanings, but the two most important are:

1) The Father is the Son, the Word. That is, Ishwara is an emanation or expansion of Brahman. The early Christian writer Tertullian said exactly this, too.

2) The Name of God is God. A mantra is not a common word, but the embodiment of what it designates. Inherent in the mantras used by yogis for meditation is the Consciousness they are meant to invoke. Japa and meditation convey the Divine Consciousness to the yogi's consciousness and unites them with the Divine Being. Japa and meditation "beget" gnosis in the individual who is constant in them. (Again, see *Soham Yoga*.)

He Who created wisdom is wiser than his works.

As stated in the Gita: "I know all beings: past, present and to come. But no one knows me" (Bhagavad Gita 7:26). "Therefore, be a yogi" (Bhagavad Gita 6:46). *And he Who created me when yet I was not, knew what I should do when I came into being.*

It is not uncommon for saints to know when we are thinking good thoughts and for them to respond to them. This is a happy event, but if we are reflective then we will realize that they know when we are thinking wrong thoughts, yet they still retain a positive attitude towards us. From this we can realize that before we enter into relative existence God knows every silly and negative thought and deed we are ever going to think and do. Yet he loves us and provides for us even the things we need for those wrong thoughts and acts! This should give us hope when, regretting our past follies, we wish to turn around and tread the upward path out of the "valley of the shadow of death" in which such ways prevail. We need not dislike ourselves nor waste time in condemning ourselves. We need to become intent on reforming our minds and lives. For God has provided all we need to do that, as well. We have come into this world to learn, and learn we will, eventually. The seed of all we shall ever do or be is present from the beginning.

Wherefore he pitied me in his abundant grace, and granted me to ask from him and to receive from his sacrifice.

For the sake of our evolution, God has poured out himself in the form of the cosmos, visible and invisible, and thus become himself "the Lamb slain from the foundation of the world" (Revelation 13:8). All the worlds through which we evolve are the "abundant grace" of God. Saint John the Baptist assures us that "God giveth not the Spirit by measure" (John 3:34). Rather, we find the totality of Being and assimilate It into our finite selves in a manner past understanding–but not past experiencing. Thus we "receive from his sacrifice."

For he it is Who is incorruptible, the perfection of the worlds and their Father.

This is an exposition of the nature of Ishwara. If we unite ourselves with him through yoga sadhana we shall become like him.

He has allowed him to appear to them that are his own, in order that they may recognize him that made them, and not suppose that they came of themselves.

One of the greatest flaws of any religion or spiritual philosophy is the presumption that spiritual truths can be figured out intellectually or by applying logic. Anyone with a modicum of self-observation is aware of both the limitations and the unreliability of the mind. This is why all authentic spiritual traditions tell us that the only viable working with the mind is that which enables us to go beyond the mind!

In the Divine Unity, the Supreme Spirit fosters the evolution of all the individual spirits which draw their being from It. Patanjali tells us in the Yoga Sutras that God himself is the Guru of all. ("Being unconditioned by time he is guru even of the ancients" 1:26.) Mostly he teaches through providing the experiences that their own higher minds determine, but he does at times teach them through intuitions that arise from the depths of their own beings where God is to be found.

The ancient tradition of India tell us that the primeval sages, the rishis, turning within in profound meditation, discovered Brahman as the essence of all Being, just as the ode says in this verse. Brahman is also our Source, the power which has enabled our manifestation within relativity and which empowers us to ascend to the Absolute.

For knowledge he hath appointed as its way; he hath widened it and extended it and brought it to complete perfection.

This is why we must persevere in the practice of japa and meditation, simple as they may seem. On the mechanical level they are simple (even childishly simple), but on the level of their effects they are as complex as relative existence itself. That is why the practice of yoga can deliver us from the nets and snares of relativity. You will find that your experience of yoga practice will be infinitely varied. On occasion, of course, your meditation and japa may seem to be the same day after day, but that is because your inner and outer bodies are adjusting to the plateau of evolution your practice has brought you to. The effects are being assimilated and permatized during such periods. But after a while you will perceive yourself moving on in the depths of meditation to new areas of development. At first the "way" of yoga may seem simple, simplistic and narrow in the sense of being minimal. But you will find it widening and extending, the path "that shineth more and more unto the perfect day" (Proverbs 4:18). "As for God, his way is perfect: the word of the Lord is tried [proven]: he… maketh my way perfect" (Psalms 18:30, 32). And he not only perfects the way, he perfects those who walk the way.

And has set over it the traces of his light, and I walked therein from the beginning even to the end.

A mantra, when continually invoked in both japa and meditation, is the light that leads us onward, further into the Light. "For with thee is the fountain of life: in thy light shall we see light" (Psalms 36:9). Literally: "Thy word is a lamp unto my feet, and a light unto my path" (Psalms 119:105). "The sun shall be no more thy light by day; neither for brightness shall the moon give light unto thee: but the Lord shall be unto thee an everlasting light, and thy God thy glory" (Isaiah 60:19). God shows us the way and *is* the way, but it is up to us to walk the way, like the chick emerging from the egg.

For by him it was wrought,…

The journeying of the way is accomplished by increasing consciousness and communication with Ishwara, who reveals us as Brahman's eternal rest, Its eternal abiding place. For we are ourselves the Sons of God in which Divinity comes to rest. As Emily Bronte wrote:

> O God within my breast,
> Almighty, ever-present Deity!
> Life, that in me has rest,
> As I, undying Life, have power in Thee!

One of the greatest reliefs of my life was the discovery that spiritual life was not a haphazard thing at all, but an exact science, that whims, human or divine, never came into it and never could, because God does not have whims and human whims are meaningless when dealing with Reality. Nor did I have to wheedle and whine before God to persuade him to let me draw near to him. I already was one with him! So all (!) I had to do was wake up and "get real." And God had anticipated that moment, and had prepared the way of awakening: Yoga. Through yoga creation itself becomes the Path of Return.

The sole purpose of the universe is the ultimate liberation of all sentient beings. They may wander for many, many years (ages, even) before reaching the goal of conscious union with Infinity and a sharing in the same Consciousness. (See *Robe of Light*.) The cosmos is a device for the enlightenment of those within it, as is the individual body temporarily inhabited by a sentient being. So God has set us upon the stream that in time returns us, but we will not be the same as we were when we first entered the stream. Rather, we shall have as a result of our pilgrimage, developed the capacity to participate in the Life Divine.

Into the fabric of creation God has woven certain strands or laws that operate unerringly and without exception to keep the individual spirit moving onward and inexorably toward the Goal, however much an individual might delay it. The three fundamental strands or laws are karma, reincarnation and evolution of consciousness. Adding to these the innate urge of the finite for the Infinite, the Way of Salvation is complete.

The Sufi poet, Rumi, wrote:

A stone I died and rose again a plant.
A plant I died and rose an animal;
I died an animal and was born a man.
Why should I fear? What have I lost by death?
As man, death sweeps me from this world of men
That I may wear an angel's wings in heaven;
Yet e'en as angel may I not abide,
For nought abideth save the face of God.
Thus o'er the angels' world I wing my way
Onwards and upwards, unto boundless lights;
Then let me be as nought, for in my heart
Rings as a harp-song that we must return to him.

Oliver Wendell Holmes, one of many great Americans whose belief in reincarnation is overlooked, wrote in his poem, *The Chambered Nautilus:*

Build thee more stately mansions, O my soul!
As the swift seasons roll!
Leave thy low-vaulted past!
Let each new temple, nobler than the last,
Shut thee from heaven with a dome more vast,
Till thou at length art free,
Leaving thine outgrown shell by life's unresting sea!

... and he rested in the Son.

God in the aspect known as Brahman transcends the creation, yet when he projects creation, he also enters into it as "the Son" or Ishwara, the Lord. His guiding presence as the Intelligence within every atom of creation is his resting "in the Son," the Christ Consciousness within all. Those who evolve their consciousness sufficiently to unite with the Son are themselves Christs, as was Jesus. Then, evolving even further, they unite with the transcendent "Father" aspect of God, themselves becoming the Father in a manner incomprehensible to us at our present stage of development. Jesus had also attained this, and was able to say: "He that hath seen me hath seen the Father" (John 14:9).

Having lost the original, mystical perspective, Christianity began wandering in the labyrinth of intellectual, speculative theology and eventually formulated a doctrine of the Trinity and of the nature of Jesus that is far wide of the mark. To return to the original perspective of Christianity it is necessary to become well acquainted with the basic scriptures of Sanatana Dharma. That is why a Saint Thomas Christian priest once said to me: "You cannot understand the teachings of Jesus unless you know the Indian scriptures." That is also why Patriarch Zachariah, the former head of the Syrian Orthodox (Jacobite) Church, kept a copy of the Gita by his bed and read it daily along with the Bible.

God within the creation guides its every atom and draws each sentient being into eventual union with him as the Son and then as the Father. Thus the way of salvation is completed for them. That is why the next verse says:

And for its salvation he will take hold of everything; and the Most High shall be known in his Saints.

God is always in charge. We claim to believe that, but our actions "speak louder" and show otherwise. We, too, are always in charge and also do not believe that. But truth is truth and we need to awaken to it. The purpose of being in charge is a single thing: evolving to perfection. God is evolving the creation and we are evolving our little universe consisting of the various energy bodies which are encasing us like the layers of a pearl around the little bit of grit that started it all. Unlike God, we have lost sight of this fact and therefore much about us that should be controlled is running amok, and that produces karma and rebirth, for cosmic law cannot be abrogated by anyone. The material cosmos will never be conscious of God, but every sentient being will eventually move out into the light of the Divine Vision and God will be known in his saints and his saints will know themselves in God: an ideal arrangement.

To announce to those that have songs of the coming of the Lord, that they may go forth to meet him and may sing to him, with joy and with the harp of many tones.

Just as the ocean can be smelled when we get near to it, and a waterfall is heard the closer we come to it, in the same way when someone evolves to a certain point spiritual intuition begins to function and he intuits that it is his destiny to return to God, to attain union with the Infinite. As cited above, Rumi wrote that "in my heart rings as a harp-song that we must return to him." The "harp" that we read about in the Bible and mystical poetry is the inner instrument of the awakening spirit.

Although a Fundamentalist Protestant, the poetess Fanny Crosby, whose poems became the basis for many of the best hymns written in America, was a great mystic who practiced a form of meditation she discovered intuitionally and which she called "Entering the Vale of Silence." Writing of her spiritual experience and ultimate destiny, she simply said: "This is my story, this is my song...." The heart sings in anticipation of that wondrous day when "faith shall be lost in sight." As Saint Methodius of Olympus wrote in the early Christian era: "Chastely I live for Thee; and holding my lighted lamps, O Lord, I go forth to meet Thee." The awakened soul realizes that its every step brings it closer to oneness with the One. That is why the poetess-nun Sister Madeleva wrote this poem she called Travel Song:

> Know you the journey that I take?
> Know you the voyage that I make?
> The joy of it one's heart could break.
>
> No jot of time have I to spare,
> Nor will to loiter anywhere,
> So eager am I to be there.
>
> For that the way is hard and long,
> For that gray fears upon it throng,
> I set my journey to a song,

And it grows wondrous happy so.
Singing I hurry on for oh!
It is to God, to God, I go.

The Seers shall go before him, and they shall be seen before him. And they shall praise the Lord for his love, because he is near and seeth.

Those who see God are ever before his Face, and wherever they go they bring with them that sacred Presence. Fortunately I have known quite a few holy people like this. If I wanted to be with God I went to spend time with them. They have been of various spiritual traditions, for God knows nothing of our artificial boundaries and foolish attempts to have an exclusive franchise on his love. When one man I knew would speak to a group there would an all-pervading sense of heavenly joy and sweetness. What he said was wise, but the inner experience was beyond all words. I was only a teenager then and had not yet read Yogananda's definition that God is joy, but I certainly experienced it. Another blessed soul was a frail little lady who literally blazed with white fire which I could feel from a distance. She lived in constant spiritual vision. It is true: God is "glorified in his saints" (II Thessalonians 1:10). He is their song and they are his. So before we see God he sends his holy ones to give us a "foretaste of glory divine" as Fanny Crosby put it. Such exalted souls dwell in God's love "because he is near and seeth" them as surely as they see him.

And hatred shall be taken from the earth, and along with jealousy it shall be drowned. For ignorance hath been destroyed upon it, because the knowledge of the Lord hath arrived upon it.

All the evil passions that are as demons tormenting humanity on this earth which they have turned into a hell spring from one cause: ignorance. This is why the great teachers of India, especially Shankara, insist that spiritual wisdom (jnana) alone brings liberation from the bonds of ignorance. When the knowledge of God (Brahmajnana) enlightens the consciousness then hell becomes heaven without our needing to go anywhere.

There was a spiritual adept in China who was a devotee of Amitabha Buddha, the Buddha of Infinite Light. Once as she was walking along softly reciting the invocation of Amitabha a spiritual wiseacre said to her contemptuously: "Tell me grandmother, do you think Amitabha Buddha is listening to you in his paradise?" To his surprise she shook her head, continuing her invocations. "Then if Amitabha is not in his paradise, where is he?" insisted the smart-aleck. She pointed to her heart and kept on walking and reciting.

The idea of peace on earth in a social and political sense is as silly as expecting mental institutions to cease having mentally ill people living there. This earth is where the spiritually crazy are put. Someone once asked Yogananda if he believed in hell. The Master smiled and asked: "Where do you think you are?" But peace and joy can prevail in the heart of God's devotee wherever he may be. It is an individual matter, but none the less glorious for that.

Let the singers sing the grace of the Lord Most High, and let them bring their songs. And their heart shall be like the day, and like the excellent beauty of the Lord their pleasant song.

In the deepest sense, the "songs" of the righteous are their very lives. So they "sing the grace of the Lord Most High" by living in his grace and embodying it in their lives. They are a message of love to both God and man. Their hearts are illumined by the "Sun of Righteousness" and shine outward into the hearts of those around them who are sensitive enough to pick up the "broadcast." Their song-life will be perfect reflections of the Face of God, the beauty of the Divine. All who hear it will rejoice in the joy it also brings to them.

And let there be nothing without life, nor without knowledge nor dumb. For (the Lord) hath given a mouth to his creation, to open the voice of the mouth towards him, and to praise him.

This is a profound counsel. The spiritual aspirant must ensure that he is truly alive on every level, that no aspect of his heart or mind is dormant, but rather is living and shining in/with the Light of God. Every atom of his being is to be conscious and fully functioning. No part of him should be unconscious or without a real effect. This is the new birth which Jesus announced to the world.

"There was a man of the Pharisees, named Nicodemus, a ruler of the Jews: the same came to Jesus by night, and said unto him, Rabbi, we know that thou art a teacher come from God: for no man can do these miracles that thou doest, except God be with him. Jesus answered and said unto him, Verily, verily, I say unto thee, Except a man be born again, he cannot see the kingdom of God. Nicodemus saith unto him, How can a man be born when he is old? can he enter the second time into his mother's womb, and be born? Jesus answered, Verily, verily, I say unto thee, Except a man be born of water and of the Spirit, he cannot enter into the kingdom of God. That which is born of the flesh is flesh; and that which is born of the Spirit is spirit. Marvel not that I said unto thee, Ye must be born again. The wind bloweth where it listeth, and thou hearest the sound thereof, but canst not tell whence it cometh, and whither it goeth: so is every one that is born of the Spirit" (John 3:1-8).

In time the entire cosmos must become awake and alive in Divine Consciousness and be manifested as consciousness Itself. For intelligence is inherent in every atom of creation so it may open itself toward God and become living praise unto him. It is this to which Jesus was referring when his enemies told him to silence those who were welcoming him into Jerusalem on Palm Sunday. He told them: "I tell you that, if these should hold their peace, the stones would immediately cry out" (Luke 19:40). And he did not mean that mute matter would be crying out in a mechanical, unconscious sense, for he had also said to these same opponents: "I say unto you, that God is able of these stones to raise up children unto Abraham" (Matthew 3:9), enunciating the metaphysical principle that every atom is a potential sentient being, as it is the body of a spark of intelligence whose destiny is to evolve upward to humanity and far beyond to divinity.

Confess ye his power, and show forth his grace.

Although we should certainly "speak the wonderful works of God" (Acts 2:11), we must also ourselves perform wonderful works and "show forth his grace." The Beloved Disciple wrote: "my little children, let us not love in word, neither in tongue; but in deed and in truth" (I John 3:18). Quoting Isaiah, Jesus had said: "This people draweth nigh unto me with their mouth, and honoureth me with their lips; but their heart is far from me" (Matthew 15:8). Again, it is the mind, heart, and life of each one of us that the ode is speaking about.

The final ten verses beginning with "And for its salvation…" have another, prophetic, meaning as well as that which we have just considered. I was told by an Orthodox rabbinical student that in Israel he had learned of a Jewish mystical tradition that the Messiah was to come two times: first as Son of Joseph and be rejected by Israel and later as Son of David and be accepted as the Messiah. Jesus was born at the beginning of the Piscean Age, and now that it is the beginning of the Aquarian Age there are those who believe that he is to appear again. To them these verses are a prophecy of this Second Coming in which he shall appear with disciples who will have taken birth to work with him in his mission. A new era will open up for those on the earth who truly "seek the kingdom," while the others will go on just as before. I say this because it is vain to suppose that the whole world is going to turn into a paradise by the mere birth of anyone, even such a Master as Jesus. The world is a vast lunatic asylum and will continue to be one. Jesus will come to heal and deliver those that "hunger and thirst after righteousness" (Matthew 5:6). The rest will in time also awake and arise, as shall every sentient being in the universe.

ODE 8

Open ye, open ye your hearts to the exultation of the Lord, and let your love abound from the heart and even to the lips.
To bring forth fruits to the Lord—a holy life, and to talk watchfully in his light.
Rise up and stand erect, ye who were sometimes brought low.
Ye who were in silence speak, for your mouth hath been opened.
Ye who were despised be lifted up, now that your righteousness has been lifted up.
For the right hand of the Lord is with you, and he will be your helper.
And peace hath been prepared for you, before your war ever happened.
Hear the word of truth, and receive the knowledge of the Most High.
Your flesh may not know what I am saying to you, nor your garment what I am showing to you.
Keep my secret ye who are kept by it; keep my faith ye who are kept by it.
And understand my knowledge, ye who know me in truth; love me with affection ye who love.
For I do not turn away my face from my own, for I know them.
Before they came into being, I took knowledge of them, and on their faces I set my seal.
I fashioned their members. my own breasts I prepared for them, that they might drink my holy milk and live thereby.

I took pleasure in them, and I am not ashamed of them.
For my workmanship are they, and the strength of my thoughts.
Who then shall stand up against my handiwork? Or who is there that is not subject to them?
I willed and fashioned mind and heart, and they are Mine. And upon my right hand I set my elect ones.
And my righteousness goes before them, and they shall not be detached from my Name, for it is with them.
Pray and increase, and abide in the love of the Lord;
And the beloved ones in the Beloved, and those who are protected in him Who lives, and those who are saved in him Who was saved.
And ye shall be found incorrupt in all ages, on account of the Name of your Father. Alleluia.

Open ye, open ye your hearts to the exultation of the Lord, and let your love abound from the heart and even to the lips.

The necessary thing here is to open our hearts, then everything will follow as it should. But what is the heart? Not the organ that pumps blood, but the very core of our being which is the pure consciousness that alone is spirit. We need to open our consciousness, our spirit, but a multitude of things are in the way: body, emotions, desires, mind, intellect and will: all of which have been distorted by our chaotic earthly experience. They are meant to be instruments for our evolution, but instead they are instruments of stagnation and often regression rather than progress. Unless they are purified and made responsive to our spirit it will never be fully opened because they are like mountains of debris under which it is buried. Not only that, but they are continually being mistaken by us for our spirit and erroneously called "me" by us daily.

What shall we do? Vigorously take up interior life through meditation and order our life scrupulously to conform to and reflect the principle found in the Bible: "Beloved, now are we the sons of God, and it doth not yet appear what we shall be: but we know that, when he shall appear, we shall be like him; for we shall see him as he is.

And every man that hath this hope in him purifieth himself, even as he is pure" (I John 3:2-3). Until we do this we shall neither exult in the Lord nor love him from the heart.

To bring forth fruits to the Lord–a holy life, and to talk watchfully in his light.

The primary things we should be offering to God are a holy life and a consciousness illumined by the Divine Light that is God himself. For "talk" is not a typographical mistake for "walk," but literally means that every word and thought are to proceed from a mind filled with God's Light: his Consciousness. Such a person can say with Saint Paul: "For to me to live is Christ" (Philippians 1:21).

Rise up and stand erect, ye who were sometimes brought low.

The force of cosmic evil and delusion is called "the Devil" and "Satan" (Revelation 12:9). Devil (diabolos) means "false accuser" or "slanderer," and Satan (satanas) means "adversary." This terrible force, called "Mara" by the Buddhists and "Maya" by the Hindus, completely undermines us in many ways, not the least of which is to get us to adopt wrong ideas about ourselves. Belief that we are weak, unable to prevail against evil or that we are evil or somehow "wrong" is a major ploy used to paralyze, conquer and dominate us. Those who have fallen and been "brought low," are fooled into thinking that they cannot rise or stand upright. But we can snap this psychic hypnosis in a moment and do exactly that, for it is our nature to rise and stand tall in body, mind, and spirit. It is delusion that is really weak, not we.

Ye who were in silence speak, for your mouth hath been opened.

At the time of Jesus it was common to speak of "having a voice" in the sense of being able to affect or direct something, to wield personal power to actual effect, as in having a voice in government. The fundamental power of human life is "the word," the ability to put forth our will and make a change in something. Many people think they are spiritually mute when they are not. One of the most brilliant minds I ever encountered was that of an elderly lady living in a tiny town in the Midwest. Intelligent as she was, she had the delusion that she was blind, and I more than once heard her tell people: "I'm sorry, I'm blind." She was not mentally ill, so I have no explanation for it. But this I can say: she had the most challenging mind I had ever met. It is the same with many people: they think they lack abilities they have abundantly. I have known intelligent people who thought they were stupid, and beautiful people who thought they were ugly. One of the most beautiful women I have ever seen told me more than once: "I am hideous," and believed it firmly. Why? Because her father told her throughout her childhood that she was ugly and "looked a sight" and "was a mess." It was impossible to get her to see herself in any other way. In the same way, the Liar tells us we cannot do what we can do easily. And in that way we become stymied and stagnated.

Ye who were despised be lifted up, now that your righteousness has been lifted up.

Of course, some of these illusions have nothing to do with this present life, but are carried over from previous lives in which we may really have been the way we now think we are. Some people develop abilities they did not seem to have in the previous parts of their lives. One day it just surfaces, having been there all along but unseen. I have witnessed people suddenly manifesting artistic and musical abilities–some of them in their early sixties.

It is the same with spirituality. Even if in the past we were filled with faults and "sins," in time we can become "lifted up" and free of those old bonds. Saint Francis had nothing in his past that indicated his future holiness. Saint Catherine of Genoa was a empty-headed worldling, and one day after receiving the blessing of a priest she jumped up and shouted: "No more world! No more sin!" and was a saint from that moment on. Most of us, though, have to lift our own inner righteous up and bring it into the light of day. That is what spiritual practice, especially meditation, is all about.

For the right hand of the Lord is with you, and he will be your helper.

This is the secret: the power of God is within us to accomplish all things. "Because greater is he that is in you, than he that is in the world" (I John 4:4). "Christ in you, the hope of glory" (Colossians 1:27).

And peace hath been prepared for you, before your war ever happened.

Before we even began the "war" to overcome ignorance and sin and attain wisdom and holiness, our success was assured. "In all these things we are more than conquerors through him that loved us" (Romans 8:37).

Hear the word of truth, and receive the knowledge of the Most High.

The Word of Truth is spoken in the depths of our spirit; it is not something spoken by any human being: it is the voice of God that has always been speaking to us, but which we were unable to hear. Again we see that interior life is absolutely indispensable, otherwise we will remain blind, deaf and mute in the inner kingdom of the spirit. Therefore: "Let this mind be in you, which was also in Christ Jesus.… Work out your own salvation,… for it is God which worketh in you both to will and to do of his good pleasure" (Philippians 2:5, 12-13). And God does not fail.

Your flesh may not know what I am saying to you, nor your garment what I am showing to you.

To be "carnally [fleshly] minded" (Romans 8:6) is to be blind to things of the spirit. "As it is written, Eye hath not seen, nor ear heard, neither have entered into the heart of man, the things which God hath prepared for them that love him" (I Corinthians 2:9). So our five body-garments: body, emotions, desires, mind, intellect and will, have no idea what awaits the liberated spirit. But our spirit even now knows, because "we have the mind of Christ" (I Corinthians 2:16).

Keep my secret ye who are kept by it; keep my faith ye who are kept by it.

However, when we do come to know the full life of the spirit, we are not to speak of it, for it is a secret between us and God. What we need is not to brag about it and expound our spiritual life to others, but to "keep faith" with God, Who will then keep us secure in the spirit.

"my beloved is mine, and I am his" (Song of Solomon 2:16). "I am my beloved's, and my beloved is mine" (Song of Solomon 6:3). It is between the spirit and God alone.

And understand my knowledge ye who know me in truth; love me with affection ye who love.

"Understand my knowledge" is an interesting expression, because we mistakenly think that if we know something we understand it, but that is hardly ever true. We know that petroleum is flammable, but how many of us know why? We use electricity constantly and have some idea of how it is generated, but just what it is and how it works is a complete mystery to nearly everyone. The same is true of our life; we know next to nothing about it really, so no wonder our lives are vague, disordered, disoriented and even destructive either to ourselves or others. No one commits suicide because they really know their life, for if they did they would be able to cope with it and direct it to conform to their will.

Those who seek higher evolution must first search outwardly and obtain knowledge of the facts of spiritual life; they must familiarize themselves with the teaching of the masters of spiritual life, not mere philosophers or theologians. At the same time, through cultivation of inner consciousness they must develop the faculty of intuitive and intellectual understanding through meditation. In this way they will both know and understand. There is no place in spiritual life for stupidity and sheep-wittedness. Believe me, there are no stupid yogis, for yoga develops the intellect as well as the intuition.

As this verse implies, it is those who know God (not just about God) who understand through their spiritual experience which is totally inward and has nothing to do with emotions, feelings, or "faith." To "believe," "trust," and "hope" is meaningless. And please understand that psychic experience is not spiritual experience. A lot of experiences and phenomena that supposedly indicate spiritual development and enlightenment are merely psychic. Even in the East these lesser things are considered to be of a value they intrinsically lack.

We can only value and love what we know. To know God is to love God in the truest sense: not emotional or ego-based. It is common for people to love something or someone only because of a false impression of them, and when they see them for what they really are the love evaporates. But with God it is just the opposite. Those who do not know God do not really love him, but those who come to know him do indeed love him with all their heart, soul and mind (Matthew 22:37).

The love of God is not blind, but "most secret knowledge combined with realization" (Bhagavad Gita 9:1).

For I do not turn away my face from my own, for I know them.

In the Bhagavad Gita the Lord says: "I am the Omniscient" (10:33). Since God is omniscient there is nothing and no one he does not know. But his knowing is not intellectual, just a kind of inventory sheet. He truly knows, and therefore he loves just as we shall love when we know him, for "God is love" (I John 4:8). And this will never change. He shall "face" us forever, for he is "the Father of lights, with whom is no variableness, neither shadow of turning" (James 1:17). "He abideth faithful: he cannot deny himself" (II Timothy 2:13).

This citation from Timothy is most important because it implies that we are part of the Divine; therefore he cannot deny us because it would be denying himself. The word *arneomai* also means to refuse, disregard or reject. These things can only occur in relation to someone other than the subject of the sentence. Such cannot occur on the part of God because we are an integral part of his very Being. The mystic Angelus Silesius said that the very existence of God and his existence were interdependent, and Meister Eckhart said much the same. When God looks at us he sees himself, for we are his images, his likenesses. "And God said, Let us make man in our image, after our likeness.... And Adam begat a son in his own likeness, after his image" (Genesis 1:26; 5:3). That is why we can call him "Father." "I said, Thou shalt call me, my father" (Jeremiah 3:19).

Before they came into being, I took knowledge of them, and on their faces I set my seal.

God did not create us from nothing (ex nihil), for we are co-eternal with him. But he did send us forth into manifestation.

"All this world is pervaded by me in my unmanifest aspect. All beings dwell within me, but I do not dwell within them. And yet beings do not dwell within me: behold my Divine Yoga. Sustaining beings and yet not dwelling in them, I myself cause all beings to come into manifestation. As mighty winds move everywhere, yet always dwell in the ether, know that even so do all beings dwell within me. At the end of a kalpa, all beings merge into my Prakriti: at the beginning of another kalpa, I myself send them forth. Resting on my Prakriti, I send forth again and again this entire multitude of beings" (Bhagavad Gita 9:4-8).

We were known by God from eternity and he put his seal upon us. As Saint Paul wrote: "And we know that all things work together for good to them that love God, to them who are called according to his purpose. For whom he did foreknow, he also did predestinate to be conformed to the image of his Son, that he might be the firstborn among many brethren. Moreover whom he did predestinate, them he also called: and whom he called, them he also justified: and whom he justified, them he also glorified" (Romans 8:28-30).

I fashioned their members. my own breasts I prepared for them, that they might drink my holy milk and live thereby.

Just as the child grows in the womb and after birth is nursed by the mother, so God the Mother has given us our bodies and even now sustains them through the life-power that ever flows from her to us. The entire realm of relativity is dual in order for us to manifest; the cosmos, material and subtle, can be considered the "breasts" of our Mother God in whom we live.

I took pleasure in them, and I am not ashamed of them.

So intimate and irrevocable is our relationship with God that he said through the prophet Isaiah: "Can a woman forget her sucking child, that she should not have compassion on the son of her womb? yea, they may forget, yet will I not forget thee. Behold, I have graven thee upon the palms of my hands" (Isaiah 49:15-16). This is the truth. All talk of separation from and rejection by God is based on misunderstanding of God with Whom there is no "shadow of turning" in relation to us.

For my workmanship are they, and the strength of my thoughts.

All creation is the Thought-Power of God; the cosmos and our bodies within it are dreams of God in which we dwell and through which we are dreaming within his greater dream. We, too, are "Words" of God, his Living Thoughts in which his Power resides even if at this moment things seem otherwise. We are not weak and helpless sinners, we are divine sons of the Divine Being.

Who then shall stand up against my handiwork? Or who is there that is not subject to them?

Nothing can stop our evolution and eventual return to God; nothing can prevent forever the revelation of our innate divinity. As the poem says in Mahler's *Resurrection Symphony*, "I came from God and I shall return to God!" That is why Saint Paul wrote: "In all these things we are more than conquerors through him that loved us" (Romans 8:37).

It is only the dream-illusion of weakness and vulnerability that is holding us back. "Wherefore he saith, Awake thou that sleepest, and arise from the dead, and Christ shall give thee light" (Ephesians 5:14).

I willed and fashioned mind and heart, and they are Mine. And upon my right hand I set my elect ones.

Not only is the universe an evolutionary device, so also is the makeup of the individual person. We are so constituted that we shall absolutely awaken in time and return to our Source. God has put certain mechanisms in our gross and subtle bodies that will ensure this. Externally the law of cause and effect (karma) also works to the same end. Those who defy the laws inherent in themselves and in the cosmos eventually run into an impenetrable wall, and their only option is to change direction in their life. Certainly it is a slow and sometimes painful process with many setbacks involving what the Bhagavad Gita (2:40) calls "great fear" (*mahato bhayat*). Yet, since the core of it all is the spirit, it shall prevail. After all, it has eternity to wait for its unveiling, just as does God. We always belong to God and are on his right hand of liberating consciousness, for we are all his elect.

"I am the same to all beings. There is no one who is disliked or dear to me. But they who worship me with devotion are in me, and I am also in them. If even an evildoer worships me single-heartedly, he should be considered righteous, for truly he has rightly resolved. Quickly he becomes a virtuous soul and goes to everlasting peace. Understand: no devotee of me is ever lost" (Bhagavad Gita 9:29-31). This is the correct perspective.

Notice how the scriptures of India coincide with these Odes. In the West Jesus truly has become, as Bruce Barton proposes in his small book, "The Man Nobody Knows."

And my righteousness goes before them, and they shall not be detached from my Name, for it is with them.

From eternity it has been the intention of God that we shall be revealed as eternal sons of the Eternal Father. This intention was perfectly realized in Jesus, who is referred to as the "firstfruits" of humanity. "Now is Christ risen from the dead, and become the firstfruits of them that slept" (I Corinthians 15:20). *Aparche*, firstfruits, does not just refer to produce, but to intended offerings to God that were first taken or marked out from the ordinary things. For example, when bread was made, a portion was first taken out that would be made into bread-offerings. Whatever the nature of the firstfruits, it would be exactly the same as those it was separated from, though sometimes more perfect. Applying this term to Jesus implies that he, too, was human like us and attained to perfection in spirit: total union with God. To underscore this, exemplary Christians are also referred to as firstfruits. "Of his own will begat he us with the word of truth, that we should be a kind of firstfruits of his creatures" (James 1:18). "These were redeemed from among men, being the firstfruits unto God" (Revelation 14:4).

What is the Name of God in this verse? It is the nature and will of God, the idea being that nothing can alienate us from the fact that we are eternally part of the Divine Life which we are destined to manifest perfectly on the finite level. The Divine Name is the Divine Plan for all sentient beings. It is also our name because we, too, are both unity and trinity as image-reflections of God. We cannot be separated from It because it is the essential nature of both us and God. (Once more, see *Soham Yoga*.)

Pray and increase, and abide in the love of the Lord.

"Pray" (proseuchomai) means to come before someone and speak to them, usually in petition of some sort. In Sanskrit the word is *upasana*, which means "draw near." Saint James wrote: "Draw nigh to God, and he will draw nigh to you" (James 4:8). The supreme mode of prayer is meditation. Just as an object becomes warmer the nearer and longer it is by or in the fire, so it is with us and God. Continually invoking the Divine Consciousness in meditation, the reflection of that Consciousness increases in us and reveals itself as a permanent state. Thus we shall abide in the love of God and be transmuted into the Beloved, for God Is Love.

And the beloved ones in the Beloved, and those who are protected in him Who lives, and those who are saved in him Who was saved.

Since we are beloved of God it is preordained that we shall be united to him, the Beloved. Since he protects and watches over us, we shall live in him who protects and fosters our life from within and without. He ordained that we shall be "saved," freed in and by him.

And ye shall be found incorrupt in all ages, on account of the Name of your Father.

Throughout eternity as cycles of creation come and go, we shall abide free from all taint of ignorance and bondage while countless spirits not yet liberated will find themselves cycling and suffering in a seemingly endless process that shall, however, end in their liberation as it has with us. This is because the Name of the Father shall have prevailed in us as our eternal Self. "For whatsoever is born of God overcometh the world" (I John 5:4).

ODE 9

Open your ears, and I will speak to you.
Give me your souls, that I may also give you my soul.
The Word of the Lord and his good pleasures, the holy thought that he has thought concerning his Messiah.
For in the will of the Lord is your life, and his intention is everlasting life, and your perfection is incorruptible.
Be enriched in God the Father, and receive the intention of the Most High, be strong and redeemed by his grace.
For I proclaim peace to you his holy ones, so that none of those who hear may fall in battle.
And that also those who have known him may not perish, and that those who receive him may not be ashamed.
An everlasting crown is Truth, blessed are they who set it on their head.
A stone of great price it is, and the wars were on account of the crown.
And righteousness hath taken it, and hath given it to you.
Put on the crown in the true covenant of the Lord, and all those who have conquered shall be inscribed in his book.
For their book is the victory which is yours, and she sees you before her and wills that you shall be saved. Alleluia.

The prevailing view in nearly all religion is that human beings are helpless, pathetic messes, if not outright evil, and that unless there is an intervention through the advent of a "savior," whether God, god, prophet, avatar, guru, astral master or astrological configuration, there is simply no hope for them whatever unless they accept and follow said savior. Modern Christianity is a major advocate of this doctrine, but it was not always so, as this and other Odes demonstrate. Having spent over half of his life in India, Jesus brought back to his homeland the eternal verities of Eternal (Sanatana) Dharma.

One of the main principles of Eternal Dharma is the total responsibility of the individual for his present status and condition in this world: karma. We are not really helpless, but we think we are and so we continue in that illusory state. Jesus, like the primeval sages of India, sounded the call of the spirit to awakening and freedom.

Open your ears, and I will speak to you.

How is it we have the power to open our deaf ears? Because we used the same power to close them. No one else did this to us; it all lies at our door. This fact was not unknown to Jesus even in previous lives. For example, as Isaiah, "the Messianic Prophet," he relayed the words of God: "Is my hand shortened at all, that it cannot redeem? Or have I no power to deliver?" (Isaiah 50:2). Then he explained their meaning to his hearers: "Behold, the Lord's hand is not shortened, that it cannot save; neither his ear heavy, that it cannot hear: But your iniquities have separated between you and your God, and your sins have hid his face from you" (Isaiah 59:1-2). God has not turned from us or hidden his face; we have separated our consciousness from God and blinded our inner eyes to his omnipresence. Lady Macbeth was quite wrong when she said: "What's done cannot be undone." Duality being a fundamental condition of all relative existence, what comes will most certainly go and what has been done will indeed be undone: we alone decide whether it will be sooner or later. We did it and we can undo it.

Every aspect of our existence in this world is according to our will. We can say, "Oh, why doesn't God take me now like Elijah?" But the reason lies in our will, not God's. Two friends of mine had some truly precocious grandchildren, and at the beginning of December one year Anne said to Elwood: "I told them you would write a Christmas play for them and we would record it and send it to them." Elwood was amazed and chagrined, but he put his mind to it and wrote a two-person play about the birth of Jesus. Elwood was one of the shepherds the angel told about Jesus' birth, and Anne was an angel who helped him go into Bethlehem and find where the Child was. At the end, the angel tells the shepherd she must return to heaven, and he says: "How I wish I could go to heaven!" She asks: "Do you *really* want to go to heaven?" He says, "Of course," and there comes a great whooshing sound and that is the end of the play. He really wanted it, so he went there. Only intensity of desire had been lacking, and once he had it… whoosh!!!

Usually we need to be shown the way to open our ears, and that is what yoga is all about.

Give me your souls, that I may also give you my soul.

James Charlesworth translates: "Give me yourself, so that I may also give you myself." Just this morning I was reading in Hilton's *Ladder of Perfection* this very thing: that if we give ourselves to God, God will give himself to us. Long before either the Odes or the *Ladder* were written, Patanjali said that the method to attain supreme consciousness was Ishwarapranidhana, the giving of our life to God. Again, we have the power to do so because ages ago we "separated" ourselves from God and claimed that our life really was *our* life, and no one else's. So, trying desperately to live out such a colossal folly, we have been miserable and subject to continual birth and dying with all their attendant suffering, and it will stay that way until we stop the charade and reunite our consciousness (spirit) with God.

A fully liberated (perfected) being is one with God in full awareness and capacity. Jesus not only said: "I and my Father are one" (John 10:30), he further said: "He that hath seen me hath seen the Father" (John 14:9). Nor did he intend to claim for himself a unique status, for in the closing hours of his life he prayed: "that they all may be one; as thou, Father, art in me, and I in thee, that they also may be one in us" (John 17:21).

The Word of the Lord and his good pleasures, the holy thought that he has thought concerning his Messiah. For in the will of the Lord is your life, and his intention is everlasting life, and your perfection is incorruptible.

This is a very literal translation and sounds like it just got put in here at random, but in Aramaic it is perfectly all right. It is a statement regarding the previous two sentences about the opening of our ears by us and the giving of ourselves to God.

"Word" in ancient usage commonly meant intention, purpose and will to accomplish that intention or purpose. So our spiritual awareness and dedication to God is the fundament intention and will of God. That is why the universe exists: for our spiritual perfection. God delights in our progress toward total, conscious union with him. The Messiah, the Christ, is the Only-Begotten Son of God: God within all creation as the guiding Intelligence that brings it to fruition in the revelation of the sons of God such as Jesus, who is *a* Christ, not *the* Christ. "For the earnest expectation of the creature [creation] waiteth for the manifestation of the sons of God.… Because the creature itself also shall be delivered from the bondage of corruption into the glorious liberty of the children of God" (Romans 8:19, 21). "For in the will of the Lord is your life, and his intention is everlasting life, and your perfection is incorruptible." What a glorious vision God has of man's eternal destiny. May we always keep that in mind.

Be enriched in God the Father, and receive the intention of the Most High, be strong and redeemed by his grace. For I proclaim peace to you his holy ones, so that none of those who hear may fall in battle.

"O the depth of the riches both of the wisdom and knowledge of God! how unsearchable are his judgments, and his ways past finding out!" (Romans 11:33). Saint Paul speaks of the necessity of "the eyes of your understanding being enlightened; that ye may know what is the hope of his calling, and what the riches of the glory of his inheritance in the saints,… That in the ages to come he might shew the exceeding riches of his grace in his kindness toward us through Christ Jesus.… unto me,… is this grace given, that I should preach among the Gentiles the unsearchable riches of Christ.… that he would grant you, according to the riches of his glory, to be strengthened with might by his Spirit in the inner man" (Ephesians 1:18; 2:7; 3:8, 16). For we, too, are intended to be Christs, revelations of God, just as was Jesus.

"For I proclaim peace to you his holy ones, so that none of those who hear may fall in battle. And that also those who have known him may not perish, and that those who receive him may not be ashamed." Since it is the express will and purpose of God, what hinders our attainment of Christhood? Only *our* lack of understanding and will.

An everlasting crown is Truth, blessed are they who set it on their head.

The greatest philosopher of India, Shankaracharya, was one asked: "What is truth [satya]," and he replied: "There is no such thing as truth; there is only the True [Sat]," meaning that God is the only absolute Truth. It is not a philosophy or dogmatic system that is the crown of spirit, but God himself. That is why the very first Ode of Solomon is:

The Lord is on my head like a crown, and I shall not be without him.
They wove for me a crown of truth, and it caused Thy branches to bud in me.
For it is not like a withered crown which buddeth not.
But Thou livest upon my head, and Thou hast blossomed upon me.
Thy fruits are full-grown and perfect; they are full of Thy salvation.
Alleluia.

A stone of great price it is, and the wars were on account of the crown.

"The kingdom of heaven is like unto a merchant man, seeking goodly pearls: who, when he had found one pearl of great price, went and sold all that he had, and bought it" (Matthew 13:45-46). All the struggles and spiritual warfare of the saints against ignorance and sin were to win the crown of God Consciousness which is Divinity Itself.

And righteousness hath taken it, and hath given it to you.

True righteousness ("rightness") is perfect conformity to God, the erasure of all in us that is not of God. Union with God is its "gift" to us. Therefore: "Every man that hath this hope in him purifieth himself, even as he is pure" (I John 3:3).

Put on the crown in the true covenant of the Lord, and all those who have conquered shall be inscribed in his book.

The true covenant of the Lord is revealed in the previous verses of this Ode. It is not simple: it requires conquering and banishing all that conflicts with God Consciousness, but its reward is inscription in the Book of Life. (See Philippians 4:3 and Revelation 21:27.)

For their book is the victory which is yours, and she sees you before her and wills that you shall be saved.

Because God wills it we can say that victory is ours even now, we need only put forth our entire strength and will to "lay hold on eternal life" (I Timothy 6:12).

"She" is the Holy Spirit, the deifying Power of God, the Mother that brings all her children, all the sons of God, to birth in the heavenly Kingdom. This is salvation in God, the Eternal Kingdom.

ODE 10

The Lord hath directed my mouth by his Word, and he hath opened my heart by his Light.
And he hath caused to dwell in me his deathless life, and permitted me to speak the fruit of his peace.
To convert the souls of those who are willing to come to him, and to lead captive a good captivity for freedom.
I was strengthened and made mighty and took the world captive, and the captivity became to me for the praise of the Most High and of God my Father.
And the Gentiles were gathered together who had been scattered abroad, but I was not polluted by my love (for them), because they had praised me in high places.
And the traces of the light were set upon their heart; and they walked in my life and were saved, and they became my people for ever and ever. Alleluia.

Whether this Ode was written by Jesus or by someone writing what Jesus would have said, we cannot know. But we can certainly appreciate its truth as the testimony of one who has attained enlightenment in Christhood.

The Lord hath directed my mouth by his Word, and he hath opened my heart by his Light.

Two of the basic factors of our existence are Sound and Light. The Word, the Cosmic Creative Vibration, is manifesting as our various levels of vibratory energy. Inherent in that Vibration is the impulse to evolve to perfection. Therefore our personal Word in the sense of will and intelligence is guided by that greater Word which draws us ever upward along the scale of evolution that culminates in the realization of our divine nature. At first we only know the realm of the Word, of Vibration, but in time the second factor begins to reveal itself. And that factor is the Light of Consciousness which is our inmost reality, for light and spirit are the same. When the heart opens at the touch of Divine Light just as does the flower at the touch of sunlight, then realization is near. The Word is outside and the Light is inside, yet they are the one Spirit. We are all the Work of God, the *Opus Dei*.

And he hath caused to dwell in me his deathless life, and permitted me to speak the fruit of his peace.

We are always immortal, but we experience mortality and identify with it, fearing death that is only a mirage. So the "dwelling" in us of God's deathless life is the advent of spirit-consciousness into our awareness. It is a discovery rather than an attainment.

The "fruit" of this realization is "spoken" inwardly and outwardly through our inner and outer lives. It is not speaking, but demonstration-manifestation.

To convert the souls of those who are willing to come to him, and to lead captive a good captivity for freedom.

Neither God nor gods (perfected masters) can convert anyone who is not willing to tread the upward path to God-realization. Those who have any other interests may pursue them until they realize there is only one truly attainable goal: liberation of the spirit. That is just the nature of things. But when our will is aligned with God, when we say with Jesus: "Not my will, but thine, be done" (Luke 22:42), our transformation becomes possible

Three times in the Bible we find the expression "captivity captive" (Judges 5:12; Psalms 68:18; Ephesians 4:8). It means to vanquish all that which enslaves or captivates us, to capture and banish it forevermore from our life sphere. Then we will be established in total freedom of spirit. Psalms and Ephesians refer to "ascending on high" to accomplish this. Simply put, when we evolve our consciousness into higher levels we will gain the mastery over that which presently masters us. Yoga is the means of our evolution.

I was strengthened and made mighty and took the world captive, and the captivity became to me for the praise of the Most High and of God my Father.

We ourselves can become the glory that is given to God when we become "more than conquerors through him that loved us" (Romans 8:37).

And the Gentiles were gathered together who had been scattered abroad, but I was not polluted by my love (for them), because they had praised me in high places.

"The Gentiles" refers to the uncontrolled and often chaotic energies that disrupt our attempts at higher life and consciousness, but if they, too, are "lifted on high" through their purification and refinement, they will be our praise and glory whereas once they were our shame.

And the traces of the light were set upon their heart; and they walked in my life and were saved, and they became my people for ever and ever.

When all aspects of our makeup are touched by the light of the spirit-self, they enter into harmony with our upward development and are themselves carried upward and liberated in/with us and become "ours" forever in our complete mastery over them.

ODE 11

My heart was cloven and its flower appeared, and grace sprang up in it, and it brought forth fruit to the Lord.
For the Most High uncovered my inward being towards him, and filled me with his love.
And this became my salvation, and I ran in the Way in his peace, in the way of truth.
From the beginning and even to the end, I received his knowledge.
And I was established upon the rock of truth, where he had set me up.
And speaking waters drew near my lips, from the fountain of the Lord plenteously.
And I drank and was inebriated with the living waters that do not die.
And my inebriation was not one without knowledge, but I forsook vanity.
And I turned to the Most High my God, and I was enriched by his bounty.
And I forsook the folly cast away over the earth, and I stripped it off and cast it from me.
And the Lord renewed me in his garment, and possessed me by his light.
And from above he gave me rest without corruption, and I became like the land which blossoms and rejoices in its fruits.
And the Lord was like the sun, shining upon the face of the land.
My eyes were enlightened, and my face received the dew.

And my soul was refreshed, by the pleasant fragrance of the Lord.
And he carried me into his paradise, wherein is the abundance
　　of the pleasure of the Lord.
I beheld blooming and fruit-bearing trees.
And self-grown was their crown.
Their branches were sprouting, and their fruits were shining.
From an immortal land were their roots.
And a river of joy was watering them
And round about them in the land of eternal life.
And I worshipped the Lord on account of his glory.
And I said, Blessed O Lord, are they who are planted in Thy
　　land, and those who have a place in Thy Paradise,
And who grow in the growth of Thy trees, and have changed
　　from darkness to light.
Behold! all Thy laborers are fair, who work good works, and
　　turn from wickedness to Thy pleasantness.
And they have turned away from themselves the bitterness of
　　the trees, when they were planted in Thy land.
And everything was like Thy remnant–(Blessed are the workers of
　　Thy waters)–and an eternal memorial of Thy faithful servants.
For there is abundant room in Thy Paradise, and nothing is
　　useless therein, but everything is filled with fruit.
Glory be to Thee, O God, the delight of Paradise for ever.
　　Alleluia.

My heart was cloven and its flower appeared, and grace sprang up in it, and it brought forth fruit to the Lord.

　　Spiritual progress involves change which may entail drastic alteration. Consider a seed. When it germinates, the tiny living plant breaks open its shell and begins its journey upward to the light. The seed cannot manifest its potential without in a sense destroying its original form and status. That is what Jesus was speaking about when he said: "Except a corn [grain] of wheat fall into the ground and die, it abideth alone: but if it die, it bringeth forth much fruit" (John 12:24).

Interestingly, the breaking forth of the seedling reveals the dual nature of the seed, coming out from between the two halves. In time the single plant absorbs the halves and only the one growing entity remains. In the same way spiritual progress is a movement from duality to unity, a unity that disrupts and annihilates the duality. That is why Jesus further said: "He that loveth his life shall lose it; and he that hateth his life in this world shall keep it unto life eternal" (John 12:25). *Miseo*, the word translated "hateth" here, can mean to dislike intensely, but it also means "to love less," and that is its meaning here. Our external life should be of lesser value to us than our internal life of the spirit. If we hold these correct priorities, considering the spiritual life more important to us than the material life, we will find that we shall ascend into the consciousness that is "life eternal." Unfortunately we often cling to the status quo, and that clinging is often the basis for spiritual failure: we refuse to grow and change.

In this verse we see that the aspirant's very heart was burst apart so the flower of spiritual consciousness and power could appear and divine grace arise. Just as hard earth must be broken up by the plough so seed can be successfully planted in it, in the same way, the Psalmist said that "The Lord is nigh unto them that are of a broken heart" (Psalms 34:18), prepared for the advent of the life in the spirit. The result will be the offering of the entire life to God so the individual can henceforth live in a state of union with God, having left even the capacity for separation behind. But along with that capacity is also left behind all that drew its existence from separation. That is why Jesus said: "No man can serve two masters: for either he will hate the one, and love the other; or else he will hold to the one, and despise the other. Ye cannot serve God and mammon" (Matthew 6:24). "Mammon" is material consciousness and all that it seeks after and embraces. The yogis call it Maya: Cosmic Delusion. It is only a dream, yet everyone runs after it, turning away from God the sole Reality.

For the Most High uncovered my inward being towards him, and filled me with his love.

Our consciousness, our "inward being," languishes beneath innumerable veils of ignorance accumulated through past lives beyond number, many of them pre-human. The only solution to our present dilemma is the removal of those veils. Therefore the odist tells us that God himself removed those coverings and turned his inner consciousness toward himself.

Enlightenment is a divine action upon the individual spirit, but the individual must know the way to fulfill the aspiration: "my soul thirsteth for God, for the living God: when shall I come and appear before God?" (Psalms 42:2). For the prophet Micah asked: "Wherewith shall I come before the Lord, and bow myself before the high God?" (Micah 6:6). And Saint Paul exhorts us: "Let us therefore come boldly unto the throne of grace, that we may obtain mercy, and find grace to help in time of need" (Hebrews 4:16). At the core (kardia: heart) of our being God is enthroned as our divine Source and Sustainer. Therefore our spirit-consciousness itself is his throne, and when we enter it the Divine Light will begin dissolving the veils of ignorance along with the karmas they caused us to incur. Meditation that directly invokes the divine Power and Consciousness that is God, is the way to uncover our own eternal divinity.

And this became my salvation, and I ran in the Way in his peace, in the way of truth.

The great non-dual philosopher of India, Shankara, insisted in his many writings that jnana, knowledge, was the single factor of enlightenment, although obviously countless other things were assists and even essentials. Here we have the same principle expressed poetically: at the vanishment of ignorance came the dawning of divine, spiritual knowledge: and that was salvation. But enlightenment was not the end, it was a virtual beginning, for "I ran in the Way in his peace, in the way of truth." The dawning of knowledge may be salvation, but dawn itself is a beginning. We have to sprint unerringly "in the way of truth" to become fully united with the Truth.

From the beginning and even to the end, I received his knowledge.

Here Shankara is again vindicated. Jnana is the alpha and omega of true salvation.

And I was established upon the rock of truth, where he had set me up.

What is this rock of truth upon which God wills us to be established? It is the sure knowing revealed to us by our spiritual intuition–not dogma or intellectual belief. The direct knowing of spiritual realities, either spontaneously from within or upon hearing of them, are both deep responses from the inmost reality, the spirit of the individual. Those who do not have such intuitions can gain them by cultivating their innate spirit-knowledge through the diligent practice of meditation.

And speaking waters drew near my lips, from the fountain of the Lord plenteously.

Those who are established on the rock of meditation will find that "living water" about which Jesus spoke in the Gospel of Saint John (7:38), saying that his disciples will find rivers of living water flowing out from their inmost being. In this verse of the ode, the speaker is describing how that water flowed to his lips, inspiring him to speak the words of eternal truth, and it flowed abundantly. There have been many instances in which yogis have gained tremendous knowledge spontaneously from within as a result of their sadhana.

In the thirty-fifth chapter of *Autobiography of a Yogi* mention is made of Brinda Bhagat, a postman. Brinda could not read and write, but when he aspired to be a postman he learned the Bengali alphabet and numbers so he could puzzle out the names and addresses on the letters. But that was all. Yet in time he came to possess vast, detailed knowledge without any study. Once when he was present at a very heated debate between outstanding scholars who could not be reconciled, Brinda said he wanted to say something. Everyone told him to be quiet, but he proceeded to completely clarify the question by making many quotations in Sanskrit from very technical and obscure texts.

A sadhu in Rishikesh, Swami Satchidananda, had only received an elementary public education. But one night in the nineteen-sixties, after having prayed fervently, he instantly knew the entire four Vedas by heart.

Around the same time in Greece it was the custom for senior students at the theological school in Thessalonika to be taken to Mount Athos to visit a monastery whose librarian was a remarkable monk. The students would ask him very involved and subtle theological questions. He would point to various books that contained the answers and quote the relevant passages to them. But he had never read those books. In fact, he never read anything at any time.

And I drank and was inebriated with the living waters that do not die.

Yogananda often said that two things were experience of the Divine: seeing light in meditation and feeling profound bliss. This is the holy inebriation of the truly sober who will not die, having been made immortal by the living waters from within.

And my inebriation was not one without knowledge, but I forsook vanity.

Many people think the purpose of meditation is to "get high," but the sole purpose of meditation is liberation of the spirit, the expansion of consciousness. And expansion of consciousness manifests as illumined intelligence. That is again why Shankara continually emphasized that the prime necessity is jnana: knowledge gained by direct spiritual experience. Vijnana, the Supreme Knowledge, is inseparable from liberation. Therefore the search for knowledge is essential. The speaker in this ode is showing us that spiritual life is not getting "blissed out," but gaining the knowledge which the Living Waters of Spirit bestow. Further, his knowledge was not theoretical or philosophical but practical. And it manifested through enabling him to see through ordinary "reality" as illusion and impelling him to turn away from it to the Real. We must all be sannyasis through yoga: renouncers of all that engender ignorance and bondage.

And I turned to the Most High my God, and I was enriched by his bounty.

Some people who made a business out of yoga once told me with great seriousness: "People do not want anything that hints of renunciation." That may be so, but Jesus' words in Matthew 6:33: "*Seek ye first* the kingdom of God, and his righteousness" still apply. So also do his very next words: "And all these things shall be added unto you." Those who do not seek God first are the real renouncers: they renounce everything, for only in God can anything be really gained or held on to. In chapter seven of *Autobiography of a Yogi*, Yogananda gives us this example of wisdom:

"Master, you are wonderful!" A student, taking his leave, gazed ardently at the patriarchal sage [Nagendranath Bhaduri]. "You have renounced riches and comforts to seek God and teach us wisdom!" It was well-known that Bhaduri Mahasaya had forsaken great family wealth in his early childhood, when single-mindedly he entered the yogic path.

"You are reversing the case!" The saint's face held a mild rebuke. "I have left a few paltry rupees, a few petty pleasures, for a cosmic empire of endless bliss. How then have I denied myself anything? I know the joy of sharing the treasure. Is that a sacrifice? The shortsighted worldly folk are verily the real renunciates! They relinquish an unparalleled divine possession for a poor handful of earthly toys!"

Those who turn to God will be enriched by his bounty; those who turn to the world will be impoverished by its poverty. The choice is simple and clear.

And I forsook the folly cast away over the earth, and I stripped it off and cast it from me.

This is wisdom. Icons of Saint Anthony the Great, the patriarch of Christian monks, often show him holding a scroll with these words: "I saw the snares of evil spread out upon the earth." Nearly three hundred years before Saint Anthony the odist had the same vision. Folly is broadcast like seed over the whole earth. Now the odist perceived that he was clothed or covered in it, so he did not go around pointing the finger at others, like drunks who go around saying "You're drunk" to everyone else. He knew the problem lay with him. So he ruthlessly stripped it all off and threw it away. Saint Francis began his spiritual life in a court of law before a crowd of people by taking off all his clothes and tossing them to his father, saying that henceforth God alone was his father and support. And see what great results he got by doing that.

We are of heaven, not of earth, but intellectually knowing that is not enough: we must free ourself of all it entails and transcend the wheel of earthly birth and death. It is all a matter of consciousness.

And the Lord renewed me in his garment, and possessed me by his light.

The Psalmist tells us that God covers himself with Light as with a garment (Psalms 104:2), and Saint Paul says that God is "dwelling in the light which no man can approach unto; whom no man hath seen, nor can see" (I Timothy 6:16). Yet, when the odist stripped off the world God clothed him in his unapproachable and unseeable light. God's Light cannot be seen or approached by earthbound, human consciousness, but the eternal spirit of each one of us can see, enter and unite with It. God will clothe us with himself and make us one with him. This is an excellent exchange for a perishable world filled with infinite possibilities for suffering, decay and death.

And from above he gave me rest without corruption, and I became like the land which blossoms and rejoices in its fruits.

"Peace I leave with you, my peace I give unto you: not as the world giveth, give I unto you" (John 14:27), said the Lord Jesus. Regarding the spiritual rest intended for those who seek it, Saint Paul wrote: "There remaineth therefore a rest to the people of God. For he that is entered into his rest, he also hath ceased from his own works, as God did from his" (Hebrews 4:9-10). Actually the first word translated "rest" is *sabbatismos*: Sabbath. This implies that the seventh "day" or level of consciousness that is God Consciousness is possible of attainment, an attainment that cannot be lost to any degree ("without corruption"). Those who attain this level of divine realization blossom and rejoice in their possession of the "kingdom that knows no end."

And the Lord was like the sun, shining upon the face of the land. my eyes were enlightened, and my face received the dew. And my soul was refreshed, by the pleasant fragrance of the Lord. And he carried me into his paradise, wherein is the abundance of the pleasure of the Lord.

This is of course all symbolic, employing very Biblical language. The idea is that the odist was enlightened, renewed, made aware of the presence of God and lifted into the highest level of awareness known in Sanskrit as Satchidananda, the state of blissful, conscious Reality.

I beheld blooming and fruit-bearing trees. And self-grown was their crown. Their branches were sprouting, and their fruits were shining. From an immortal land were their roots. And a river of joy was watering them, and round about them in the land of eternal life.

Now he is describing in symbols the spiritual qualities of those perfected beings who live in Satyaloka, the highest world, so we can have somewhat of an understanding of their exalted attainment.

I beheld blooming and fruit-bearing trees.

One question has often been asked by those whose philosophy affirm that human beings are meant to be raised to divinity, that such is their destiny based on their innate nature. The question is: Does the evolving individual come to an end of growth, or is there eternal progression? The answer of the saints of the East, including the Christian East, is that there is a final attainment, but it shall unfold eternally, that the illumined spirit, being finite, will explore the Infinite infinitely; that there is an end to evolution that really is only the beginning of endless manifestation. One very interesting aspect of this is the assertion that the perfect ones can choose to be either unchanging or ever-changing: ever-changingly unchangeless or changelessly ever-changing. This sounds like mere word juggling for mystification, but when we realize that we are destined for a state of divinity, it only follows that we will be as inexpressible and incomprehensible as God, who continually manifests contradictory modes of being: at least so it appears to his finite observers. For we will remain ever finite, God alone being infinite. God is always God and we are always god within God.

And self-grown was their crown.

This is extremely important. The "crown" of our evolution is totally self-produced. Neither God nor any other being in the entire range of existence can bring about our enlightenment and liberation. Nor can any outer event or condition make it happen. It is all up to us. It truly is "the flight of the alone to the Alone." To be as truly one as God is, we must complete our spiritual journey by our self-effort alone. As God is one without a second, we have to approximate that situation and also be *as though* we are the sole existent being. We must do it all on our own. This is an inviolable law. That is why from the beginning the aspirant must strive to be independent and self-sufficient, even though relying on the grace and power of God. It is like when we were children and our parents gave us the money with which we bought their Christmas presents. The money came from them, but the buying was exclusively ours.

Now some people do not like growing up and accepting adult responsibility. We see it all the time, and can find the trait in ourselves on occasion when the situation evokes it. Religion is especially prone to induce childishness, if not outright infantilism, in its adherents. There is constant insistence on our helplessness, weakness, ignorance, unworthiness and sinfulness in contrast to God, who is exactly the opposite of all these things. So the conclusion is that God has to do it all for us, we need only take refuge or "surrender" and all will be done for us, otherwise we are guilty of egotistical presumption and over-confidence. This nonsense is blasphemy of both God and man. As Krishna says: "Stand up resolved to fight" (2:37).

The Bhagavad Gita is a perfect illustration of the right attitude. The *Mahabharata* from which it is extracted tells us that when it was obvious after years of Krishna's attempt at peace that war was inevitable, Arjuna his friend and Duryodhana his enemy went to see what side Krishna would take in the war. He astounded them by saying that one of them could have his army and the other could have him, but he would not fight. Duryodhana was in a sweat, sure that Arjuna would ask for the army and he would be left with Krishna, whom he hated. But Arjuna chose Krishna and asked that he would be his charioteer. Krishna agreed, but again said that he would not fight. Arjuna said he understood, but Krishna's presence was enough for him.

Krishna represents God's presence in our heart, and Arjuna represents each one of us. God will illumine us as to how we should fight, but the fighting will be all up to us. Of course, in God's wisdom we will conquer, but still the conquering will be ours to do. Substituting God or a "savior" is mere evasion and if we insist on it we will lose the battle and then whine about how God knows that we are "but dust" and sinners by nature. As long as we cling to that hardly-comforting delusion we will never manage anything but our own defeat.

Their branches were sprouting, and their fruits were shining.

The saints live in eternal springtime: it is always the season for growth and fruitfulness. There is no time when growth cannot or should not take place. For the aspirant there must always be a forward movement.

There is a legend, perhaps truth, that in one battle of the American Civil War the drummer boy was killed. Another took his place and when the commander told him to sound the retreat he said that he only knew how to sound a really good charge. The commander considered it a sign and told him to go ahead. He did, and they won the battle.

From an immortal land were their roots.

This is the secret of spiritual success: our roots, our inmost consciousness must be in our immortal part, our divine spirit. Our minds and hearts must draw on the intuition and inspiration of spirit. That is why Krishna told Arjuna in the Gita: "They speak of the eternal ashwattha tree with roots above and branches below" (15:1).

And a river of joy was watering them, and round about them in the land of eternal life.

They were immersed in the water of life, so how could they be anything but living? The Bible has a bit to say about living waters, and so did Jesus. On one occasion "Jesus stood and cried, saying, If any man thirst, let him come unto me, and drink. He that believeth on me, as the scripture hath said, out of his inmost being shall flow rivers of living water" (John 7:37-38).

And I worshipped the Lord on account of his glory.

This is possible only for those that have seen the divine glory. Only such persons can intelligently and rightly worship God. How to see the glory? Through purification of body, mind and soul and meditation.

And I said, Blessed O Lord, are they who are planted in Thy land, and those who have a place in Thy Paradise.

Originally our consciousness was in God, but long, long, long ago it got transplanted to the earth. This was necessary, but we lost our way and now wander. We must replant ourselves in the world, the consciousness, of God and begin to live in Paradise, the true home of humanity. Then we can grow into the next level of angelic evolution. (See *Robe of Light*, which explains this.)

And who grow in the growth of Thy trees, and have changed from darkness to light.

There is a pattern for our growth inherent in us from the moment we entered into the realm of relative existence. But we have lost touch with that–and it with us. So we fail to become what we were supposed to be. Once again, it is meditation that will put us back on the right way to proceed and grow "from darkness to light."

Behold! all Thy laborers are fair, who work good works, and turn from wickedness to Thy pleasantness.

Here we are given two prime traits of those who succeed in spiritual life: they do the good and turn from the evil. It also tells us that happiness is in God. The real "pursuit of happiness" is the pursuit of God-realization. "We are labourers together with God" (I Corinthians 3:9; see II Corinthians 6:1), and are told to: "work out your own salvation" (Philippians 2:12).

And they have turned away from themselves the bitterness of the trees, when they were planted in Thy land.

The "trees" planted in an alien world, the mortal world, partake of bitterness until they become replanted in the divine world.

And everything was like Thy remnant–(Blessed are the workers of Thy waters)–and an eternal memorial of Thy faithful servants.

Dr. James Charlesworth (who advised our Brother Simeon in his translation that I am using for this commentary) renders the first part of this verse: "And everything becomes a remnant of Yourself." The idea is that we are eternally part of God: he is the whole and we are the parts. Yet, we are one with him in an inexplicable manner which we cannot intellectually comprehend but which we can experience for ourselves through meditation. Knowing we are part of God's infinite Life is true salvation. It is our blessed privilege to be "workers" in the waters of life, keeping the example of the saints, God's faithful servants, before us as worthy patterns and examples.

For there is abundant room in Thy Paradise, and nothing is useless ["barren" according to Charlesworth] *therein, but everything is filled with fruit.*

To ensure our place in the Paradise of God we must be useful and not barren of spiritual fruit. Indeed, we must be filled with the fruits of the Spirit: "love, joy, peace, longsuffering, gentleness, goodness, faith, meekness, temperance:… For the fruit of the Spirit is in all goodness and righteousness and truth" (Galatians 5:22-23; Ephesians 5:9). For in Paradise there is "abundant room." That is, there are no limits to the scope of the consciousness of those who dwell there. Infinity is theirs for the experiencing.

Glory be to Thee O God, the delight of Paradise for ever.

Those who live in Paradise live in the consciousness of God, and in that is their delight. For, as Yogananda often emphasized: God is ever-new joy, eternally the delight and rejoicing of the perfected spirits.

ODE 12

He hath filled me with words of truth, so that I may speak it.
And like the flowing of waters truth flows from my mouth, and my lips show forth his fruits.
And he has caused his knowledge to abound in me, because the mouth of the Lord is the true Word, and the door of his light.
And the Most High hath given him to his worlds, (which are) the interpreters of his beauty, and the repeaters of his praise, and the confessors of his thought, and the heralds of his mind, and the chasteners of his servants.
For the swiftness of the Word is inexpressible, and like his expression is his swiftness and his sharpness, and his course has no limit.
Never (doth the Word) fall, but ever it standeth; his descent and his way are incomprehensible.
For as his work is so is his expectation, for he is the light and the dawn of thought.
And in him the worlds spoke one to the other, and those that were silent acquired speech.
And from him came love and concord, and they spoke one to the other that which they had (to tell).
And they were goaded by the Word, and they knew him that made them, because they came into concord.
For the mouth of the Most High spoke to them, and the clarification of himself moved quickly by his hand.
For the dwelling-place of the Word is man, and his truth is love.

Blessed are they who by it have comprehended everything, and who have known the Lord by his truth. Alleluia.

Before beginning comment on this ode I want to point out how all the odes are consistently positive in their view of the nature of human beings and their ultimate goal. Over and over the odist speaks of his liberation from ignorance, "giving thanks unto the Father, which hath made us meet to be partakers of the inheritance of the saints in light: who hath delivered us from the power of darkness, and hath translated us into the kingdom of his dear Son" (Colossians 1:12-13). These marvelous hymns show us the glory in store for all the sons of God and reveal the attitude we should always have: confidence in God rather than in our "sinfulness." How can we be disciples of Christ unless we live moment by moment in the consciousness: "now are we the sons of God" (I John 3:2)?

He hath filled me with words of truth, so that I may speak it.

In the seed is the entire plant. In each one of us cosmic consciousness and omniscience is inherent eternally. But we must grow into "the knowledge of the Son of God, unto a perfect man, unto the measure of the stature of the fulness of Christ" (Ephesians 4:13) in order to be consciously established in our true being and able to manifest it. Within the seed is everything, but without the right conditions it will not germinate, grow and flourish. These processes, in the spiritual sense, constitute true religion.

Everything is within us because we are not just in the image of God, we are part of the being of God in a manner incomprehensible, but nonetheless real. That is why Yoga Sutras 1:25 says regarding God: "In him is the highest limit of omniscience." This is very important, for by perfect union with God the individual can come to share or participate in his omniscience. That is, the finite can experience the consciousness of the Infinite, just as God already experiences the consciousness of each individual being. In God is everything, and that all-encompassing being is reflected in us. That is why we are yogis: to reveal the truth of that.

And like the flowing of waters truth flows from my mouth, and my lips show forth his fruits.

The more a person's consciousness is opened, the more he thinks, speaks and acts from his spirit rather than the body and mind. Jesus has declared to us: "He that believeth on me, as the scripture hath said, out of his inmost being shall flow rivers of living water. (This spake he of the Spirit, which they that believe on him should receive" (John 7:38-39). Jesus told the Apostles when he promised them the Holy Spirit: "She dwells *with* you and shall be *in* you" (John 14:17). That is, from thenceforth the Holy Spirit manifests from within us, not outside.

So the odist says the Water of Truth, the Holy Spirit, flows from within him and he manifests the action of the Holy Spirit Who resides in him. Certainly the Odes present a high ideal, but that is in keeping with Jesus' authentic teaching.

And he has caused his knowledge to abound in me, because the mouth of the Lord is the true Word, and the door of his light.

This is an extremely important verse, informing us that the Word manifests in and through us, because It is the mouth of God, the Only-begotten of the Father, the door to the Kingdom of Light. The opening verses of Saint John's Gospel are about the Word as the Eternal Christ which manifested in Jesus Christ and is to be manifested in us in time. It is speaking of both God and deified humanity. This ode is surely the words of Jesus or someone who in the earliest days of the Church attained to the same Christhood.

And the Most High hath given him to his worlds, (which are) the interpreters of his beauty, and the repeaters of his praise, and the confessors of his thought, and the heralds of his mind, and the chasteners of his servants.

In the Gloria of the Liberal Catholic Church we find these words: "O Lord Christ, alone-born of the Father; O Lord God, Indwelling Light, Son of the Father, Whose wisdom mightily and sweetly ordereth all things, pour forth Thy love: Thou Whose strength upholdeth and sustaineth all creation, receive our prayer; Thou Whose beauty shineth through the whole universe, unveil Thy glory." The worlds are the handiwork of the Only-Begotten of the Father, and like the words of all great men they are his praise, the revelations of his glory. God can be known to some extent from his creations. But the worlds are also the means of discipline and learning for us under the law of karma. There is no doubt that there are pain and suffering, but just as we learn not to touch fire because it hurts, in the same way we learn what to avoid as we move from life to life, and hopefully learn what to pursue. So these worlds serve to keep us in line and on the right track, eventually.

For the swiftness of the Word is inexpressible, and like his expression is his swiftness and his sharpness, and his course has no limit.

Both the Only-Begotten and his Word-Being are quick [*dzao*: living] and powerful in operation. So what is true of Ishwara, the Son of God, is true of the Divine Word. Both are limitless in their transformation of the creation and all the sentient beings within it. "For the word of God is quick [living: *dzao*], and powerful [*energes*: effectual], and sharper than any two-edged sword, piercing [*diikneomai*: penetrating] even to the dividing asunder of soul [*psychi*: psyche] and spirit [*pneuma*], and of the joints and marrow, and is a discerner of the thoughts and intents of the heart" (Hebrews 4:12). The Only-Begotten knows us, and the Divine Word reveals us to ourselves.

Never (doth the Word) fall, but ever it standeth; his descent and his way are incomprehensible.

The Only-Begotten is the supreme avatar (a Sanskrit word that means to come down, to descend.) That is, he "incarnates" in the creation. His descent and his way may be incomprehensible to us at the moment, but he has revealed both through the great masters of all ages, and if we follow their direction we shall ascend in that way and become ourselves all-comprehending sons of God.

For as his work is so is his expectation, for he is the light and the dawn of thought. The creation is itself the purpose of God: the liberation and enlightenment of all. Just as a person builds a factory because he intends to manufacture, in the same way the cosmos is a divine factory that produces sons of God. "For the earnest expectation of the creature [creation] waiteth for the manifestation of the sons of God.… Because the creature itself also shall be delivered from the bondage of corruption into the glorious liberty of the children of God" (Romans 8:19, 21). Both creation and those conscious entities within it are to be restored to the bosom of the Father (John 1:18), the Divine Being, for both are evolving under the call of the Son and the Holy Spirit. "And the Spirit and the bride say, Come. And let him that heareth say, Come. And let him that is athirst come. And whosoever will, let him take the water of life freely" (Revelation 22:17).

And in him the worlds spoke one to the other, and those that were silent acquired speech.

Even in the Old Testament there are many passages indicating that what is commonly called "dead matter" is both consciousness and will. How is this? Because all things are the Holy Spirit in manifestation. Therefore intelligence is inherent in the essence of all things. Since God is manifesting himself in and as all things, how could it be otherwise?

The idea of this verse is that all the worlds are integrated with one another, that they function in a cosmic synergy whose purpose is evolution, that they are conscious wombs that gestate the spirits incarnate in them and bring them to birth in a series of higher and higher worlds in a series of increasingly complex bodies which provide for them an increasingly wider scope of consciousness and mastery in those worlds.

The Byzantine Orthodox prayers of Matins often affirm that in the Holy Spirit the worlds are made alive and fulfilling the work of God: the manifestation of sentient beings as perfect sons of God. Such is not just the original Christian view of creation, but also that of the psalmists and prophets of Judaism.

And from him came love and concord, and they spoke one to the other that which they had (to tell).

Here we must remember that ultimately love is a divine force that draws a sentient being into union with the Supreme Being: not just nearness, but union in which distinction of being remains in perfect unity. We can guess at its nature, but human beings are presently unable to comprehend it intellectually. What we need is to evolve beyond the human condition.

The worlds "speak one to the other" in the communication necessary for the furtherance of the evolution of those within them. It is of course a metaphysical process which does not at all involve words, but creative impulses and interactions. Right now this is a mystery to us, but one which we can believe since the enlightened of all ages have assured us of its reality.

And they were goaded by the Word, and they knew him that made them, because they came into concord.

Working from within them, Christ the Word stimulates the worlds to come into perfect harmony with God, their Source. That is why Jesus taught: "The kingdom of heaven is like unto leaven, which a woman took, and hid in three measures of meal, till the whole was leavened" (Matthew 13:33). The three measures are the physical, astral and causal bodies of both the individual and the cosmos.

For the mouth of the Most High spoke to them, and the clarification of himself moved quickly by his hand.

It is a matter of divine revelation. As God said through the prophet: "So shall my word be that goeth forth out of my mouth: it shall not return unto me void, but it shall accomplish that which I please, and it shall prosper in the thing whereto I sent it" (Isaiah 55:11). From this as well as all the verses of this ode and all the other odes, we can see that original Jewish and Christian mysticism were nothing like those of today, but were identical with that of the sages of India which originally inspired and formed both religions.

For the dwelling-place of the Word is man, and his truth is love.

This does not say that man shall be the dwelling-place of the Word, but that man *is* Its dwelling-place. It is our eternal nature to embody the Word just as did Jesus and all the other great masters of human history. The truth of our being itself is God Who is Love (I John 4:8).

Blessed are they who by it have comprehended everything, and who have known the Lord by his truth.

God is himself the way to God. That is, in our meditation and throughout the day and night we must live in the consciousness of God, not prepare for it or be working up to it. To end with Spirit we must begin with Spirit. Then we can say with Saint Paul: "I know even as also I am known" (I Corinthians 13:12).

ODE 13

> Behold! the Lord is our mirror. Open (your) eyes and see them in him.
> And learn the manner of your face, and declare praises to his Spirit.
> And wipe off the filth from your face, and love his holiness and clothe yourselves therewith.
> And you will be without stain at all times with him. Alleluia.

Behold! the Lord is our mirror. Open (your) eyes and see them in him.

Here we see how incredibly far contemporary Christianity has drifted from Original Christianity, which was a firmly non-dual philosophy rooted in the enlightened consciousness of the Indian sages with whom Jesus lived for over half of his life before beginning his mission. It would seem that today the more "Christian" a person is, the less they have to do with the real Christ and his teachings.

Normally we think that the illumined mystic sees through or into the world around him and sees God. But the Isha Upanishad opens with the words: "[Know that] all this, whatever moves in this moving world, is enveloped by God." That is, we should be seeing God first and the world only secondarily. Instead of God being seen inside the world of matter, we should be seeing God as pervading the world and filling all space. Further, since we are eternally one with God, in him we see our true Self. We reflect him and he reflects us in perfect unity. If we see anything outside God it is unreal. Only when we open our spiritual eyes in God will we see things as they are.

And learn the manner of your face, and declare praises to his Spirit.

When we see divinity we see the reality of humanity, and see that our face is Brahmamayi–formed of God. Then we can really praise God, not as some mighty universal potentate but as Infinite Consciousness, Infinite Spirit of which we are an integral and inseparable part.

And wipe off the filth from your face, and love his holiness and clothe yourselves therewith.

We must remove all vestiges of relative, illusory existence from the face of our mind and clothe ourselves with the holiness that is God. Saint Paul was referring to this mystical reality when he wrote: "As many of you as have been baptized into Christ have put on Christ" (Galatians 3:27).

And you will be without stain at all times with him.

Awake in God we will be perpetually pure with his purity. There is no place here for the "poor miserable sinner" attitude of corrupted Christianity. "I have said, Ye are gods; and all of you are children of the most High" (Psalms 82:6), is the true Gospel of Christ, of "Christ in you, the hope of glory" (Colossians 1:27).

Ode 14

As the eyes of a son upon his father, so are my eyes, O Lord, at all times towards Thee.
For with Thee are my breasts and my pleasure.
Turn not away Thy mercy from me, O Lord, and take not Thy sweetness from me.
Stretch out to me my Lord at all times Thy right hand, and be my guide even to the end according to Thy will.
Let me be well-pleasing before Thee because of Thy glory, and because of Thy Name let me be saved from the Evil One.
And let Thy gentleness, O Lord, abide with me, and the fruits of thy love.
Teach me the Odes of Thy truth, that I may bring forth fruits in Thee.
And the harp of Thy Holy Spirit open to me, that with all [its] notes I may praise Thee, O Lord.
And according to the multitude of Thy mercies so shalt Thou give to me. And hasten to grant our petitions.
And Thou art able for all our needs. Alleluia.

As the eyes of a son upon his father, so are my eyes, O Lord, at all times towards Thee.

The son looks toward the father for many reasons which apply here. First, he does so because of his intimate connection with his father, which includes the fact of the father being the archetype of the son. This is why it is said in the East and Middle East that "the father is born in the son." Therefore the eyes of our soul and spirit are upon God because we are not creations, but offsprings (emanations) of the very being of God. God is the sun and we are the rays.

Ideally, the son looks to the father because he understands what is in the foregoing paragraph, and therefore looks to the father to see what he should be modeling himself upon, observing and imitating in order to unfold the inherent likeness to the father. It is so with each one of us and God. We are to be godlike and then become god. (Not God, but god: a perfect image-likeness.) We are meant to be on a finite scale just what God is on an infinite scale. We see few people attaining this, but how many are really trying, either in the right way or to the right degree? The fact still remains that is it our unalterable destiny.

The son looks toward the father because he desires a response from the father, a communication and a moving into a unity of life between himself and the father. It is the same with the individual spirit as it relates to the Cosmic Spirit. "Unto thee lift I up mine eyes, O thou that dwellest in the heavens. Behold, as the eyes of servants look unto the hand of their masters, and as the eyes of a maiden unto the hand of her mistress; so our eyes wait upon the Lord our God" (Psalms 123:1-2).

This is a familiar theme in the Bible:

"I waited patiently for the Lord; and he inclined unto me, and heard my cry. He brought me up also out of an horrible pit, out of the miry clay, and set my feet upon a rock, and established my goings. And he hath put a new song in my mouth, even praise unto our God" (Psalms 40:1-3).

"I wait for the Lord, my soul doth wait, and in his word do I hope. my soul waiteth for the Lord more than they that watch for the morning" (Psalms 130:5-6).

"The Lord is good unto them that wait for him, to the soul that seeketh him. It is good that a man should both hope and quietly wait for the salvation of the Lord" (Lamentations 3:25-26).

It is because we are eternally part of God that we ever look toward God in the essence of our being. Oneness with God is our whole being, therefore it is the prime subject that should occupy our thought and life.

For with Thee are my breasts and my pleasure.

Another translation (from *The Lost Books of the Bible and the Forgotten Books of Eden*) says: "For with thee are my consolations and my delight."

Only God can really soothe and calm the troubled soul to the extent that real healing and restoration take place and the soul becomes increasingly immune to all that troubles and distracts the ordinary person. In the same way, only communion with God gives real happiness or peace that keeps increasing to the point where nothing can disturb a continual state of joyful quiet in which the soul begins to permanently abide.

Turn not away Thy mercy from me, O Lord, and take not Thy sweetness from me.

This verse continues the idea of the previous one. We crave healing and peace and the blessed joy of continual contact with God.

It is an absolute necessity that the questing soul develops the conviction that only in God is there any fulfillment that can last and be meaningful. Being ourselves eternal beings, only Eternal Being can satisfy and glorify us. Jesus, our example, prayed: "O Father, glorify thou me with thine own self with the glory which I had with thee before the world was" (John 17:5). It is not heaven we should desire, but God alone.

Stretch out to me my Lord at all times Thy right hand, and be my guide even to the end according to Thy will.

Not remembering how we got into this mess (see *Robe of Light*), we have no idea how to get out. Therefore we need the guidance of God and our own awakened spirit to ascend the ladder of evolution "even to the end" in the attaining of Divine Consciousness which is the essence of our very existence. At the same time we need to heed the counsels of those great souls (mahatmas) who have gone on before us and reached the Goal. Daily we should be reading their biographies and words and applying them to our own lives. This is because it is God who guides us through those that show us the way by their example and teaching.

Let me be well-pleasing before Thee because of Thy glory, and because of Thy Name let me be saved from the Evil One.

We are part of God, and God's glory is within us, waiting for us to awaken, uncover and bring it forth into every atom of our life. True spiritual life has various aspects, but the most important is that which enables us to come into touch with our eternal spirit. And that is profound and continual meditation which enables us to maintain outside of meditation the state of consciousness produced by meditation. (See *Soham Yoga: The Yoga of the Self*.) May the awareness of God be so developed and established in us that no evil can touch us, not even the cosmic evil known as "Satan."

And let Thy gentleness, O Lord, abide with me, and the fruits of thy love.

The true spiritual ideal is not to be floating around in some exalted state of self-satisfaction, hoping that others will see and admire us and maybe even follow us, but rather that the qualities of God such as love and mercy will abound in us and bless those around us–that our mere presence will spread healing and awakening wherever we go. Many great souls are walking among us right now, changing lives by just being near us. They are never recognized by those they are blessing, but great change results from their presence. I have observed such people, even in places considered hopelessly negative, and spiritual friends have reported seeing them also.

Teach me the Odes of Thy truth, that I may bring forth fruits in Thee.

This verse is not referring to these Odes of Solomon, but is a petition for the same insight and inspiration that produced them. For this, no human teacher is possible. This is the direct teaching of Spirit to spirit, of God to us. When we have this divinely imparted knowledge, then we shall ourselves be trees of life in Paradise, bearing abundant fruit to the glory of God and the glorification of the world around us. For always there is the corollary: "Thy neighbour as thyself" (Matthew 19:19).

And the harp of Thy Holy Spirit open to me, that with all [its] notes I may praise Thee, O Lord.

The harp of the Holy Spirit is our inner being, the subtle levels we call spiritual "bodies." Through yoga meditation our inner spiritual machinery (*antahkarana*) comes into operation and we become of aware of it and develop it fully so we may use all its aspects ("notes") to praise God. We thereby become living harps of the Holy Spirit in the glorification of God.

And according to the multitude of Thy mercies so shalt Thou give to me. And hasten to grant our petitions.

It is God's will to bestow all these mercies and graces upon us, so we can be sure that we will receive them abundantly when we ask aright and prepare ourselves to be capable of receiving them. And it will not be lifetimes away, but the glory will begin even now. "O taste and see that the Lord is good" (Psalms 34:8).

And Thou art able for all our needs. God wills to do all good things for us, and is able to do all good things for us. "That ye may have lack of nothing.... And being fully persuaded that, what he had promised, he was able also to perform.... And this is the confidence that we have in him, that, if we ask any thing according to his will, he heareth us" (I Thessalonians 4:12; Romans 4:21; I John 5:14).

ODE 15

As the sun is the joy to them that seek its daybreak, so is my joy the Lord.
Because he is my Sun, and his rays have lifted me up, and his light hath dispelled all darkness from my face.
In him I have acquired eyes, and have seen his holy day.
Ears I have acquired, and I have heard his Truth.
The thought of knowledge I have acquired, and I have been delighted by him.
The way of error I have left, and I went towards him and have received Salvation from him abundantly.
And according to his bounty he hath given to me, and according to his excellent beauty he hath made me.
I have put on incorruption by means of his Name, and I have put off corruption by his grace.
Death hath been destroyed before my face, and Sheol hath been abolished by my word.
And there hath gone up deathless life in the Lord's land, and it hath become known to his faithful ones, and hath been given without stint to all those that trust in him. Alleluia.

As the sun is the joy to them that seek its daybreak, so is my joy the Lord.
To how many people is God really a joy, though he is said to be bliss (ananda) itself? He may be awesome and inspiring reverence and gratitude, but do people really rejoice in the Lord as their rising sun? Certainly many people rejoice in what God gives them and even in

the exalted feeling occurring in worship or the "high" produced by certain "yogic" techniques, but who rejoices in God and not just in what he gives?

As Yogananda said: "God is just as much a beggar as we are. He is begging for our attention. The Master of the Universe, who has everything–suns, moons, stars, worlds–quivering at the glance of His being, is begging for our love. He is running after the devotee and He is begging for the devotee's love. He is saying, 'Won't you give Me your love? Will you seek Me? Do you like Me better than all the things I have made for you?' But the devotee says, 'I am too busy now. I have work to do. I can't look after You.' And the Lord says, 'I will wait.'"

But this ode shows us that when for us God is the joy above all others, his advent in our consciousness is like the dawning of the sun beside which all else is darkness and emptiness. Then we have some relation with God and are on the path to liberation.

Because he is my Sun, and his rays have lifted me up, and his light hath dispelled all darkness from my face.

Water comes down to the earth in rain and then the sun draws them back upward into the heavens. In the same way we have come forth from God into this earthly life, and God is drawing us back to him, to our source. God alone has this power, and the more we align ourselves with God, especially through meditation, the more quickly will we return. Once we break through the clouds of material existence and experience, the divine light will dispel all darkness from our consciousness, our true face.

In him I have acquired eyes, and have seen his holy day.

Since "God is light and in him is no darkness at all" (I John 1:5), in him alone do we acquire eyes with which to see truly. In this world all we see are dreams, for God alone is Real. The holy day of God is the advent of God in our consciousness, just as the rising of the sun brings the day. How utterly different, even contradictory, is this view of spiritual life from that dispensed by the churches! Where is Christianity to be found at this point in time? Only where the message of Light and the means to rise into It are proclaimed. Hindu, Buddhist and Taoist teachers are far more of Christ than most Christian preachers and teachers. Only those who see the Day of God in their inmost depths are true believers, true theists.

Ears I have acquired, and I have heard his Truth. The thought of knowledge I have acquired, and I have been delighted by him.

In God alone is there true knowledge, and only through the ears of spiritual knowing, spiritual intuition, is he known. For truth is not just "of" God, God himself is Truth. And he is met face-to-face in meditation. Only when God is known can God be delighted in. So here we are given the how-to of the first verse.

The way of error I have left, and I went towards him and have received Salvation from him abundantly.

There are two "ways" in this world: the way that leads away from God consciousness and the way that leads toward God consciousness. Many who are walking away from God try to substitute religion, philosophy, philanthropy and the like, but only those who go toward him can ever reach him. John Oxenham wrote:

> To every man there openeth
> A Way, and Ways, and a Way,
> And the High Soul climbs the High Way,
> And the Low Soul gropes the Low,
> And in between, on the misty flats,
> The rest drift to and fro.
> But to every man there openeth
> A High Way, and a Low.
> And every man decideth
> The way his soul shall go.

We must see through the clouds of delusion and turn out of the way that led us into those clouds, into "the misty flats" where "the rest drift to and fro." Then we must "run with patience the race that is set before us" (Hebrews 12:1) and break out into Light that is God; for that alone is salvation which is infinite in its glory.

And according to his bounty he hath given to me, and according to his excellent beauty he hath made me.

Infinity is ours in God, and total transformation into the divine likeness.

I have put on incorruption by means of his Name, and I have put off corruption by his grace.

By continually uniting ourselves in ascending degrees with God through meditation and yogic disciplines, we can become as immortal as he, leaving change, decay, and death behind by his grace: the call upward to the divine revelation of "Christ in you, the hope of glory" (Colossians 1:27).

Death hath been destroyed before my face, and Sheol hath been abolished by my word.

"For this corruptible must put on incorruption, and this mortal must put on immortality. So when this corruptible shall have put on incorruption, and this mortal shall have put on immortality, then shall be brought to pass the saying that is written, Death is swallowed up in victory" (I Corinthians 15:53-54). "The sleep of death" (Psalms 13:3), the state of being unconscious of God in this world, the world of the dead, the grave of the spiritually unconscious, is to be awakened from in a moment like the temporary dream it really is.

And there hath gone up deathless life in the Lord's land, and it hath become known to his faithful ones, and hath been given without stint to all those that trust in him.

Immortality does not come from outside, but arises from within those whose enlightenment has made them "the Lord's land," the place of his abode. In this Light no shadows remain and nothing remains to be known or attained, for Infinity is from thenceforth their only dwelling for eternity.

ODE 16

As the work of the ploughman is the ploughshare, and the work of the helmsman is the steering of the ship, so also my work is the Psalm of the Lord in his praises.

My craft and my work are in his praises, because his love hath nourished my heart, and even to my lips he hath brought forth his fruits.

For my love is the Lord, and therefore I will sing unto him.

For I am made strong in his praise, and I have faith in him.

I will open my mouth, and his spirit will utter in me the glory of the Lord and his beauty,

The work of his hands and the labor of his fingers;

For the multitude of his mercies, and the strength of his Word.

For the Word of the Lord searches out the unseen thing, and scrutinizes his thought.

For the eye sees his works, and the ear hears his thought.

It is he who spread out the earth, and placed the waters in the sea.

He expanded the heavens, and fixed the stars.

And he fixed the creation and set it up, and he rested from his works.

And created things run in their courses, and work their works, and they know not how to stand still and to be idle.

And the hosts are subject to his Word.

The treasury of the light is the sun, and the treasury of the darkness is the night.

> And he made the sun for the day so that it will be light, but the night brings darkness over the face of the earth.
> And by their reception one from the other, they speak the beauty of God.
> And there is nothing that is outside of the Lord, for he was before anything came into being.
> And the Worlds were made by his Word, and by the thought of his heart.
> **Glory and Honor to his Name. Alleluia.**

As the work of the ploughman is the ploughshare, and the work of the helmsman is the steering of the ship, so also my work is the Psalm of the Lord in his praises.

To fix the mind on and in God is the purpose of life itself. Those who would truly live, not just rush around in distraction, can do so if they diligently apply themselves to the purification of their life and thought, especially through the practice of meditation. God is Life, and immersion of the consciousness in him is the way to really live life to the full.

My craft and my work are in his praises, because his love hath nourished my heart, and even to my lips he hath brought forth his fruits.

Applying our intelligence to every aspect of our life in order to conform them to our spiritual aspiration is also praise of God in action. It is the presence of divine love in our heart that brings us to life and inspires us to speak and live in the remembrance of God at all times. my first spiritual teacher was one of my aunts. One of her cousins said to her: "Some people talk about God some of the time, but you always speak about him." And that cousin had known her from birth. Regarding Saint John Maximovitch of San Francisco someone once said: "Archbishop John never begins to pray because he never stops praying at any time."

For my love is the Lord, and therefore I will sing unto him.

We only love what we know; therefore if we know God, even a bit, we will spontaneously love him, and our hearts will always sing the hymn of his love for us.

For I am made strong in his praise, and I have faith in him.

A friend of mine had a motto hanging on her wall: "I remember God and I live; I forget God and I die." This is absolutely true. To remember God is to be alive and to grow and evolve and become strong in our spirit. Then, being aware of his presence in and around us we will have the true faith that is really a manifestation of knowing the reality of God.

I will open my mouth, and his spirit will utter in me the glory of the Lord and his beauty.

The Holy Spirit of God moving within us as the Water of Life will raise our awareness to him, and will speak in us the glory of God and show us his beauty.

The work of his hands and the labor of his fingers.

Everywhere the awakened seeker sees the hand of God and his continual action within and without.

For the multitude of his mercies, and the strength of his Word.

All that God does is motivated by love and mercy; he reveals to us his purpose and plan, his Word, and we become strong in loving and following it.

For the Word of the Lord searches out the unseen thing, and scrutinizes his thought.

The Word of the Lord is the revelation of the Lord within our consciousness, revealing to us that which none but those with opened inner eyes can see. And that includes the thought of God toward us and all sentient beings. Life itself is a vast panorama of sentient beings moving upward to the goal of conscious union with God.

For the eye sees his works, and the ear hears his thought.

It is the inner eyes and ears that the odist speaks of here, the eyes and ears of the spirit. This is a foreshadowing of the state of union with God.

It is he who spread out the earth, and placed the waters in the sea. He expanded the heavens, and fixed the stars. And he fixed the creation and set it up, and he rested from his works.

The inner secret of all this is that the creation is really the Eternal God in extension, in manifestation. He alone is. And best of all, we are the most important of his works for we are part of him.

And created things run in their courses, and work their works, and they know not how to stand still and to be idle.

Since we, too, are his manifestation, we should always be "running in our course" by following the divine plan and ever evolving toward "the manifestation of the sons of God" (Romans 8:19), that is our work. Because this is such a great, virtually infinite destiny, we must never stand still or be idle, but ever run "the race that is set before us" (Hebrews 12:1). For the race ends in God.

And the hosts are subject to his Word.

"For while all things were in quiet silence, and that night was in the midst of her swift course, thine Almighty word leaped down from heaven out of thy royal throne, as a fierce man of war into the midst of a land of destruction, and brought thine unfeigned commandment as a sharp sword, and standing up filled all things with death; and it touched the heaven, but it stood upon the earth" (Wisdom 18:14-16). This Word is the divine will and intention of God for the creation and all things within it. It is the entire divine plan for the evolution of the universe. The angels, being wise and more highly evolved than us, are ever in conformity with that plan, and we, being blind and ignorant, are usually in conflict with it. But if we intend to evolve beyond this human condition into the angelic realms we must right now do everything we can to embody the divine will and word: "Ye are gods" (Psalms 82:6; John 10:34).

The treasury of the light is the sun, and the treasury of the darkness is the night. And he made the sun for the day so that it will be light, but the night brings darkness over the face of the earth. And by their reception one from the other, they speak the beauty of God.

It is commonly thought that light is good and darkness is bad, but both are of positive value, and their alteration is necessary for evolution. Both are of benefit to sentient beings and are fundamental to their well-being.

And there is nothing that is outside of the Lord, for he was before anything came into being.

There is no such thing as separation from God, only the illusion of separation. Therefore any attempt to reconcile ourselves with God, to "reach" him or "find" him is doomed to failure or further delusion, because separation does not exist. What we need is to awaken to the reality of the situation.

In the Bible the prophet Isaiah, a prior incarnation of Jesus, expresses this very well, just as do the sages of India: "Behold, the Lord's hand is not shortened, that it cannot save; neither his ear heavy, that it cannot hear: But your iniquities have separated between you and your God, and your sins have hid his face from you" (Isaiah 59:1-2). The word translated "separated" is *badal*, which means to produce a difference, a dual consciousness that divides what is one into the semblance of many. It also means to alienate the consciousness. That is why people in the grip of delusion continually say: "It is *my* life; I will do with it what *I* please." Such people are very big on independence and self-sufficiency, not in the positive sense but in the sense of selfishness and ego-domination. As a result the truth of things is hidden from us. The word translated "hid" is *cathar*, which means to hide, conceal and close away. The fact that this is a delusion in no way alleviates the terrible consequences of this blindness of heart. That is why religiosity accomplishes nothing; yoga is the prime essential.

And the Worlds were made by his Word, and by the thought of his heart.

The entire creation is the Thought of God, the "Dream" of God. So also is our presence within it. As Poe said in one of his poems: "All that we see or seem is but a dream within a dream." That is why David, another previous incarnation of Jesus, sang: "As for me, I will behold thy face in righteousness: I shall be satisfied, when I awake, with thy likeness" (Psalms 17:15). And simply: "When I awake, I am still with thee" (Psalms 139:18).

Glory and Honor to his Name.

As Bishop Wedgwood told a choir that was rehearsing the *Gloria* for Mass: "*Be yourself* that glory that is offered to 'God In The Highest.'"

Ode 17

Then I was crowned by my God, and my crown is living.
And I was justified by my Lord, for my salvation is incorruptible.
I was loosed from vanities, and am not condemned.
My choking bonds were cut off by his hands; I received the face and the likeness of a new person, and I walked in him and was saved.
And the thought of truth led me, and I walked after it and did not wander.
And all that have seen me were amazed, and I was supposed by them to be a stranger.
And he Who knew and brought me up, is the Most High in all his perfection.
And he glorified me by his kindness, and raised my mind to the height of Truth.
And from thence he gave me the way of his steps, and I opened the doors that were closed.
And I broke in pieces the bars of iron, for my own iron (bonds) grew hot and melted before me.
And nothing appeared as closed to me, because I was the opening of everything.
And I went towards all my bondsmen to loose them, that I might not leave any man bound or binding.
And I gave my knowledge without grudging, and my prayer through my love.
And I sowed my fruits in hearts, and transformed them through Myself.

And they received my blessing and lived, and they were gathered
 to me and were saved.
Because they became my members, and I was their head.
Glory to Thee our head, O Lord Messiah. Alleluia.

Then I was crowned by my God, and my crown is living.
This takes us right back to the very first Ode:

The Lord is on my head like a crown, and I shall not be without him.
They wove for me a crown of truth, and it caused Thy branches to
 bud in me.
For it is not like a withered crown which buddeth not.
But Thou livest upon my head, and Thou hast blossomed upon me.
Thy fruits are full-grown and perfect; they are full of Thy salvation.

So we will examine this Ode keeping the first in mind as the theme-setter for the entire series of Odes.

And I was justified by my Lord, for my salvation is incorruptible.

Salvation (*sotiria*) is a state, not an event or a reward. Rather, it is our eternal nature. Therefore there is no question of our being acceptable to God when we seek to regain awareness of that nature. Nor is there any such thing as God being pleased or displeased with us, since his nature, like ours, is unchanging. Saint James described him as "the Father of lights, with whom is no variableness, neither shadow of turning" (James 1:17). Therefore our justification by the Lord is absolutely assured. All we need do is turn our will in the right direction and pursue it.

I was loosed from vanities, and am not condemned.

The odist was loosed from the vanities of ignorance and folly when he turned himself around and, like Buddha said, beheld the "other shore" of enlightenment and went toward it. There was no condemnation directed toward him, because he was leaving behind all that was reprehensible in his past. As the Bhagavad Gita says: "If even an evildoer worships me single-heartedly, he should be considered righteous, for truly he has rightly resolved. Quickly he becomes a virtuous soul and goes to everlasting peace. Understand: no devotee of me is ever lost" (Bhagavad Gita 9:30-31).

Sin and ignorance, the root of sin, are only overlays, not our true nature. Therefore they are essentially illusions; how can they mean anything to God? He knows what we truly are because we are part of him.

My choking bonds were cut off by his hands.

All that binds us stifles us, paralyzing and blinding us. In that condition what hope have we? Utter confusion is our continual state. But when we turn back to our divine origin and move ever deeper into that Light, all our bonds are dissolved like the dreams they really are. It is our consciousness of Spirit that frees us. That is why we are yogis. Yoga is the path of restoration through awareness of our own and God's reality.

I received the face and the likeness of a new person.

In the growing consciousness of our spirit within the Supreme Spirit we are renewed.

"Ye have put off the old man with his deeds; and have put on the new man, which is renewed in knowledge after the image of him that created him" (Colossians 3:9-10).

"Be renewed in the spirit of your mind; and put on the new man, which after [the likeness of] God is created in righteousness and true holiness" (Ephesians 4:23-24).

"Be ye transformed by the renewing of your mind" (Romans 12:2).

"If any man be in Christ, he is a new creature: old things are passed away; behold, all things are become new" (II Corinthians 5:17).

"He that sat on the throne said, Behold, I make all things new" (Revelation 21:5).

This renewal is a restoration of our original consciousness in order that we may begin evolving from that point unto the revelation of our innate divinity.

I walked in him and was saved.

Living in the consciousness of God and living in the world as a god, we are truly saved: delivered from ignorance and mortality.

And the thought of truth led me, and I walked after it and did not wander.

We must to the best of our ability fix firmly in our mind the truth as we understand it, and then we must conform our entire life, thought and actions, to it. This must be done without wavering or any break in our application to its realization. Then we shall undoubtedly succeed in our pursuit.

And all that have seen me were amazed, and I was supposed by them to be a stranger.

This is the experience of all who seriously and effectively strive to attain the highest. First there is shock and disbelief that they could possibly be serious and "believe all that" and "think all that is necessary." Then come the accusations of negative change and no longer being the person formerly known by the accusers. Hypnotism, brainwashing and even drugs are bandied about as the cause, of course, with speculation as to who had influenced them so. (Credit is never given to the accused of having any ideas of their own.) Threats of disowning and expelling them from the family or group naturally follow. Get ready. In time it will all seem rather sad and at the same time rather funny.

And he Who knew and brought me up, is the Most High in all his perfection.

This we must realize: it is God who calls us to higher life and helps us along the path to conscious eternal life. As Patanjali says, God is the Teacher (Guru) of all human beings (Yoga Suras 1:26). No external teacher can substitute, though God can certainly use them to help us. We need not doubt or fear when "the Most High in all his perfection" is our guide.

And he glorified me by his kindness, and raised my mind to the height of Truth.

In loving-kindness God has already made the way for us to ascend "to the height of Truth." He has set his divine seal upon it, and our success is assured.

And from thence he gave me the way of his steps, and I opened the doors that were closed.

Yoga is such an essential of spiritual life because it is the only direct and sure means of elevating our consciousness and refining (evolving) the mind. Spiritual life can only be guessed at by an earthbound mind, however good the intentions may be. Just as from a mountaintop we can see the surrounding area, so only from a high level of consciousness can we comprehend either the ways of God or our way to God. Intellectual insight is certainly a blessing in spiritual life, but it is even more necessary to open the doors of inner perception to intelligently and effectively carry on the spiritual life. Opening those doors is the true beginning of our pathway to God-realization.

And I broke in pieces the bars of iron, for my own iron (bonds) grew hot and melted before me.

This is very important: we bound ourselves, no one else, and we must free ourselves. With the same will with which we put on the shackles, we must break them off. It both can and must be done. This is part of what it takes to be a true Master. How do the bonds grow hot and melt away? Through *tapasya*: spiritual discipline and practice. In Sanskrit *tapasya* means "the generation of heat." We must burn the seeds of karma and their binding power in the fires of yoga, of God-consciousness. "For our God is a consuming fire" (Hebrews 12:29).

And nothing appeared as closed to me, because I was the opening of everything. Here is another tremendously important truth: All things are open to him who abides in the consciousness of the Self and sees as the Self sees. To him there will be no mysteries in the universe because he has solved the supreme mystery: Self-knowledge.

See how identical the teachings of these first hymns of Christianity, some of them such as this one perhaps authored by Jesus himself, are with the teachings of the Gita and the Upanishads. (See *The Bhagavad Gita For Awakening* and *The Upanishads For Awakening*.) These odes themselves are proof that original Christianity was really the Sanatana Dharma of India. Those who would truly follow Jesus will adopt and follow his religion: the Eternal Dharma of the sages of India. (See *The Christ of India*.)

And I went towards all my bondsmen to loose them, that I might not leave any man bound or binding.

Liberation (moksha) is not abstract. It is realized and demonstrated on all levels, including the most practical and objective. All the aspects of our being and existence, our "bondsmen," are loosed when we ourselves become truly free. If a single aspect of our makeup remains bound, then the whole of us is still bound.

Unhappily there are many illusions and delusions about spiritual progress and liberation. The test of the reality of our freedom is our ability to truly be free outwardly as well as inwardly. I have met a lot of deluded yogis and gurus that were total wrecks but so clouded by their illusions that they could not see their sad state. Many false yoga practices cause such illusions, and most others are worthless. Few things are more perilous than the decision to become a yogi and learn meditation. That is a terrible thing to have to say, but it only reflects the truth of the situation.

And I gave my knowledge without grudging, and my prayer through my love.

"Jesus said unto him, Thou shalt love the Lord thy God with all thy heart, and with all thy soul, and with all thy mind. This is the first and great commandment. And the second is like unto it, Thou shalt love thy neighbour as thyself" (Matthew 22:37-39). Having become established in the knowledge of the Self, the enlightened person then begins to enlighten others by sharing his knowledge of the way to self-realization. Loving all beings, he prays for their welfare fervently. We see this is the examples of all the saints and masters.

And I sowed my fruits in hearts, and transformed them through Myself. And they received my blessing and lived, and they were gathered to me and were saved. Because they became my members, and I was their head.

These certainly sound like the words Jesus would have written, but they can be said by all the anointed saviors that have arisen throughout the history of the world. Those who take refuge with such true way-showers and follow their example and teachings will attain the same spiritual status as theirs.

Glory to Thee our head, O Lord Messiah.

Either this is an exclamation added by Christians to what they considered were the words of the Lord Jesus, or are an acclamation addressed to the Christ, the Only-begotten Son, who is the prototype of all Christs of earth. In *The Aquarian Gospel of Jesus the Christ* we find the correct teachings of Jesus regarding the Cosmic Christ and an individual Christ. For example, in one place he says: "Men call me Christ, and God has recognized the name; but Christ is not a man. The Christ is universal love, and Love is king. This Jesus is but man who has been fitted by temptations overcome, by trials multiform, to be the temple through which Christ can manifest to men. Then hear, you men of Israel, hear! Look not upon the flesh; it is not king. Look to the Christ within, who shall be formed in every one of you, as he is formed in me" (Aquarian Gospel 68).

ODE 18

My heart was lifted up and enriched in the love of the Most High, that I might praise him by my name.

My members were strengthened, that they might not fall from his power.

Sickness removed from my body, and it stood firm for the Lord by his will; for his kingdom is firm.

O Lord, for the sake of them that are deficient, do not cast off from me Thy Word.

Nor for the sake of their works do Thou withhold from me Thy perfection.

Let not the light be conquered by the darkness, nor let truth flee away from falsehood.

Let Thy right hand bring our salvation to victory, and receive from all quarters, and preserve (us) from all who are held in bonds.

Thou art my God—falsehood and death are not in Thy mouth, only perfection is Thy will.

And vanity Thou knowest not, for neither doth it know Thee.

And error Thou knowest not, for neither doth it know Thee.

And ignorance appeared like dust, and like the scum of the sea.

And vain people supposed that it was great, and they came to resemble it and became empty.

And those who knew understood and meditated and were unpolluted in their meditations, because they were in the mind of the Most High.

And they mocked those who were walking in error.
Then they spoke the truth, from the inspiration which the Most high breathed into them.
Praise and great beauty to his Name. Alleluia.

My heart was lifted up and enriched in the love of the Most High, that I might praise him by my name.

In every traditional liturgy, whatever the form, there is always a point before the Sanctus ("Holy, holy, holy,...") when the celebrant calls out to the people: "Lift up your hearts." Spiritual laziness (rooted in spiritual indifference) wants God to come down to us, but the whole idea of all authentic religion is our elevation for the purpose of communion with God. So even though the Holy Eucharist is a descent of the divine upon the earth, we are exhorted to continually lift our consciousness into the heights, into the Light of the Son (and sons) of God which is our true home, our intended dwelling-place for eternity.

How is this done? By purifying our entire being and entering our inmost Self where we can commune with God directly. Meditation is the process of both purification and entry: meditation supported by the purification and conformity of all the external aspects of our existence to the laws of God. Without this purification spiritual life is impossible.

This elevation of our awareness will result in increase of love for God and the ability to make our life an entire hymn of praise to him. Obviously this can only be done when God is the prime focus of our entire life at all times.

My members were strengthened, that they might not fall from his power.

This is very important to know: right meditation makes us stronger and more stable, not over-sensitive, fragile and incapable of meeting life head-on successfully. Because of the negative religious currents of both East and West, it is common for people to think that spiritual people are unworldly and even anti-world, needing to keep away from nearly everything and live withdrawn and indrawn: spiritually inbred. It is also considered that incompetence is somehow a mark of spirituality, as is poverty and shabbiness. This is completely wrong, and opposite to the truth.

Spiritual life makes us able to hold firmly to the life of the spirit which is the life of power, because all power emanates from spirit. If we look at the genuine saints of all traditions we will see that they accomplished far more than ordinary people, and their influence continues after their earthly life for centuries and even millennia. They were extremely active and creative in their action. Further, they kept going until the end, never letting up or retiring. We must be and do the same.

Sickness removed from my body, and it stood firm for the Lord by his will; for his kingdom is firm.

Here is another common myth exploded. Saints do not languish and suffer, feeble and holding to life by a frayed thread. There have been exceptions, but the majority of saints, even if ill, are filled with vigor and free from weakness. Their bodies are vessels of the power of God. God is not weak and ineffectual, so it is not godly to be so ourselves.

I can tell you from decades of experience that right meditation is the supreme corrective and healer. Weakness and illness are banished by prolonged meditation practice. I have never seen authentic meditation weaken or waste the body: just the opposite.

Healing and health are indications of spiritual life. I know that religions like to hold the opposite view because their negativity produces misery and suffering, which they claim ennobles the human being, but this is just a cover for the truth that they are false, worthless and even destructive. Jesus said: "Beware of false prophets, which come to you in sheep's clothing, but inwardly they are ravening wolves. Ye shall know them by their fruits. Do men gather grapes of thorns, or figs of thistles? Even so every good tree bringeth forth good fruit; but a corrupt tree bringeth forth evil fruit. A good tree cannot bring forth evil fruit, neither can a corrupt tree bring forth good fruit. Every tree that bringeth not forth good fruit is hewn down, and cast into the fire. Wherefore by their fruits ye shall know them" (Matthew 7:15-20).

After having healed the man at the pool of Bethesda, "afterward Jesus found him in the temple, and said to him, See, you have been made well. Sin no more, lest a worse thing come unto you" (John 5:14). This indicates that physical illness and deficiency come from personal negativity. Spiritual life, however, is a life of purification and therefore frees us from the effects of negativity. There is no virtue in the continued results of sin: indeed it is impossible for those correctly treading the spiritual path. True religion frees from sin and therefore from sickness and limitation.

O Lord, for the sake of them that are deficient, do not cast off from me Thy Word. Nor for the sake of their works, do Thou withhold from me Thy perfection.

Now we come to the hazards of dealing with spiritually incompetent people. Sri Ramakrishna said that we can exhaust all our spiritual resources just getting unqualified people to take up spiritual life, and then they will fall back into their former condition, leaving us devoid of the inner strength we expended on them. Association with the unfit can render us unfit. So the odist prays not to fall into the pit along with the unworthy he might try to help. All viable spiritual traditions tell us to be careful in our dealings with others that are unfit for spiritual life. The best thing for them and us is to leave them alone. As the prophet said: "Ephraim is joined to idols: let him alone" (Hosea 4:17). Jesus agreed, saying: "Give not that which is holy unto the dogs, neither cast ye your pearls before swine, lest they trample them under their feet, and turn again and rend you" (Matthew 7:6).

Let not the light be conquered by the darkness, nor let truth flee away from falsehood.

This is a serious insight. The light we possess can be conquered by darkness if we do not firmly hold to it. Further, the truth we now know can be vanquished by falsehood if we accede to it and do not resist it. I have seen this throughout my life: people's "light" being extinguished by turning back to their former darkness, forgetting the truth they had learned and returning to their discarded ignorance and delusion.

Let Thy right hand bring our salvation to victory, and receive from all quarters, and preserve (us) from all who are held in bonds.

Spiritual life in all its forms is essentially the invoking of the divine Light which is our only true nature. It is this Light and its inherent power that is the right hand of God. By attuning ourselves to it and being filled with it ever more and more, the spiritual growth we have attained will ultimately result in permanent victory over all that covers and hinders our innate divinity. "For this corruptible must put on incorruption, and this mortal must put on immortality. So when this corruptible shall have put on incorruption, and this mortal shall have put on immortality, then shall be brought to pass the saying that is written, Death is swallowed up in victory.… Thanks be to God, which giveth us the victory through our Lord Jesus Christ. Therefore, my beloved brethren, be ye stedfast, unmoveable, always abounding in the work of the Lord, forasmuch as ye know that your labour is not in vain in the Lord" (I Corinthians 15:53-54, 57-58).

Even more, this divine Light draws more light to itself and therefore to us "from all quarters," ever increasing our spiritual strength. We need to be strong to be safe from the onslaughts of all the forces of bondage and those that are enslaved by them. For it is a fact that to ascend in consciousness we must overcome the gravitational pull of ignorance and bondage that prevails in ourselves and others. We will be opposed by our own inner negativity and that of the world and those who are in bondage to it. And of those who are not strong and vigilant it will be as Saint Peter wrote: "It is happened unto them according to the true proverb, The dog is turned to his own vomit again; and the sow that was washed to her wallowing in the mire" (II Peter 2:22). All the whining and accusation in the world on their part cannot cover up this simple fact: They are back in the mud. (And maybe never really got out of it.)

The word *dioko* that is translated "persecution" means that which is intended to overcome and pressure us into failure and defeat through surrender of our ideals and our adherence to them. This comes in many forms and in many manners. But come it does, we can be assured. However, "in all these things we are more than conquerors" (Romans 8:37) if we persevere in our pursuit of higher consciousness.

It is a plain fact that those who are bondservants of ignorance and illusion are oftentimes bitter and determined opponents of those who seek to be free. They do not enter into the kingdom of light and do all they can to prevent the entry of others (Matthew 23:13). Jesus told his disciples: "If the world hate you, ye know that it hated me before it hated you" (John 15:18). And the Beloved Disciple: "Cain slew his brother because his own works were evil, and his brother's righteous. Marvel not, my brethren, if the world hate you" (I John 3:12-13). So we will be in good company. However, we should mind our own business and do our best, not seeking the opposition of those of a different cast of mind. As Saint Paul counsels us: "If it be possible, as much as lieth in you, live peaceably with all men" (Romans 12:18).

Thou art my God–falsehood and death are not in Thy mouth, only perfection is Thy will.

Here is an amazing principle: falsehood in any form is equated with death. Why? Because we will forfeit our spiritual life if we are not honest and forthright at all times, including our resistance to opposition from the children of darkness who detest the children of light.

Nothing should deflect us from the divine purpose for us. "For this is the will of God, even your sanctification" (I Thessalonians 4:3). "As he which hath called you is holy, so be ye holy in all manner of conversation; Because it is written, Be ye holy; for I am holy" (I Peter 1:15-16).

And vanity Thou knowest not, for neither doth it know Thee.

"Vanity" is translated from four words in the Bible: three Hebrew and one Greek. *Hebel* means that which is totally insubstantial like mist. *Shav* means that which is empty and therefore false, nothingness in the absolute sense. *Reek* means that which is empty, to no purpose, idle and vain. *Mataiotes* means that which is devoid of truth and therefore insubstantial and thoroughly weak. Frankly, all these are applicable to our illusions and delusions as well as to the world of ignorance and evil. Those who cling to vanity and abide in it as a mode of life and thought cannot know the Reality which is God.

And error Thou knowest not, for neither doth it know Thee.

"Error" is translated from six words in the Bible: five Hebrew and one Greek. *Shal* means something that is both a mistake and a fault. *Meshugah* means to stray. *Shegagah* means ignorance and unawareness. *Towah* means hindrance, wandering, and confusion. *Shaluw* means failure and neglect. *Plane* means deceit, deception, delusion, straying and wandering about, and wrong opinion which leads into error, deceit or fraud. As Isaiah said: "All we like sheep have gone astray; we have turned every one to his own way" (Isaiah 53:6) rather than the way of God.

The ordinary human condition is one of confusion, delusion, illusion, self-deception and outright unconsciousness. In fact the human condition can be summed up in a single word: unconscious. Since a human being does not know himself, there is no hope of his knowing God, or even having a right idea about God, his nature, his purpose for mankind and his relationship to humanity. This is not a criticism but a lament, for Western religion does nothing but compound the tragedy, and Eastern religion often does little to alleviate the situation. This is why Jesus said that few would be saved. "Many, I say unto you, will seek to enter in, and shall not be able" (Luke 13:24) due to the prevailing condition of man. He did not mean that ultimately only few would be saved, for it was a fundamental tenet of original Christianity that all will eventually be saved, but that at this point in the evolutionary cycle of humanity in general only a comparatively few at a time are escaping the grinding wheel of rebirth.

And ignorance appeared like dust, and like the scum of the sea.

The happy aspect of this is the fact that dust and scum are only overlays, not part of what they overlie. Therefore ignorance obscures our vision but cannot obliterate our sight. All that is needed, then, is for the dust and scum to be cleared away and the innate perfection and awareness is made manifest. No matter how terrible the condition of man and society may be, it never is the reality, only the appearance. This is is why yoga meditation is the hope of the world, for it reveals the truth of ourselves to us. We do not need a voice from heaven, a new scripture or another teacher. We only need Self-knowledge. Then freedom is gained.

And vain people supposed that it was great, and they came to resemble it and became empty.

Someone once said: "The trouble with ignorance is that it picks up confidence as it goes along." This is nowhere more evident than in religion. The less people know, the more they think they know; the less they have a reason to believe, the more confident they are. It is a colossal monument to a colossal egotism equaled only by its ignorance. The more false a thing is the more the ignorant love it, and the more foolish a thing is the more the ignorant pursue it. We have actually come to a point in time where really good frauds are never successful, but the cheap, silly and obvious frauds are acclaimed on all sides. Only "bad acts" are acceptable, and trash of all sorts is tremendously popular.

Speaking of reputation and fame, Jesus said: "These are but worthless baubles of the day; they rise and sink, like empty bottles on a stream; they are illusions and will pass away; they are the indices to what the thoughtless think; they are the noise that people make; and shallow men judge merit by noise" (Aquarian Gospel 27:8-9).

Just as there will always be those who prefer the fake to the genuine, so it will be in spiritual matters. People may be deluded, but they have an unerring sense of the true and the false: they avoid the true and flock to the false. It is very much like *Lady From Lisbon*, a motion picture made in the 1940's. The "Lady" was the Mona Lisa which had been stolen from the Louvre during the upheavals of the Second World War. The thieves took it to Lisbon where people were able to travel freely, usually to the Western hemisphere. Once the news of the theft went out, several people made fake copies of the Mona Lisa and also came to Lisbon to sell them. Every one of the fakes sold readily, but no one would buy the real item. The reason? It looked fake to the prospective buyers, and the fakes looked real. In the photographic negative of an object the light areas are dark and the dark areas are light. The same is true in the judgment of negative, ignorant people. You can judge something by their reaction to it, knowing that the truth will be exactly the opposite to their opinion. Popularity and "public confidence" truly are only "the noise that people make." And it is also true that "shallow men judge merit by noise."

And those who knew understood and meditated and were unpolluted in their meditations, because they were in the mind of the Most High.

Here we find the contrast made between the knowers (gnostics) and the unknowers (agnostics). The ignorant idolize their ignorance and do everything they can to confirm and increase it. The gnostics do the same in relation to true knowledge, especially by meditation which elevates their consciousness above the ordinary levels into the Light that is the "mind of the Most High." Thus their minds become purified from the darkness of ignorance and they "walk in the light of the Lord" (Isaiah 2:5).

And they mocked those who were walking in error.

The wise do not despise the ignorant, for they, too, were once as they, but they do point out their folly. Sri Ramakrishna used to make very funny jokes about those who were devoid of spiritual wisdom, but he loved them.

Then they spoke the truth, from the inspiration which the Most High breathed into them.

Illumined by their meditation, the wise can speak the truth; not from mere intellect, but "from the inspiration which the Most High breathed into them" in meditation.

Praise and great beauty to his Name. Certainly this is the response of those who follow the ways of the wise and come to know the Most High.

Ode 19

A cup of milk was offered to me, and I drank it in the sweetness of the delight of the Lord.
The Son is the cup, and he who was milked is the Father, and the Holy Spirit is She Who milked him.
Because his breasts were full, and it was not desirable that his milk should be spilt to no purpose.
And the Holy Spirit opened her bosom, and mingled the milk of the two breasts of the Father.
And She gave the mixture to the world without their knowing, and those who take it are in the fulness of the right hand.
The womb of the Virgin took it, and She received conception and brought forth.
And the Virgin became a mother with great mercies.
And She labored and bore the Son but without pain, for it did not happen without purpose.
And She had not required a midwife, because he caused her to give life.
And She brought forth as a man by her own will, and She bore according to the manifestation, and acquired with great power.
And She loved with redemption, and guarded with kindness, and declared with grandeur. Alleluia.

A cup of milk was offered to me, and I drank it in the sweetness of the delight of the Lord.

It was the practice of the early Christian Church to give the newly-baptized a cup of milk mixed with honey to drink as a symbol of the new and continuing life given them in baptism and the sweetness that would be theirs as they advanced in it, "from glory to glory, even as by the Spirit of the Lord" (II Corinthians 3:18).

At every moment we live in God and draw upon his infinite Life, making it our individual, finite life. The more consciously we do this, the greater our happiness will be.

The Son is the cup, and he who was milked is the Father, and the Holy Spirit is She Who milked him.

In his essential being God is transcendent; so to communicate himself to us he has expanded or emanated himself as both the creation and the guiding intelligence within it. These are the Holy Spirit and the Son. Having entered into this creation for the purpose of spiritual evolution we are living on and in the Life of the Father through our connection with the Son, who therefore is called "the Cup." To partake of this life we have taken on many layers or "bodies" of relative existence formed of the vibrating Light that is the Holy Spirit. Our consciousness lives in the Son and our bodies live in the Holy Spirit, are actually formed of her Divine Light. Since the Life of the Father is conveyed to us through the Holy Spirit, the author of this ode says she "milks" him.

Because his breasts were full, and it was not desirable that his milk should be spilt to no purpose. And the Holy Spirit opened her bosom, and mingled the milk of the two breasts of the Father.

The Son and the Holy Spirit are "the two breasts of the Father," full of his Life in a mode that can be communicated to all evolving, sentient beings. But it is the Holy Spirit who causes us to drink of that Life by means of our evolving bodies.

And She gave the mixture to the world without their knowing, and those who take it are in the fulness of the right hand.

All sentient beings live on and in the Life of God, most of them being unaware of that. But those evolved enough to "take" in that Life consciously and intentionally are gods within God, "in the fulness of the right hand" of God, the evolutionary stream that is flowing upward back to the transcendent "bosom of the Father" (John 1:18) which is the state of perfect reunion with the Father. For, all of us being "sons" of the Father, we have come forth from him. But "Deep calleth unto deep" (Psalms 42:7). The Infinite perpetually calls out to the finite: "Return, ye children of men" (Psalms 90:3). This is the impulse of universal evolution, the "right hand" of God.

Now we are going to have to consider two very different manifestations of the divine Life. It is very obvious that the Odes of Solomon are not just the earliest hymns of Christianity, they are definitely in the Gnostic, the mystical and esoteric, tradition of Christianity. In Gnostic Christian writings there are references to the Virgin of Light, the living, conscious creation that is a manifestation of the Holy Spirit and *is* the Holy Spirit. However, the Virgin is an aspect of the Holy Spirit, not the infinite totality of the Holy Spirit. So we need to avoid confusion in this matter. Also the rest of the verses of this Ode certainly apply to the Virgin Mary, the perfect image of the Holy Spirit Mother, just as Jesus was the perfect image of the Son of the Father, Ishwara. So we will be considering the ode's application to both the Life of the Universe and the virgin mother of Jesus.

The womb of the Virgin took it, and She received conception and brought forth.

The will of the Father is reflected in the cosmos which "takes" it and in response shapes itself according to the plan of evolution. The story of the cosmos is the story of unfolding evolution.

Various spiritual traditions tell us that originally human beings were "mind-born," they were conceived through the spiritual power and will-intention of both father and mother. It was the same with the Virgin Mary at the time of Jesus' conception, except it was a co-operation of humanity and divinity. This was necessary because Jesus himself was going to be both divine and human, manifesting divinity and humanity in his incarnation to a unique degree because of the purpose of his advent among humanity, which was to be both savior of humanity and savior of the world.

It is important for us to keep in mind that Jesus was not born mechanically through the Virgin, nor was she just one of many who could have been the mother of the Messiah. She possessed unique development, intelligence and will to fulfill her purpose. She herself had been conceived super-normally, although her father was human, each of her parents being sages honored among the Essenes. (See *Robe of Light*.) Jesus and Mary were both one-of-a-kind in the entire realm of relative existence.

And the Virgin became a mother with great mercies.

The universe is the embodiment of divine mercies extended to all sentient beings, for without the universe there would be no field of energies within which their vehicles and consciousnesses could evolve.

The Virgin Mary is called Mother of Mercies because of the tremendous blessing and potential brought into the world through Jesus. Furthermore, she continues to actively impart those mercies in union with Jesus, so in the Western Church she has been recognized as co-redemptress of the world. This is extremely significant.

And She labored and bore the Son but without pain, for it did not happen without purpose.

This is a very interesting statement, for it implies that pain is a result of disharmony with the divine/cosmic purpose, that wherever there is suffering it is an indication of some violation or opposition of divine law. The common adage "No Pain, No Gain" is true only within an all-embracing condition of being out of sync with God and divine order. The cessation of suffering can be accomplished through complete conformity with the inner and outer spiritual principles and laws. That which fulfills the eternal purpose of all things will always be free of conflict and pain. Since the Virgin Mary was fulfilling the divine intention, her giving birth was totally painless.

And She had not required a midwife, because he caused her to give life.

Neither the universe nor the Virgin needed any assistance or direction from another to accomplish the divine will, because the will of God is the power of God and was manifesting through them both.

And She brought forth as a man by her own will, and She bore according to the manifestation, and acquired with great power.

The creation is not inert, but essentially intelligent, being a manifestation of the Holy Spirit, the Holy Breath of God. So the evolution of the universe and the birth of Jesus were accomplished by intelligent will. Because the will of the Father was manifesting through the evolving universe and the Virgin, their actions were not their own, but God's. "And Mary said, Behold the handmaid of the Lord; be it unto me according to thy word" (Luke 1:38).

And She loved with redemption, and guarded with kindness, and declared with grandeur.

Nature itself embodies the loving, maternal care of God, redeems through evolving those within her "womb," watches over them constantly, and reveals to them her secrets that are theirs as well. Spiritually, the Virgin Mary does the same for the disciples of Jesus. They can both say the words of Ecclesiasticus 24:18: "I am the mother of fair love, and reverence, and knowledge, and holy hope: I therefore, being eternal, am given to all my children which are named of him."

ODE 20

I am a priest of the Lord, and to him I do priestly service.
And to him I offer the offering of his thought.
For his thought is not like the world, nor like the flesh, nor like them who worship according to the flesh.
The offering of the Lord is righteousness, and purity of heart and lips.
Offer thy inward being faultlessly, and let not thy compassion oppress compassion, and let not thyself oppress anyone.
Thou shouldest not purchase a stranger by the blood of thy soul, nor seek to deceive thy neighbor, nor deprive him of the covering for his nakedness.
But put on the grace of the Lord without stint, and come into his Paradise, and make for thyself a crown from his tree.
And put it on thy head and be joyful, and recline upon his rest.
And his glory shall go before thee, and thou shalt receive of his kindness and his grace, and thou shalt be anointed in truth with the praise of his holiness.
Praise and honor to his Name. Alleluia.

I am a priest of the Lord, and to him I do priestly service.
In the book of Revelation we find these relevant verses: "[Jesus Christ] hath made us kings and priests unto God and his Father" (Revelation 1:6). "[Thou] hast made us unto our God kings and priests" (Revelation 5:10). "Blessed and holy is he that hath part in the first resurrection… they shall be priests of God and of Christ" (Revelation 20:6).

Saint Peter wrote to all Christians: "Ye also are… an holy priesthood, to offer up spiritual sacrifices, acceptable to God by Jesus Christ" (I Peter 2:5). "Ye are a royal priesthood" (I Peter 2:9).

And to him I offer the offering of his thought.

This would be impossible to understand if we did not know what was meant by someone's "thought" at the time the odes were written. "Thought" was the state of consciousness in which a person continually dwelt. That is why one of the earliest desert fathers said that no one in the entire desert could "hold the thought" of Saint Anthony the Great. He did not mean intellectual concepts, but the level of spiritual consciousness in which the saint ever dwelt. Yogis use the Sanskrit term *bhava*, which *A Brief Sanskrit Glossary* defines as: "subjective state of being (existence); attitude of mind; mental attitude or feeling; state of realization in the heart or mind."

Divine (or divinized) consciousness is the only thing we can really offer God, for it is the only thing that is the same as Divine Being. Words and feelings mean nothing, for they are far from the heights of Divine Consciousness.

The priestly service we owe to God, then, is the attaining of the highest spiritual consciousness, linking ourselves to the Divine Consciousness and remaining in that Consciousness. Anything less is unacceptable. "Therefore, be a yogi" (Bhagavad Gita 6:46).

For his thought is not like the world, nor like the flesh, nor like them who worship according to the flesh.

"For my thoughts are not your thoughts, neither are your ways my ways, saith the Lord. For as the heavens are higher than the earth, so are my ways higher than your ways, and my thoughts than your thoughts" (Isaiah 55:8-9). This description of God's thought is important for us, because our consciousness must become the same.

Not like the world.

This is profound, and so far-reaching that I could never encompass it completely. So the best thing is for us to think of any characteristic of the world, both the material world and the artificial world of human society, and realize that any consciousness corresponding to it is not just unacceptable, it is incompatible with the Divine.

Nor like the flesh.
The same analysis should be done regarding the material body.
Nor like them who worship according to the flesh.
Fleshly (material) religion disqualifies us for divine contact. As Saint John says: "They are of the world: therefore speak they of the world, and the world heareth them" (I John 4:5). They orient themselves entirely toward the world because it is the world they want to recruit. (Or recruit themselves to the world; sometimes you cannot tell the difference.) Realizing that people rarely actually change, their whole approach is to accommodate the ignorance and delusions of the world while offering a veneer of religiosity that is usually comprised of platitudes and momentary emotional highs. The higher they fly, the lower they fall, but it does not matter, because "they have their reward," just like the religionists of Jesus' day (Matthew 6:2).

"God is a Spirit: and they that worship him must worship him in spirit and in truth" (John 4:24). Only by going within and contacting him can we worship God, for we ourselves are the temples of God (I Corinthians 6:19), who "dwelleth not in temples made with hands" (Acts 17:24).

The offering of the Lord is righteousness, and purity of heart and lips.
Righteousness is not the following of external rules and parroting of theological formulas, it is the learning and applying of the spiritual laws that lead us to communion with God. One of the "ten commandments of yoga" is Purity (Yoga Sutras 2:32). "Every man that hath this hope in him purifieth himself, even as he is pure" (I John 3:3). Our lips cannot be pure if our heart is not pure, "for out of the abundance of the heart the mouth speaketh" (Matthew 12:34). Our consciousness itself must be purified thoroughly. Then: "Blessed are the pure in heart: for they shall see God" (Matthew 5:8). How can we accomplish all this, raising ourselves to such spiritual heights?

Offer thy inward being faultlessly.
This is impossible without meditation and holding on to the level of consciousness produced by meditation. Our meditation, to be a worthy offering, must be faultless both in method and result. The purpose of

meditation must be completely realized; nothing can be lacking, nor can anything extraneous be intruded. We must know the way, follow the way and be established in the way.

And let not thy compassion oppress compassion.

Paramhansa Yogananda's guru often said: "Too much of a good thing is no longer good." It is not uncommon to see virtues turned into vice through misapplication or misplacement. There comes to mind the old joke about the boy scout who came to the scout meeting bruised, scratched and with his clothes torn. "What happened to you?" demanded the scoutmaster. "I helped an old lady cross the street," was the answer. "But how did you get like this?" asked the scoutmaster. "She didn't want to go across the street!"

A lot of do-gooders and would-be helpers of others create a lot of misery and oppression in this world. English and American literature of the nineteenth and early twentieth centuries abounded in stories of "charity" that was cruelty and "helping" that was persecution and subjugation. Today's Nanny States throughout the world are busily ruining lives, blinded by their unquestioning and destructive ignorance. We must not make the same mistakes in our personal lives. Caring and wanting to help are not justifications for action (or speech). Intelligence based on spiritual insight is also essential.

And let not thyself oppress anyone.

The previous section applies here, too. It is so easy to annoy and oppress others by self-righteous assurance. "I just want what's good for you," "I am only thinking of you," and "I just want you to be happy," are rationalizations for outrageous behavior and bullying on the part of millions. And families lead the list.

When I was in high school I met an outstandingly intelligent and mature girl and we often spoke together when riding the bus to school. In her last year of high school she became acquainted with a friend of mine from church who was really an ideal young man that everyone respected. He asked her to marry him, she accepted, and her family went berserk because they had someone "better" in mind. They locked her in her room, told the school she was seriously ill, and daily beat her. She escaped, finished school and married my friend. Wisely they immediately moved to another state where a major company had heard of his abilities while he was still in high school and had recruited him.

A friend of mine knew a girl whose parents did not like her "going to church so much." So they kept her locked in her room, took her to and from school and back to the locked room. They assured her that after she graduated they would find employment for her and would continue the routine! my friend and some others reported the situation to the local authorities who removed her from her parent's house and she lived her own life.

Think what horrible trauma both of these girls went through at the hands of those who claimed they loved her and wanted the best for her. We must not do the same under the guise of righteousness and spirituality. Throughout history religion has been second only to government in the matters of repression and persecution.

Thou shouldest not purchase a stranger by the blood of thy soul.

This is a vital counsel. We dare not sacrifice our spiritual welfare, the blood of our soul, to please or placate someone. People make this terrible mistake over and over. In commerce we see it considered a virtue: do anything to make a sale or gain the good will or patronage of someone who can benefit us. Politicians lie all the time to get votes. People sell their souls to make peace with the incorrigible, insisting it is a virtue to do so. People surrender their inner life so others will like or respect them. I have seen people destroy their souls to get into the favor of others, and especially to win or keep someone they are in love with. Both men and woman continually turn from higher life because of their spouse or family. Sometimes people compromise their integrity to supposedly help others, considering this a noble thing to do. Entire spiritual groups spiritually prostitute themselves to get members, abandoning principles they know are right but which repel the shallow and selfish. I was brought up in just such a church. "Will remodel to suit tenant" applies to contemporary religion in the West as much as to real estate.

Nor seek to deceive thy neighbor.

Fooling anyone, even "for their own good," is incompatible with spiritual life. Modern life is an edifice of lies on a foundation of lies built by liars. We are so used to it that we do not see the enormity of the situation. Deception is the order of the day, from advertising to "social norms." To be truthful in word, thought and deed is imperative: this cannot be emphasized too much.

Nor deprive him of the covering for his nakedness.

There are many ways to steal, some material, some intellectual, some social and some spiritual. We must scrutinize our ways to be sure we are not ourselves socially acceptable thieves.

But put on the grace of the Lord without stint. It has astonished me from childhood that people plunge entirely into external pursuits of all sorts and become thoroughly absorbed in them, but when it comes to religion they are minimalists supreme. After all, they do not want to become extreme or fanatical! People will sacrifice anything and risk their lives to satisfy their desires and egos, but will not even inconvenience themselves for spiritual life. When I was very young I read this verse:

> No driving rain can make us stay
> If we have tickets for the play.
> But let one drop the walk besmirch
> It's far too wet to go to church.

In her autobiography Saint Teresa of Liseaux tells of how as a small child she was asked to choose something from a number of things. "I will take them all," she announced, and did so. This, she says, is how we must be in spiritual life: we should want all God intends for us and give everything to receive it. As the odist says, we must "put on the grace of the Lord without stint." This, too, requires "the uttermost farthing" (Matthew 5:26).

As a child I sang this song in church many times:

> Since Jesus gave his life for me,
> Should I not give him mine?

I'm consecrated, Lord, to Thee,
I shall be wholly Thine.

My home and friends are dear to me,
Yet he is dearer still;
In my affections first he'll be,
And first his righteous will.

My all, O Lord, to Thee I'll give,
Accept it as Thine own;
For Thee alone I'll ever live,
My heart shall be Thy throne.

My life, O Lord, I give to Thee,
My talents, time, and all;
I'll serve Thee, Lord, Thine own to be,
I'll hear Thy faintest call.

And come into his Paradise, and make for thyself a crown from his tree.
Those who unreservedly dedicate themselves to the search for God will indeed come into his paradise and make for themselves a crown from the blossoms and leaves of the tree of life. We make the crown ourselves by our daily life and spiritual practice, for God has assured us: "Be thou faithful unto death, and I will give thee a crown of life" (Revelation 2:10).

And put it on thy head and be joyful, and recline upon his rest. And his glory shall go before thee, and thou shalt receive of his kindness and his grace, and thou shalt be anointed in truth with the praise of his holiness.
This needs no commentary, only attaining!
Praise and honor to his Name. Amen.

Ode 21

I lifted up my arms on high, on account of the compassion of the Lord.
Because he had cast off my bonds from me; and my helper had lifted me up according to his compassion and his salvation.
And I put off darkness, and clothed myself with light.
And my soul acquired members, free from sorrow, or affliction or pain.
And increasingly helpful to me was the thought of the Lord, and his incorruptible fellowship.
And I was lifted up in the light, and I passed before him.
And I was constantly near him, praising and confessing him.
He caused my heart to overflow and it was found in my mouth, and it shone forth upon my lips.
And upon my face the exultation of the Lord increased, and his praise likewise. Alleluia.

I lifted up my arms on high, on account of the compassion of the Lord. This is a symbolic way of saying that the odist lifted all the powers of his being (arms) on high. Not asking God to come down to him (which is the way of most of us), the odist rose in his consciousness Godward. Since the goal is to be at one with God in the transcendent heights, it is a good idea to start working toward that right now. That is the way of the yogi.

In India they say: "He who chooses God has first been chosen by God." Of course this is true of all of us. If we were not chosen we would not be in this universe whose sole purpose is our evolution on the path to God-realization. We entered here of our free will, enlightened by the grace of God. And now we strive to elevate our consciousness to higher levels, and that is also the grace of God.

I would like to stop here to point out that although it is true that the grace of God is everything, it is also true that *everything is the grace of God.* There is no thing in all creation that is not the embodiment of grace (kripamayi). To draw the conclusion that we need absolutely nothing but invoke God's grace is foolish. *We must put that grace to use.* The ability to discipline ourselves and engage in spiritual practice (tapasya) is itself divine grace. So doing nothing but claiming to be trusting in God's grace alone is actually a defiance of God's grace, and the results will be negative, not just nil.

True compassion is not just feeling sorry for someone, but actually being affected by another person's plight or pain. God has compassion on, in and with us because: "the Lord dwells in the hearts of all beings (Bhagavad Gita 18:61). Everything we feel, think or experience is experienced by God just as it is by us. When we descended into this world, God descended right along with us. God is living the life of every single being in creation, not just the human or even the sentient beings, but all existence. He literally is nearer than the near, and therefore dearer than the dear.

Because he had cast off my bonds from me; and my helper had lifted me up according to his compassion and his salvation.

Here again we have the understanding that choosing God is a sign that God has chosen us. In line with this, Jesus told his disciples: "Ye have not chosen me, but I have chosen you" (John 15:16). Which is also indicated by Jesus telling Nathanael at their first meeting: "Before that Philip called thee, when thou wast under the fig tree, I saw thee" (John 1:48). It is said that during much of his teaching ministry Buddha would meditate very early in the morning and perceive who in that area was ready for the call to nirvana. Then he would seek them out that day and speak with them.

Until a person is developed (evolved) enough to have a sufficient degree of spiritual consciousness it is useless to bother him with spiritual teaching. (I mean real spiritual teaching, not exoteric dogmas and intellectual and emotionally bullying or enticement.) The qualified person hears about higher consciousness and life and immediately responds and wants to learn how to attain it. Anyone that has to be cajoled and assured and given pep talks is positively not ready. We are wasting time with those who have neither ears to hear (Matthew 11:15) and nor eyes to see (Deuteronomy 29:4). Jesus told his opponents: "Why do ye not understand my speech? *Even because ye cannot hear my word"* (John 8:43). The word translated "hear" is *akouo*, which means both the ability to hear with the ears and to understand with the intellect–and to be affected by it.

There is no snobbery here; it is a realistic assessment of a person's readiness. In time everyone arrives there and in time everyone attains. So we need not be anxious, aggressive or insistent with anyone. Their divine Self will reveal itself to them at exactly the right time. We are all moving toward that goal, but we must have total freedom in doing so.

And I put off darkness, and clothed myself with light.

What is darkness, and what is light? Darkness is ignorance and unconsciousness (unawareness), whereas light is understanding and consciousness. Often in the Bible "death" means lack of conscious awareness and "life" means to be conscious and aware in spiritual matters.

This is also a matter of will and effort. The odist does not say that God took away his darkness and put light upon him. Saint Paul wrote: "As many of you as have been baptized [immersed] into Christ [consciousness] have *put on Christ*" (Galatians 3:27). It was our choice and our doing. Of course we had to know how to do it, and that is the illuminating grace of of God.

We put off darkness by ridding ourself of everything that dims our spiritual vision and hinders our spiritual growth. So we have to know just what those things are to put off and put on, for spiritual life is eminently an *intelligent* life. Feelings and faith carry one only a very little distance. It is gnosis–understanding and insight resulting from spiritual awakening and development–that gets us to the goal. The key to all this is meditation and more meditation and more meditation. Unless spiritual life in the form of spiritual practice is made the heart of our life here and now we will remain unconscious and unevolved; in other words: dead.

And my soul acquired members, free from sorrow, or affliction or pain.

In Paradise Adam and Eve were clothed with light, and nothing else. When they transgressed, their consciousness was darkened. No longer clothed in light they saw they were "naked" and were ashamed. It was not their bodies they were ashamed of, but the loss of the garment of light, the spiritual body which is necessary for spiritual evolution. Falling back into the earth plane, they and all their descendants were devoid of this light body, but spiritual practice can restore it. The Taoist yogis speak of "the divine embryo" which develops into what the yogis of India call a "sadhana body." It is through this that we attain higher consciousness. It is through the sadhana body, produced by spiritual practice, that aspirants actually come to see and know God.

Obviously the sadhana body is beyond sorrow, affliction or pain, so the more we develop and live centered in it, the freer we will be from those miseries.

And increasingly helpful to me was the thought of the Lord, and his incorruptible fellowship.

One time I was visiting Swami Vidyananda Giri my sannyasa guru (the one who made me a monk), at his ashram. I told him about some of the spiritually uplifting people I had encountered since our last meeting. When I was finished he commented with a quiet fervor: "Whenever we speak of such people we have spiritual contact with them and are benefitted." This being so, consider what the thought of God must be. On the spiritual planes the remembrance of God brings us into the presence, the "incorruptible fellowship" of God. At the time of Jesus this was commonly believed, and that is why the dying thief said to him: "Lord, remember me when thou comest into thy kingdom" (Luke 23:42). He was petitioning Jesus to bring him into his kingdom. That is why Jesus replied: "Verily I say unto thee, Today shalt thou be with me in paradise" (v. 43).

There is a valuable lesson for us here. We must keep our minds fixed on God at all times; then we shall always be with God and only good can come to us.

And I was lifted up in the light, and I passed before him.

Those who live in the light by clothing themselves in it through spiritual practice will in time be lifted into the divine Light and come before God. Then they, too, can say with the odist:

And I was constantly near him, praising and confessing him.

There is a lot of "praise" and "confession" of God that is little more than tiresome cant and cheap sentimentality, especially by those that think they can flatter their way into divine favor. But the real praise and confession come from the revelation of God within us.

He caused my heart to overflow and it was found in my mouth, and it shone forth upon my lips.

In other words, being united with God we have the experience of David when he sang: "I will bless the Lord at all times: his praise shall continually be in my mouth" (Psalms 34:1). From this we can understand that any true interior experience will ultimately manifest outwardly in a natural and spontaneous manner. So the odist concludes:

And upon my face the exultation of the Lord increased, and his praise likewise.

ODE 22

He who brings me down from on high, and brings me up from the regions below;
And he who gathers what is in the middle, and throws them to me;
He who scattered my enemies, and my adversaries;
He who gave me authority over bonds, that I might loose them;
He who overthrew by my hands the dragon with seven heads, and set me at his roots that I might destroy his seed:
Thou wert there and helped me, and in every place Thy Name was round about me.
Thy right hand destroyed his wicked venom, and Thy hand levelled the way for those who believe in Thee.
And it chose them from the graves, and separated them from the dead.
It took dead bones, and covered them with bodies.
And they were motionless, and it gave (them) energy for life.
Thy way was without destruction and Thy face; [yet] Thou hast brought Thy world to destruction, that everything might be dissolved and renewed,
And that the foundation for everything might be Thy rock; and upon it Thou hast built Thy kingdom, and Thou becamest the dwelling-place of the saints. Alleluia.

He Who brings me down from on high, and brings me up from the regions below.

"He" in this and the next four verses is God. Eternally we have existed in God, the essence of our being, though we are not God but gods. There in the bosom of the Father we rested in transcendental happiness, but within our nature there was an impulse to transcend the finite scope of our consciousness. (See *Robe of Light*.) Since this was the implanted will of God, he had spread forth the entire field of relative existence for us to enter and evolve the capacity to experience and share in his infinite consciousness. With our assent God caused us to descend from those divine heights into the depths of what in India is known as the ocean of samsara. Then from both within and without God began drawing us upward back to him, and in that process we began to evolve the capacity for increasingly expanding breadth of consciousness.

And he who gathers what is in the middle, and throws them to me.

First we learned to enter in and experience life forms whose scope of awareness and ability were much beneath ours, but slowly we kept expanding until we reached the point where the evolved level of consciousness and our innate eternal status were equal. This was the level of human life, which was in the middle of the evolutionary ladder. For the first time, being self-conscious, we experienced life as something thrown at us, for we had forgotten that everything that had occurred was both our will and the will of God. So we became overwhelmed with the experience of human existence.

He Who scattered my enemies, and my adversaries.

But our evolution was moving forward, and that which opposed our growth in consciousness was slowly pushed back and eliminated from our life sphere.

He Who gave me authority over bonds, that I might loose them.

Finally we came to the point where evolution need not be a matter of blind, automatic expansion, and there arose in us the ability to begin moving forward by our own conscious volition, evolving ourselves intentionally and methodically. This was done in many forms of positive endeavor, but eventually we came to the point where the knowledge and practice of yoga became possible so we might free ourselves from our bonds. The rate of our growth then became according to the intensity and quality of our practice, by our working together with God for our liberation (II Corinthians 6:1).

He Who overthrew by my hands the dragon with seven heads, and set me at his roots that I might destroy his seed.

In the book of Revelation we read quite a bit about this dragon, the enemy of all evolving beings. When creation came forth, since "for every action there is an equal and opposite reaction" as Newtonian physics postulates, an opposing force had to arise; otherwise the creation would have dissolved since without the duality of positive and negative there is no relative existence. This force has been spoken of under many symbolic names and forms: Mara, Ahriman, Satan and the Devil being but a few. Basically it is the force of cosmic delusion opposing the purpose of creation which is the development of consciousness and wisdom (gnosis, jnana). Since everything is the light of the Holy Spirit, all things are inherently conscious, and this force is a kind of energy robot that operates on a level of cosmic intelligence.

It is both cosmic and individual. On the cosmic level it wars with the cosmic order trying to break it down and return it to its primeval formlessness. The English occultist William Gray wrote about the conflict of what he called Chaos and Cosmos. This power also wars on the individual level to halt and reverse the evolution of every sentient being. Each one of us must conquer this negative power as it works outside in our personal environment and as we find its imprint and influence within us. As miniature reflections of the cosmos, the ancient war must be fought and won by us. "But thanks be to God, which giveth us the victory through our Lord Jesus Christ" (I Corinthians 15:57), for "in all these things we are more than conquerors through him that loved us" (Romans 8:37).

This was done by uncovering the very roots of the dragon within by the practice of yoga meditation, which by its inherent force then dissolved those roots and expelled the dragon. Thus the seeds implanted by that dragon in past and present lives were burnt in the fires of divine light, melted and passed away.

Thou wert there and helped me, and in every place Thy Name was round about me.

All this was done through the power of God, especially through his invocation and continual remembrance by japa and meditation. Yoga is the infallible sword by which all evil is cut off and banished. First and foremost the questing soul must become and know itself as a yogi. Everything else is absolutely secondary, for yoga is the only real religion.

Thy right hand destroyed his wicked venom, and Thy hand levelled the way for those who believe in Thee.

The divine power of the Holy Spirit activated through the diligent practice of yoga completely neutralized the poison of evil and turned it into the elixir of immortality (amrita). Moreover it transmuted all the energies that hindered the yogi into upward-oriented powers that ensured his success in the battle. "The right hand of the Lord is exalted: the right hand of the Lord doeth valiantly" (Psalms 118:16).

And it chose them from the graves, and separated them from the dead.

Until a significant degree of spiritual awakening/evolution is attained, the human being in a sense lives in a tomb consisting of his body, mind and earthly environment. Yoga especially takes us out of the grave and separates us from the dead who yet remain fundamentally asleep in the higher reaches of their existence, unaware that they even have a higher nature. To everyone there comes the call: "Awake thou that sleepest, and arise from the dead, and Christ shall give thee light" (Ephesians 5:14). Sometimes it is heeded and sometimes not. A lot of people awake for a while but do not arise and so fall back asleep. Many awake and arise only to wander around in the dark. But eventually everyone awakes, arises and stands forth in the light revealed as a son of God.

It took dead bones, and covered them with bodies.

The Holy Spirit clothes us in her own light as Ezekiel recorded in the thirty-seventh chapter of his prophecies. "Therefore if any man be in Christ, he is a new creature" (II Corinthians 5:17). Literally the yogi becomes recreated as the levels and faculties possessed by Adam and Eve in Paradise, but which they lost through their transgression, are restored to him and he becomes fully human. Until then there is no possibility of him evolving beyond the ordinary human condition.

And they were motionless, and it gave (them) energy for life.

The Nicene Creed refers to the Holy Spirit as "the Giver of Life." Our bodies are formed of her energies and enlivened by her Life. "Ye are the temple of God, and that the Spirit of God dwelleth in you" (I Corinthians 3:16). Having such an empowerment, it can truly be said to us, as Yogananda commented to some disciples: "You have God's blessing and my blessing; all you lack is your blessing."

Thy way was without destruction and Thy face; [yet] Thou hast brought Thy world to destruction, that everything might be dissolved and renewed.

This first clause sounds very strange in all translations, but what it means is that the creation was indestructible and destruction was not part of the divine will ("face"). That is, everything is inherently imperishable since they are a manifestation of the Holy Spirit. So any degeneration or breakdown was impossible. There was no flaw or instability in creation, yet it was meant to be cyclic, to manifest and dissolve alternately in a perpetual manner. Therefore the dissolution of the world and its regeneration or renewal is the direct action of God, a deliberate "destruction." This was well known to the sages of India, and the Bhagavad Gita explains it.

"They know the true day and night who know Brahma's Day a thousand yugas long and Brahma's Night a thousand yugas long. At the approach of Brahma's Day, all manifested things come forth from the unmanifest, and then return to that at Brahma's Night. Helpless, the same host of beings being born again and again merge at the approach of the Night and emerge at the dawn of Day" (Bhagavad Gita 8:17-19).

And that the foundation for everything might be Thy rock; and upon it Thou hast built Thy kingdom, and Thou becamest the dwelling-place of the saints.

This, too, is made clear in the Bhagavad Gita: "But there exists, higher than the unmanifested, another unmanifested Eternal which does not perish when all beings perish. This unmanifest is declared to be the imperishable, which is called the Supreme Goal, attaining which they return not. This is my supreme abode" (Bhagavad Gita 8:20-21).

Because of the famous hymn, the title "Rock of Ages" for God is considered Christian, but it is equally Jewish. The idea is that God is the foundation of the entire creation and everything within it. Further,

God is the Kingdom of God and, as this verse says, the dwelling-place of the saints. "In him we live, and move, and have our being…, For we are also his offspring" (Acts 17:28). We only need realize this, experience it truly and be established in it, to attain the goal of life itself.

ODE 23

Joy is of the Saints, and who shall put it on but they alone?
Grace is of the elect, and who shall receive it but they who trust in it from the beginning?
Love is of the elect, and who shall put it on, but those who have possessed it from the beginning?
Walk ye in the knowledge of the Most High, and ye shall know the grace of the Lord without grudging, both to his exultation and to the perfection of his knowledge.
And his thought was like a letter, and his will descended from on high.
And it was sent from a bow like an arrow, which has been violently shot.
And many hands rushed to the letter, to seize it and to take it and to read it.
And it escaped from their fingers, and they were frightened by it and by the seal that was on it.
For it was not permitted to them to loose its seal, for the power that was over the seal was greater than they.
But those who saw it went after the letter, that they might know where it would land, and who should read it, and who should hear it.
But a wheel received it, and (the letter) came over it.
And there was with it a sign, of the kingdom and of the government.

And everything which was disturbing to the wheel, it mowed and cut down.
And it restrained a multitude of adversaries, and it buried rivers,
And crossed over and rooted up many forests, and made a broad way.
The head went down to the feet, for down to the feet ran the wheel, and that which had come upon it.
The letter was one of command, and hence all regions were gathered together.
And there was seen at its head a head which was revealed, even the Son of Truth from the Most High Father.
And he inherited and took possession of everything, and then the thought of the many was brought to naught.
Then all the seducers were rash and fled, and the persecutors became extinct and were blotted out.
And the letter became a large volume, which was entirely written by the finger of God.
And the Name of the Father was upon it, and of the Son and of the Holy Spirit, to rule unto the ages of ages. Alleluia.

Joy is of the Saints, and who shall put it on but they alone?

There is a lot of talk about happiness in this world, but that only proves how little there really is to be had. Distraction is to be had aplenty and buzzes, thrills, chills and excitement. But they are only coverups for the emptiness and discontent within. The rishis of India discovered that God is ever-existent, conscious bliss. And since no one is in communion with God but the saints, they alone are anandamayi: "clothed" in joy. People go out looking for happiness as though it were a kind of material object to pick up, but in reality happiness and joy are attributes of the Divine. Consequently only those who seek God have any possibility of finding them. I have witnessed this for myself. As a child I met three saints in the church I belonged to. They had a tangible aura of joy around them all the time, and just being near them made everyone happy. One of them shone with perceptible light, and when I would come within fifteen or so feet from her I would feel a kind of fiery light coming from her. She was always immersed in joy. I never saw her in any other state. Through the years, and especially after I discovered yoga and went to India, I met holy people in very unexpected places, but they all emanated a positive joy. Some were well known and others were completely unknown, but they all lived in divine joy. So the answer to the search for happiness is to seek God diligently, for Jesus has assured us: "Ask, and it shall be given you; seek, and ye shall find; knock, and it shall be opened unto you: For every one that asketh receiveth; and he that seeketh findeth; and to him that knocketh it shall be opened" (Matthew 7:7-8). This is not a promise but the enunciation of a cosmic law.

Grace is of the elect, and who shall receive it but they who trust in it from the beginning?

It is not generally known, but one of the major differences between Eastern and Western Christianity is the definition of grace. In Hebrew and Greek the words translated "grace" all mean "favor," but both East and West consider grace to be something much more than an attitude of God toward us. The West believes that grace is a power, a force or energy created by God to assist humanity in its attempts to rise above its presently prevailing condition of spiritual alienation and debilitation. The East denies this emphatically, insisting that grace is not an energy, but God himself in communication with man. That is, grace is experience of the Divine, a partaking of the Divine Life. In Genesis God tells Abraham: "I am thy shield, and thy exceeding great reward (Genesis 15:1). The spiritual search is a search for God.

In both Hebrew and Greek the words translated "elect" mean "chosen." Just who are the chosen? Saint Paul assures us that God "will have all men to be saved, and to come unto the knowledge of the truth" (I Timothy 2:4). God intends all human beings to ultimately know him, live in him and be one with him. This is not the Christianity most of us grew up in, but it is the real one.

So this verse means that those who awaken spiritually will know through their higher intuition that it is possible to seek and know God; and that will be the beginning of their divine quest. Those who seek shall find (Matthew 7:7), for as Saint Paul told the Athenian philosophers: "God... made the world and... all nations of men... that they should seek the Lord,... though he be not far from every one of us: For in him we live, and move, and have our being... for we are also his offspring" (Acts 17:24, 26-28).

The word translated "offspring" is *genos*, which means "kind" or species. So Saint Paul is saying that human beings are of the same kind of being as God! We are all a part of God: the sages of all times and traditions have said so. God is infinite and we are finite, but God is our essential substance. That is why Tennyson, a mystic and prophet, wrote:

> Flower in the crannied wall,
> I pluck you out of the crannies,
> I hold you here, root and all, in my hand,
> Little flower–but if I could understand
> What you are, root and all, and all in all,
> I should know what God and man is.

Their absolute unity is indicated by his saying: "I should know what God and man *is*." Therefore the seeking and finding of God is the most natural thing we can do.

Love is of the elect, and who shall put it on, but those who have possessed it from the beginning?

Of course we have possessed it from the beginning because God is love, and we have always been with (and within) him. As Saint John wrote: "God is love; and he that dwelleth in love dwelleth in God, and God in him (I John 4:16). "Putting on" God is the conscious awakening in God to find that, as in the parable of the Prodigal Son, God ever says to us: "Son, thou art ever with me, and all that I have is thine" (Luke 15:31).

Walk ye in the knowledge of the Most High, and ye shall know the grace of the Lord without grudging [Charlesworth: generously]*, both to his exultation and to the perfection of his knowledge.*

As the sages of India knew thousands of years ago, and countless yogis have discovered in the meantime, it is knowledge (jnana), the knowing of God, that alone liberates the spirit. From that knowledge comes abundant grace (kripa) and mercy (daya) without diminishment or cessation. This leads ultimately to the experience of divine joy (paramananda) and the attainment of perfect Knowing in God (Brahmajnana). Then the evolutionary process is completed and the individual (jiva) is established in perfect liberation (moksha).

And his thought was like a Letter, and his will descended from on high.

In the book of Zechariah (5:1-2) the message of God is symbolized as a flying scroll coming to earth from above. So perhaps the odist had this in mind.

And it was sent from a bow like an arrow, which has been violently shot.

The idea here is that the divine communication occurs very quickly, often like a lightning strike. The effects may take quite some time in manifesting and being assimilated completely, but the initial contact is swift and revolutionary, even drastic. This has been my experience several times, and from conversations with other yogis I have learned that it is nearly always that way. For example, I knew more than one person that read Yogananda's autobiography and after only a day or two found themselves on the way to Los Angeles to become his disciple.

Sister Vimala, a disciple of Swami Paramananda, founder of the Ananda Ashrama in La Crescenta, California, told me that she went with her mother to a lecture given by the Swami in Boston where he headed the Vedanta Center. Though they did not know him, as soon as they sat down in the auditorium someone came and asked that they see the Swami after the lecture. They did so and the Swami asked that they come and see him at the Vedanta Center the next day. They went and her mother did all the talking because Sister Vimala just sat there in total awe, experiencing what she had never known before. Finally her mother said to the Swami, and indicating her said: "Obviously she belongs to you." He turned and asked: "Would you like to live in my new ashram in California." She could only nod Yes. So in a short time she was on her way to a new and glorious life, instead of going to France to study the organ as she had planned and for which all arrangements had been made.

Let me tell you something very crucial regarding spiritual life: Those who hesitate and delay will lose their chance at spiritual life. You must reach out and grasp the opportunity! That is why Jesus said: "The kingdom of heaven suffereth violence [literally: is seized], and the violent take it by force" (Matthew 11:12). And Saint Paul said we should "lay hold on eternal life" (I Timothy 6:12).

And many hands rushed to the Letter, to seize it and to take it and to read it. And it escaped from their fingers, and they were frightened by it and by the seal that was on it. For it was not permitted to them to loose its seal, for the power that was over the seal was greater than they.

Now we come to a most interesting phenomenon in religion. Some people are drawn to authentic spiritual teaching at first and then they turn or even run from it, because it really is beyond them to grasp and make their own through assimilation into their consciousness and lives.

But those who saw it went after the Letter, that they might know where it would land, and who should read it, and who should hear it. But a wheel received it, and (the Letter) came over it. And there was with it a sign, of the kingdom and of the government.

There are very interesting references by the prophet Ezekiel (1:16, 19-21; 3:13; 10:2, 6, 9, 12, 16, 19; 11:22) to beings who are simply described as "Wheels." The mystical tradition of Eastern Christianity says that these beings are purely intellectual, that their wheel-like form is actually their mind which continually circles around the matrix of their awareness which is fixed on God alone: God is at the core of their consciousness. These Wheels exist only to love and to serve. So a Wheel became the bearer of the Letter and there appeared the sign of the kingdom, the rulership, of God. Thus the Letter became secure and unhindered.

And everything which was disturbing to the wheel, it mowed and cut down. And it restrained a multitude of adversaries, and it buried rivers, and crossed over and rooted up many forests, and made a broad way. The head went down to the feet, for down to the feet ran the wheel, and that which had come upon it.

The Wheel, like Saint John the Baptist, is preparing the way for the advent, the revelation, of the Letter. Everything that would oppose or hinder the Letter is being eliminated. And that includes those that are incapable of "reading" and following it–many of whom would outrightly reject it anyway once they understood its true nature which is opposed to the illusions and delusions they live in every moment. Further, its protective power encompassed its every aspect, from head to foot.

The Letter was one of command, and hence all regions were gathered together. And there was seen at its head a head which was revealed, even the Son of Truth from the Most High Father.

Now we know what the Letter is: "the revelation of the mystery, which was kept secret since the world began" (Romans 16:25). It is the Revelation of Jesus Christ (Galatians 1:12; I Peter 1:13; Revelation 1:1).

And he inherited and took possession of everything, and then the thought of the many was brought to naught. Then all the seducers were rash and fled, and the persecutors became extinct and were blotted out. And the letter became a large volume, which was entirely written by the finger of God. And the Name of the Father was upon it, and of the Son and of the Holy Spirit, to rule unto the ages of ages.

This is the true situation of the authentic Gospel, for "grace and truth came by Jesus Christ" (John 1:17).

When we look at the world around us it does not seem that the Gospel is triumphant: quite the contrary. But it is in truth triumphant in those who are willing and able to unite with it and become transmuted in their consciousness and entire being. What we see here is the glory of the Gospel on the inner levels of being. And those levels are accessed only by those who consciously *and effectively* seek their own Christhood. They dwell in an altogether different world from those who wander unaware or disinterested in the inner Christ-life. In them the Gospel is trampled underfoot. But in the worthy seekers it is exalted in triumph. For them eternal life has already been won, and they live in its continually unfolding revelation, "that they might have life, and that they might have it more abundantly" (John 10:10).

Ode 24

The Dove flew over the head of our Lord the Messiah, because he was her head.
And she sang over him, and her voice was heard.
And the inhabitants were afraid, and the sojourners trembled.
The bird began to fly, and every creeping thing died in its hole.
And the abysses were opened and closed; and they were seeking for the Lord as those who are about to give birth.
And he was not given to them for food, because he was not theirs.
And the abysses were submerged in the submersion of the Lord, and they perished in that thought which they had held from the beginning.
For they travailed from the beginning, and the end of their travail was life.
And all of them who were lacking perished, because they were not able to pronounce the word so that they might exist.
And the Lord destroyed the thoughts, of all them that had not the truth with them.
For they were lacking in wisdom, they who exalted themselves in their hearts.
And they were rejected, because the truth was not with them.
For the Lord revealed his way, and spread abroad his grace.
And those who understood it know his holiness. Alleluia.

The Dove flew over the head of our Lord the Messiah, because he was her head.

"Jesus, when he was baptized, went up straightway out of the water: and, lo, the heavens were opened unto him, and he saw the Spirit of God descending like a dove, and lighting upon him" (Matthew 3:16). The Gospels are both literal and symbolic. Being masters of karma, liberated beings who return to earth as Way-showers perfectly control their lives and bring about incidents that have profound spiritual symbolism. Early Christian texts reveal that the original Christians looked upon the life of Jesus as a kind of mystery-drama intended to reveal spiritual truths and illumine the life and path of the initiates of Christ.

Jesus is not *the* Christ, but *a* Christ. In the esoteric cosmology of mystical Judaism, one of the highest levels of creation is called Messiah. Only those who who have reached the status of a Messiah, a Christ, dwell there and if they descend to a lower world they do so as Messiah-teachers. Just as there have been many Buddhas, so there have been many Messiah-Christs.

"Because he was her head." The Holy Breath, the divine Ruach or Holy Spirit, is considered the breath or spirit of the/a Messiah. Therefore the Holy Spirit was seen at the baptism of Jesus when he was revealed to Israel as Christ. She is also called "the Spirit of Christ" in the Bible (Romans 8:9; I Peter 1:11). Consequently this ode can be looked at as both a portrayal of the divine hierarchy and as the inner meaning of Jesus' baptism. Even more to the point, it can be studied as an exposition of the way in which those who receive the Spirit of Christ will be transformed into Christs through intense and total purification.

And she sang over him, and her voice was heard.

In his commentary on parts of the Gospels, *The Second Coming of Christ* (Amrita Foundation edition), Paramhansa Yogananda wrote:

"Cosmic sound, emanating from cosmic vibration, is called the 'Holy Ghost.'... It is holy because the emanent (outflowing) consciousness of God the Father, or Christ intelligence, guides it to create all finite matter.... The Hindus speak of this 'Holy Ghost' as the 'Aum.' 'A' stands for 'Akar' or creative vibration; 'U' for 'Ukar' or preservative vibration; and 'M' for 'Makar' or destructive vibration.... So the cosmic sound of Aum or Holy Ghost creates all things..., preserves them…, and ultimately it will dissolve all things in the bosom-sea of God.

"Jesus, during his baptism, saw the cosmic energy manifested in bodily shape,… and out of that… came a voice, or intelligent, all-creative, cosmic sound, saying, or vibrating, in intelligible voice…, 'Thou art my Son (or my manifestation) I am glad thou hast risen (lifted thy consciousness from matter), and tuned in with my Omnipresence.'"

(This is just a fraction of what Yogananda wrote on this subject. The complete section is filled with invaluable information, much or most of which is not found in the writings of any other teacher. I recommend you read it all.)

Since each of us is a potential Christ, this ode is particularly relevant, for it is an exposition of the action of the Holy Spirit on the entire makeup of the individual as he is led onward to Christhood. The "song" of the Holy Spirit is the transforming power which accomplishes this ascent in evolution. The first effect is the awareness of the Holy Spirit's action by the questing soul. It is not a vague matter of "something happening," but is understood by the aspirant to be the workings of the Holy Breath, the Holy Vibration, the leaven of the kingdom of heaven within.

"Another parable spake he unto them; The kingdom of heaven is like unto leaven, which a woman took, and hid in three measures of meal, till the whole was leavened" (Matthew 13:33). The "three measures of meal" are the physical, astral and causal levels (bodies) of the initiate.

And the inhabitants were afraid, and the sojourners trembled.

Just as a ship picks up barnacles as it plies the seas, so the individual's various bodies take on conditionings and accretions from life to life. Even if these are not positively antithetical to the divine transformation, they are yet alien, not part of the Voice from heaven which declares "This is my beloved Son, in whom I am well pleased" (Matthew 3:17). Consequently they are shaken by the song of the Holy Spirit arising from within the individual being transformed. Having identified for many lifetimes with these alien elements, the person himself may become unsettled, unsure and even fearful when this process takes place. In time peace is established by this purificatory action and any anxiety ceases, but in the meantime it can arise. Some people are even inclined to abandon spiritual life because of it. The wise face it and endure; the weak fail and fall away.

The bird began to fly, and every creeping thing died in its hole.

"The earth was without form, and void; and darkness was upon the face of the deep. And the Spirit of God moved upon the face of the waters. And God said, Let there be light: and there was light" (Genesis 1:2-3).

When the Holy Spirit begins to fly over and upon the waters of the subtle energy makeup of the seeker, that movement is a kind of friction that produces light in which all that is not real and true is dissolved. The "creeping things" of ignorance and delusion are in this way cauterized from the developing consciousness of the aspirant.

And the abysses were opened and closed; and they were seeking for the Lord as those who are about to give birth.

The dark nooks and crannies of the inner bodies, particularly those of the mind, are revealed to the questing spirit and then banished (closed), for these voids, made of spiritual anti-matter, would like to encompass and swallow up the Light of Christ produced by the flight of the Dove.

And he was not given to them for food, because he was not theirs.

Those who sought to extinguish the Light were themselves extinguished by It.

And the abysses were submerged in the submersion of the Lord, and they perished in that thought which they had held from the beginning.

Baptized in the Holy Spirit they perished in their perverse response that was the very basis of their existence, and they were no more able to hide from or harm the ascending spirit. They melted away, darkness before the Light.

For they travailed from the beginning, and the end of their travail was life.

That which hinders the evolving consciousness can have only one of two fates: annihilation or assimilation and transmutation within the Holy Spirit. So out of death sometimes comes life. This is the alchemy of the Holy Spirit within each one of us.

And all of them who were lacking perished, because they were not able to pronounce the Word so that they might exist.

Here we see what determines which fate comes to anything touched by the Light of the Holy Breath, the Divine Word. That which cannot be assimilated and made to vibrate with the Word, to "pronounce" it, perish. That which can vibrate and be assimilated into the Word Itself will live.

This reveals the basis of spiritual transformation: the Divine, Eternal Word that from the beginning was inherent in God because It was God. By It were all things made, bearing within Itself the life for which all things were destined. To as many as could receive that Word was given the Power to become the sons of God, themselves "the Word made flesh." (See John 1:1-14.) It accomplishes all that is needed for the revelation of Christ in the life and consciousness of the yogi who holds to it day and night, vibrating it within the depths of his awareness and being. (To learn how to do this, see *Soham Yoga, the Yoga of the Self.*)

And the Lord destroyed the thoughts, of all them that had not the truth with them.

All things that did or could not bear within them the Divine Word were destroyed and the ascending spirit was freed for them forever.

For they were lacking in wisdom, they who exalted themselves in their hearts.

For they were themselves the embodiments of ignorance, of darkness. Slaves of egotism, they became destroyed along with their master, the ego.

And they were rejected, because the truth was not with them.

Incapable of vibrating along with the Word and being transmuted into It, they were exorcised from the life sphere of the yogi forever.

For the Lord revealed his way, and spread abroad his grace.

This he did through (and as) the Word.

And those who understood it know his holiness.

To fully know the Word by uniting themselves with It is the secret of holiness, the secret of the saints. The way is simple and clear: "A highway shall be there, and a way, and it shall be called The way of holiness; the unclean shall not pass over it; but it shall be for those: the wayfaring men, though fools, shall not err therein. No lion shall be there, nor any ravenous beast shall go up thereon, it shall not be found there; but the redeemed shall walk there. And the ransomed of the Lord shall return, and come to Zion with songs and everlasting joy upon their heads: they shall obtain joy and gladness, and sorrow and sighing shall flee away" (Isaiah 35:8-10).

Ode 25

I was rescued from my bonds, and unto Thee O my God I fled.
For Thou art the right hand of salvation, and my helper.
Thou hast restrained those who rise up against me, and they were seen no more.
Because Thy face was with me, which saved me by Thy grace.
But I was despised and rejected in the eyes of many, and I was in their eyes like lead.
And I acquired strength from Thee, and help.
Thou didst set me a lamp at my right and at my left, so that there might not be in me anything that is not light.
And I was covered with the covering of Thy Spirit, and I removed from me my garments of skin.
For Thy right hand lifted me up, and removed sickness from me.
And I became mighty in Thy truth, and holy in Thy righteousness.
And all those who are against me were afraid of me; and I became the Lord's by the Name of the Lord.
And I was justified by his kindness, and his rest is for ever and ever. Alleluia.

I was rescued from my bonds, and unto Thee O my God I fled.
This is not always the case. Many times when people are freed from bonds and limitations they simply run after more of the same and become as bound as before. For many, terrible as it is, this bondage seems to b stability and security. Many times it has been observed that people who were virtual slaves of invalid relatives, with no life of their own

whatsoever and pitied by all that knew them, upon the death of the invalid immediately sought out a similar person and became their total slave. This is so common that Agatha Christie put such a character in at least one of her plots, and another was featured in an episode of *Mama's Family* on television.

However, there are the wise who, when their bonds are dissolved, go running to take refuge in God and seek to become established in the consciousness of God, not just formal religious piety. Such was the odist.

In the Gospel of Luke Jesus spoke an entire parable about the bonds that keep human beings from going to God and fulfilling their eternal destiny:

"A certain man made a great supper, and bade many: And sent his servant at supper time to say to them that were bidden, Come; for all things are now ready. And they all with one consent began to make excuse. The first said unto him, I have bought a piece of ground, and I must needs go and see it: I pray thee have me excused. And another said, I have bought five yoke of oxen, and I go to prove them: I pray thee have me excused. And another said, I have married a wife, and therefore I cannot come. So that servant came, and shewed his lord these things. Then the master of the house being angry said to his servant, Go out quickly into the streets and lanes of the city, and bring in hither the poor, and the maimed, and the halt, and the blind. And the servant said, Lord, it is done as thou hast commanded, and yet there is room. And the lord said unto the servant, Go out into the highways and hedges, and compel them to come in, that my house may be filled. For I say unto you, That none of those men which were bidden shall taste of my supper" (Luke 14:16-24).

I have heard and observed a great number of excuses to shirk spiritual life, among them every single one of these in the parable. Basically these excuses fall into two categories: material possessions and personal relationships. Like many excuses I have heard, the first two are pretty silly. Will not the ground be there the next day? Or the oxen? What is so urgent about the seeing and the proving? And are they saying that they have bought the property and the oxen completely unseen and unexamined? That is impossible. So what they are really saying is: "I am not interested in your benevolence and hospitality." And that is the most common reason I have encountered over several decades.

The third excuse is extremely tragic, for someone is forfeiting their spiritual life (and therefore their only possibility of real happiness, security and fulfillment) for the sake of another person who will certainly not be benefitted by their refusal. In fact, it is obvious that the host in the parable would welcome the man's wife at his great supper. So both are deprived and the responsible one has turned from life unto death, from freedom unto bondage.

I have been observing this for over half a century: When you give up spiritual life for anything or anyone, you lose that thing or person and do not take up spiritual life afterward. Instead you wander empty and unaware until death. In the thirty-eighth ode there is a description of those who commit this grave error:

"And they [the forces of delusion] make them vomit up their wisdom and intelligence, and they make them mindless. And then they leave them, and so these go about like madmen and corrupt. For they are without heart, and do not seek it" (Ode 38).

So if we are wise we flee unto God, not after more enslavement.

For Thou art the right hand of salvation, and my helper.

In Mahayana Buddhist writings it is said that the moment a person decides to seek enlightenment, a host of buddhas and bodhisattwas become of aware of it and being helping him toward Nirvana. That is certainly true, but those holy beings are motived by the will of God who is the prime helper of all who seek higher consciousness. Our own divine nature also becomes our helper. So we and God in unison become "the right hand of salvation" and our "helper." Success is ours as long as we maintain that desire and that unanimity.

Thou hast restrained those who rise up against me, and they were seen no more. Because Thy face was with me, which saved me by Thy grace.

There are many ways in which the spiritual aspirant can protect and further his spiritual life, but the surest way is by entering into the Divine Presence, for that alone ensures complete success, especially in the annihilation of that which hinders his spiritual development. Meditation is the surest means of coming into God's Presence.

But I was despised and rejected in the eyes of many, and I was in their eyes like lead.

Few things are as disregarded or despised by the world than a dedicated spiritual aspirant. First of all, he is considered daft and unreasonable. Second, he is worthless as a lump of lead because he is of no use to the world, and even turns from it and hopes to end rebirth within it. So of course those who seek God and not the world are viewed as worse than useless. They are a detriment lest they infect others with their "folly."

And I acquired strength from Thee, and help.

To God the seeker is not foolish or worthless. Those who take refuge in him unwaveringly will become strong in his strength and wise in his wisdom. Safety and peace will be theirs, for they trust in God alone in this untrustworthy world.

Thou didst set me a lamp at my right and at my left, so that there might not be in me anything that is not light.

God is the source of wisdom for those who turn from the folly of the world. They will find that whenever they need help and understanding it will come to them. If they follow that, they shall increase in understanding. If they neglect or refuse it, then the lamp goes out. Spiritual life is not easy, and often the wisdom of God is bitter to those that relish the illusions of the world. Often that which is required to carry on one's spiritual progress is also distasteful and even painful to them. "Many therefore of his disciples, when they had heard this, said, This is an hard saying; who can hear it?… From that time many of his disciples went back, and walked no more with him" (John 6:60, 66).

"And when he was gone forth into the way, there came one running, and kneeled to him, and asked him, Good Master, what shall I do that I may inherit eternal life? Then Jesus beholding him loved him, and said unto him, One thing thou lackest: go thy way, sell whatsoever thou hast, and give to the poor, and thou shalt have treasure in heaven: and come, take up the cross, and follow me. And he was sad at that saying, and went away grieved: for he had great possessions." (Mark

10:17, 21-22). This sad story has been repeated over and over since the beginning of time.

Regarding his master, Sri Yukteswar, Yogananda wrote in his autobiography: "Students came, and generally went. Those who craved a path of oily sympathy and comfortable recognitions did not find it at the hermitage. Master offered shelter and shepherding for the aeons, but many disciples miserly demanded ego-balm as well. They departed, preferring life's countless humiliations before any humility. Master's blazing rays, the open penetrating sunshine of his wisdom, were too powerful for their spiritual sickness. They sought some lesser teacher who, shading them with flattery, permitted the fitful sleep of ignorance." So it has always been. We must see that it does not apply to us. It is not easy to become all light, but it is the only worthwhile thing to do.

And I was covered with the covering of Thy Spirit, and I removed from me my garments of skin.

When Adam and Eve fell from Paradise, "unto Adam also and to his wife did the Lord God make coats of skins, and clothed them" (Genesis 3:21). That is, God created the human form for them to live in until they transcended the compulsion of the continual cycle of birth and death.

Those who persevere in their pursuit of spiritual life will become clothed in the Light of the Holy Spirit. And those who persist in that state shall find that the material side of their existence will become less and less until they are spirit and no longer matter. (This does not happen overnight!)

For Thy right hand lifted me up, and removed sickness from me.

Having aligned themselves with the will, the "right hand," of God, the faithful seekers begin to rise in their consciousness and the terrible affliction of ignorance and their addiction to it lessens until it exists no more for them.

And I became mighty in Thy truth, and holy in Thy righteousness.

The loyal seeker becomes increasingly real, in proportion to the degree he divests himself from the falsehood of this unreal world. Passing increasingly from the unreal to the real, the light of holiness increases until righteousness is revealed as his true nature.

"They who worship me with devotion are in me, and I am also in them. If even an evildoer worships me single-heartedly, he should be considered righteous, for truly he has rightly resolved. Quickly he becomes a virtuous soul and goes to everlasting peace. Understand: no devotee of me is ever lost. Having come to this impermanent and unhappy world, devote yourself to me. With mind fixed on me, devoted, worshipping, bow down to me. Thus steadfast, with me as your supreme aim, you shall come to me" (Bhagavad Gita 9:29-31, 33-34).

And all those who are against me were afraid of me; and I became the Lord's by the Name of the Lord.

Although we continually feel small and weak in this vast and mostly incomprehensible world, we are not so. All that opposes us is really weak when we stand up and walk the way of higher life. For we are in the strength of spirit before which all opposition flees.

Most important is the second clause because it give us practical information. By the invocation and meditation of the Divine Word we become the Lord's own. This is the essence of the higher life.

In the Bhagavad Gita we are told: "Among the virtuous, four kinds seek me: the distressed, the seekers of knowledge, the seekers of wealth and the wise. Of them, the wise man, ever united, devoted to the One, is pre-eminent. Exceedingly dear am I to the man of wisdom, and he is dear to me. All these indeed are exalted, but I see the man of wisdom as my very Self. He, with mind steadfast, abides in me, the Supreme Goal" (7:16-18).

And I was justified by his kindness, and his rest is for ever and ever.

Drawing near to a fire makes us warm, and drawing near to God makes us just and true. Then we enter into the very heart of God and have perfect rest for ever and ever.

Ode 26

I poured out praise to the Lord, for I am his.
And I will speak his holy Ode, for my heart is with him.
For his harp is in my hands, and the odes of his rest shall not be silent.
I will cry unto him from my whole heart, I will praise and exalt him with all my members.
For from the East and unto the West, is his glory.
And from the South and unto the North is his praise.
And from the top of the hills unto their farthest part is his perfection.
Who can write the odes of the Lord, or who read them?
Or who can train his soul for life, that his soul may be saved?
Or who can press upon the Most High, that from his mouth he may speak?
Who is able to interpret the wonders of the Lord? For he who interprets would be dissolved, and that which was interpreted will remain.
For it suffices to know and to rest, for in the rest the singers stand.
Like a river which has an increasingly gushing spring, and flows to the relief of them that seek it. Alleluia.

I poured out praise to the Lord, for I am his.
Loving and praising God is not some unnatural or artificially applied practice. Rather, those whose inner reality is becoming manifest will naturally, even automatically, begin loving and praising because they

belong to God, being a part of his Eternal Being. In this way we can distinguish those that are truly drawing near to God from those who are merely philosophizing and discussing, those whom Paramhansa Yogananda often spoke of as having philosophical indigestion. So when you meet someone who thinks they have "gone beyond duality" and therefore have so place in their life for love or devotion directed to God, remember this Ode.

And I will speak his holy Ode, for my heart is with him.

Again we find it is a matter of nature, not of intellectual choice or a sense of duty. Our heart and are Self (Atma) is the same thing. When we find our Self we naturally find God because they are ever in union. Therefore Self-realization is God-realization.

For his harp is in my hands, and the odes of his rest shall not be silent.

Elsewhere in the Odes it is stated that the Holy Spirit is the harp of the Lord. Since that Spirit is giving us life at every moment, it is accessible to us. And the peace, the rest, of our own spirit will shine forth and manifest itself. That is why "when Jesus was come nigh, even now at the descent of the mount of Olives, the whole multitude of the disciples began to rejoice and praise God with a loud voice for all the mighty works that they had seen, saying, Blessed be the King that cometh in the name of the Lord: peace in heaven, and glory in the highest. And some of the Pharisees from among the multitude said unto him, Master, rebuke thy disciples. And he answered and said unto them, I tell you that, if these should hold their peace, the stones would immediately cry out" (Luke 19:37-40).

Therefore Jesus said: "Ye are the light of the world. A city that is set on an hill cannot be hid. Neither do men light a candle, and put it under a bushel, but on a candlestick; and it giveth light unto all that are in the house. Let your light so shine before men, that they may see your good works, and glorify your Father which is in heaven" (Matthew 5:14-16).

Once again, it is a matter of spontaneous nature, like an artesian well: "Jesus stood and cried, saying, If any man thirst, let him come unto me, and drink. He that believeth on me, as the scripture hath said, out of his inmost being shall flow rivers of living water" (John 7:37-38).

I will cry unto him from my whole heart, I will praise and exalt him with all my members.

When the totality of our being is pervaded by the Divine Light of God, praise and exaltation will become our very nature. We will seek, find and rejoice. Just as the river flows to the sea, so each one of us seeks and finds our Self in God. Every atom of our being will radiate his praise.

For from the East and unto the West, is his glory. And from the South and unto the North is his praise.

Not just ourselves, but all the creation is a manifestation of the Infinite Life that is God. "Blessed be his glorious name for ever: and let the whole earth be filled with his glory" (Psalms 72:19). "Holy, holy, holy, is the Lord of hosts: the whole earth is full of his glory" (Isaiah 6:3). "The Lord shall arise upon thee, and his glory shall be seen upon thee" (Isaiah 60:2). "And every creature which is in heaven, and on the earth, and under the earth, and such as are in the sea, and all that are in them, heard I saying, Blessing, and honour, and glory, and power, be unto him that sitteth upon the throne, and unto the Lamb for ever and ever" (Revelation 5:13).

And from the top of the hills unto their farthest part is his perfection.

There is no place where the perfection of God is not to be found by those who have the eyes of their spirit open and are therefore able to directly perceive it.

Who can write the odes of the Lord, or who read them?

Only those whose consciousness has been opened in God can write or read the eternal truths found in these inspired Odes, some of whom seem to be written by Jesus himself, and perhaps some by his mother, Mary.

Or who can train his soul for life, that his soul may be saved?

Life is ours from eternity. It cannot be gotten or produced like a material object. We cannot train our soul for life or do anything to ensure our salvation because those things are present realities, only we are blind to them. That is why Ode Thirteen says: "Behold the Lord is our mirror. Open (your) eyes and see them in him. And learn the manner of your face, and declare praises to his Spirit."

"God created man in his own image, in the image of God created he him; male and female created he them. And God blessed them, and God said unto them, Be fruitful, and multiply, and replenish the earth, and subdue it: and have dominion over the fish of the sea, and over the fowl of the air, and over every living thing that moveth upon the earth (Genesis 1:27-28). The message is clear: God has created us for mastery over all things. We need only uncover and release that inherent nature.

Jesus "cried with a loud voice, Lazarus, come forth. And he that was dead came forth, bound hand and foot with graveclothes: and his face was bound about with a napkin. Jesus saith unto them, Loose him, and let him go" (John 11:43-44). Like Lazarus, we are alive but bound. When we free ourselves of the bonds then our journey is ended. Nirvana literally means "no binding." It is all a matter of awakening, of seeing. "As for me, I will behold thy face in righteousness: I shall be satisfied, when I awake, with thy likeness" (Psalms 17:15). "When I awake, I am still with thee" (Psalms 139:18). "For with thee is the fountain of life: in thy light shall we see light" (Psalms 36:9).

Or who can press upon the Most High, that from his mouth he may speak?

Neither God nor man imposes their will upon the other. This is hard to realize because we are so conditioned by coercive, sociopathic religion that goes on and on about God's will and God's law, not to mention all kinds of gimmicks by which we can supposedly win (or force) God's attention and favor. But we must shake off all such conditioning through study of true scriptures and meditation. By this means we will come to understand the real meaning of the divine will and law and what is the actual interaction between God and man, an interaction governed by the fact of their unity. Again: it is all a matter of inherent nature.

Who is able to interpret the wonders of the Lord? For he who interprets would be dissolved, and that which was interpreted will remain.

All that is not eternal about us will certainly be dissolved in the Divine Vision. Only our true Self and the Self of our Self, God, will remain. That is why, as recorded in the *Gospel of Sri Ramakrishna*, Sri Ramakrishna said: "In samadhi one attains the Knowledge of Brahman–one realizes

Brahman. In that state reasoning stops altogether, and man becomes mute. He has no power to describe the nature of Brahman.

"Once a salt doll went to measure the depth of the ocean. It wanted to tell others how deep the water was. But this it could never do, for no sooner did it get into the water than it melted. Now who was there to report the ocean's depth?" And: "There is a sign of Perfect Knowledge. Man becomes silent when It is attained. Then the 'I', which may be likened to the salt doll, melts in the Ocean of Existence-Knowledge-Bliss Absolute and becomes one with It. Not the slightest trace of distinction is left.... That which could have told about its depth had melted. Reaching the seventh plane, the mind is annihilated; man goes into samadhi. What he feels then cannot be described in words."

For it suffices to know and to rest, for in the rest the singers stand.

To know and experience the Self that is a part of God is sufficient. For in that peace and stability we are enabled to act. The real part of us does not melt away—only the unreal we have mistaken for reality, for ourself. In that freedom and peace ("rest") we will be established ("stand").

Like a river which has an increasingly gushing spring, and flows to the relief of them that seek it.

True liberation (nirvana or moksha) lasts forever, and is not a static condition but an ever-expanding scope of awareness in which the liberated live in total Satchidananda: Reality, Consciousness and Bliss. "There is a river, the streams whereof shall make glad the city of God, the holy place of the tabernacles of the most High" (Psalms 46:4).

ODE 27

> I extended my hands, and I sanctified my Lord.
> For the expansion of my hands is his sign.
> And my extension is the upright cross. Alleluia.

I extended my hands, and I sanctified my Lord.

How can God be sanctified? To understand that we must look to the roots of Jesus' teaching: India. There we find that God is both transcendent and immanent. He is beyond creation, but also within creation, which means that he is within us. In the Bhagavad Gita, which Jesus knew well and cited in his teaching, we find these words: "The Lord dwells in the hearts of all beings.... Fly unto him alone for refuge with your whole being. By that grace you shall attain supreme peace and the eternal abode" (Bhagavad Gita 18:61-62). "Those in whom this ignorance of the Self has been destroyed by knowledge–that knowledge of theirs, like the sun, reveals the Supreme Brahman. Those whose minds are absorbed in That, whose Selves are fixed on That, whose foundation is That, who hold That as the highest object, whose evils have been shaken off by knowledge, attain the ending of rebirth" (Bhagavad Gita 5:16-17).

God is within each one of us, and we must take refuge in that inner Presence. To know him we must turn within. And when we do so with diligence in the practice of yoga meditation, then his presence within us will be "sanctified" and revealed. Saint Nectarios, the great twentieth-century wonderworker of Greece, said: "Seek God every day, but in your heart, and not outside of it." That is exactly what the Gita says. The saint knew this same truth because he was an Eastern Christian.

For the expansion of my hands is his sign.

"The expansion of my hands" refers to the ancient custom of praying with elevated hands on cheek level with the palms upward. This is still the usual prayer position in the Coptic Orthodox Church of Egypt, and was the same in pre-Christian Egypt. Among esotericists this is called "the thymus position" because it actually stimulates the action of the thymus gland which controls the immune system. So it is not only spiritual, it is physically beneficial.

Thus standing in prayer with uplifted hands is the sign of God and of Jesus our Lord. "When thou saidst, Seek ye my face; my heart said unto thee, Thy face, Lord, will I seek" (Psalms 27:8). "I will therefore that men pray every where, lifting up holy hands" (I Timothy 2:8).

And my extension is the upright cross.

"Praying in the Cross" is an ancient Christian practice, standing with the arms outstretched at shoulder level so the body become a living cross. I used to see the Franciscan sisters praying this way in their chapel at Saint Joseph's Hospital in Bloomington, Illinois. For we are not just to carry our cross, we are to become the Holy Cross itself, a throne of Christ from which he reigns.

Ode 28

As the wings of doves over their nestlings, and the mouths of their nestlings towards their mouths, so also are the wings of the Spirit over my heart.

My heart is delighted and leaps up, like the babe who leaps up in the womb of his mother.

I believed and because of this I was at rest, for faithful is he in whom I have believed.

Blessing he has blessed me, and my head is with him.

And the sword shall not divide me from him, nor the scimitar.

For I was ready before destruction came, and I have been set on his immortal wings.

And deathless life embraced me, and kissed me.

And from that (life) is the Spirit within me, and it cannot die because it is life.

Those who saw me were amazed, because I was persecuted.

And they thought that I had been swallowed up, for I seemed to them as one of the lost.

But my oppression became my salvation.

And I was their scorn, because there was no jealousy in me.

Because I did good to every man I was hated.

And they surrounded me like mad dogs, who ignorantly attack their masters.

For their thought is corrupt, and their mind devious.

But I was carrying water in my right hand, and their bitterness I endured by my sweetness.

And I did not perish for I was not their brother, nor was my birth like theirs.

And they sought for my death and could not (accomplish it), for I was older than their memory, and vainly did they cast lots against me.

And those who came after me, sought in vain to destroy the memorial of him who was before them.

For the mind of the Most High cannot be anticipated, and his heart is superior to all wisdom. Alleluia.

As the wings of doves over their nestlings, and the mouths of their nestlings towards their mouths, so also are the wings of the Spirit over my heart.

This is expressing the intense attention of God for the devotee and of the devotee for God. God the Infinite is completely intent on us, and if we are wise, we the finite will be completely intent on him. That is why David sang: "Deep calls unto deep" (Psalms 42:7). "Behold, as the eyes of servants look unto the hand of their masters, and as the eyes of a maiden unto the hand of her mistress; so our eyes wait upon the Lord our God" (Psalms 123:2). "When thou saidst, Seek ye my face; my heart said unto thee, Thy face, Lord, will I seek" (Psalms 27:8). And his son, Solomon wrote: "my beloved is mine, and I am his" (Song of Solomon 2:16).

Total absorption in God is the secret of the saints and angels.

My heart is delighted and leaps up, like the babe who leaps up in the womb of his mother.

Obviously the odist is thinking of the Visitation of the Virgin Mary: "Mary arose in those days, and went into the hill country with haste, into a city of Juda; and entered into the house of Zacharias, and saluted Elisabeth. And it came to pass, that, when Elisabeth heard the salutation of Mary, the babe leaped in her womb; and Elisabeth was filled with the Holy Ghost: And she spake out with a loud voice, and said, Blessed art thou among women, and blessed is the fruit of thy womb. And whence is this to me, that the mother of my Lord should come to me? For, lo, as soon as the voice of thy salutation sounded in mine ears, the babe leaped in my womb for joy" (Luke 1:39-44).

Rejoicing in the thought of God, in the awareness of his presence, we are the sons of God striving upward in the womb of the Cosmic Mother, the Holy Spirit, seeking for total union with him as our very Life. And the remembrance is not bitter medicine, but our joy. Outside of God there is no joy, no peace and no real meaning.

I believed and because of this I was at rest, for faithful is he in whom I have believed.

True faith is an intuition of the reality of God as our life. When this arises in us we have peace, for God alone is unchanging and ever-abiding. As Saint James wrote, God is "the Father of lights, with whom is no variableness, neither shadow of turning. Of his own will begat he us with the word of truth, that we should be a kind of firstfruits of his creatures" (James 1:17-18). God intends that we should attain the fullest level of evolution within this cosmos, so we may then pass upward to a higher world and then an even higher, until we reach the eternal heart of God and merge with him forever.

Blessing he has blessed me, and my head is with him.

Through the blessing of God our minds should be ever with him. In fact, it is impossible without the blessing of God. So this should ever be our aspiration and our prayer with Isaiah: "Thou wilt keep him in perfect peace, whose mind is stayed on thee" (Isaiah 26:3).

And the sword shall not divide me from him, nor the scimitar.

Neither persecution nor death itself can separate us from God. Separation from God is an illusion based on ignorance, but when we have spiritual experience through spiritual practice, especially meditation, then we will know our perpetual union with God.

For I was ready before destruction came, and I have been set on his immortal wings.

We often do not call upon God until troubles come, but the wise are well acquainted with God and link their consciousness with his before trouble comes. And then usually trouble will not come at all. For when we are established in divine awareness we will rest in him and will be lifted up and carried onward by means of his own power and light. With his wings we will fly to him.

And deathless life embraced me, and kissed me.

In the Song of Solomon, a purely mystical and symbolic writing, the first verse is: "Let him kiss me with the kisses of his mouth" (Song of Solomon 1:2). What is the "mouth" of God? It is the divine power of communication between God and man; and the "kisses" of his mouth are the communications of his love for us: his blessing and imparting to us of his own Life and Light. So the odist tells us that he was enwrapped in the very Presence of God and his finite heart entered into communion with the infinite heart of God.

Jesus said: "It is written, Man shall not live by bread alone, but by every word that proceedeth out of the mouth of God" (Matthew 4:4). The devotee of God lives on every communication which God bestows on him in direct heart-to-heart, spirit-to-spirit experience. God is love, therefore love for God is the life-cord that binds us to him, just as his love for us binds him to us. These are mystical matters and transcend the merely human experience. They are precursors of the experience of non-duality in which all such anthropomorphic thought and experience are dissolved.

Many insist that personal concepts of God are mistaken, but they are actually steps which the aspirant uses while still conditioned by relativity. They lead to higher and higher insights until the seeker's own divinity is revealed and he experiences being one with the One Life. Then of course much that was essential to him in his journey to the Infinite is no longer relevant, but that does not mean it was not at one time completely legitimate. The mockers of a personal approach to God as a Person are spiritually childish and by their words betray that they are hardly on the way to Oneness with the All. Paramhansa Yogananda often spoke of such people as having philosophical indigestion: they have "swallowed" philosophical principles which they are not evolved enough to understand. So they choke and gag on them, and that comes out in the form of falsely sophisticated denials of basic truths.

And from that (life) is the Spirit within me, and it cannot die because it is life.

God is Life and Existence Itself; and being part of God, we are immortal just as is he. In fact, we are living spirits because he is Life and Spirit. God will never cease to exist or live, and neither shall we. For we are one.

Those who saw me were amazed, because I was persecuted.

There are those who insist that enlightened people cannot undergo suffering, oppression or persecution; that they should be able to defend themselves or wise enough to avoid those things. For example, on his second visit to England Swami Vivekananda was told that some people who were his most fervent admirers during his first visit had actually fled London so they would not have to meet him. The reason? They had heard that he had been seriously ill in India, and they declared that a Master could never become sick, therefore Vivekananda was a fraud. There are many variations on this theme, but it all distills down to the fact that such "seekers" are seeking someone to end all their troubles and vulnerabilities, so a person who undergoes such things himself cannot do that for them, so he cannot be a Master.

In the same way observers condemned Jesus when he was arrested, imprisoned and executed. Such things could not happen to a Son of God, they insisted, because they expected God to make sure it could never happen to them. Ego is always at the center.

And they thought that I had been swallowed up, for I seemed to them as one of the lost.

At the crucifixion, "they that passed by reviled him, wagging their heads, and saying, Thou that destroyest the temple, and buildest it in three days, save thyself. If thou be the Son of God, come down from the cross. Likewise also the chief priests mocking him, with the scribes and elders, said, He saved others; himself he cannot save. If he be the King of Israel, let him now come down from the cross, and we will believe him. He trusted in God; let him deliver him now, if he will have him: for he said, I am the Son of God" (Matthew 27:39-43).

But my oppression became my salvation.

For through his persecutions Jesus conquered death and rose from the dead, Master of Life and Death, having turned death into life.

And I was their scorn, because there was no jealousy in me. Because I did good to every man I was hated.

Because he was not ruled by ego as they were, and because his only thought was to do good to as many as he possibly could, thinking not of himself but of others, he was despised and hated because his example revealed his enemies for what they were: irreligious, selfish and vicious.

And they surrounded me like mad dogs, who ignorantly attack their masters. For their thought is corrupt, and their mind devious.

Their own actions proved the truth of these words.

But I was carrying water in my right hand, and their bitterness I endured by my sweetness.

But Jesus possessed the water of life. "And he said unto me, It is done. I am Alpha and Omega, the beginning and the end. I will give unto him that is athirst of the fountain of the water of life freely" (Revelation 21:6). Furthermore, he was "carrying" it in his "right hand" in order to give it to others so they, too, could live forever. For he had promised: "He that believeth on me, as the scripture hath said, out of his inmost being shall flow rivers of living water" (John 7:38). This loving-kindness was the sweetness by which he endured and overturned their machinations.

And I did not perish for I was not their brother, nor was my birth like theirs.

"And he said unto them, Ye are from beneath; I am from above: ye are of this world; I am not of this world. I said therefore unto you, that ye shall die in your sins: for if ye believe not that I am he, ye shall die in your sins. Then said they unto him, Who art thou? And Jesus saith unto them, Even the same that I said unto you from the beginning. I have many things to say and to judge of you: but he that sent me is true; and I speak to the world those things which I have heard of him. They understood not that he spake to them of the Father. Then said Jesus unto them, When ye have lifted up the Son of man, then shall ye know that I am he, and that I do nothing of myself; but as my Father hath taught me, I speak these things. And he that sent me is with me: the Father hath not left me alone; for I do always those things that please him" (John 8:23-29).

And they sought for my death and could not (accomplish it), for I was older than their memory, and vainly did they cast lots against me.

Jesus said to his enemies: "I know that ye are Abraham's seed; but ye seek to kill me, because my word hath no place in you. I speak that which I have seen with my Father: and ye do that which ye have seen with your father.

"They answered and said unto him, Abraham is our father. Jesus saith unto them, If ye were Abraham's children, ye would do the works of Abraham. But now ye seek to kill me, a man that hath told you the truth, which I have heard of God: this did not Abraham. Ye do the deeds of your father.

"Then said they to him, We be not born of fornication; we have one Father, even God. Jesus said unto them, If God were your Father, ye would love me: for I proceeded forth and came from God; neither came I of myself, but he sent me. Why do ye not understand my speech? even because ye cannot hear my word. Ye are of your father the devil, and the lusts of your father ye will do. He was a murderer from the beginning, and abode not in the truth, because there is no truth in him. When he speaketh a lie, he speaketh of his own: for he is a liar, and the father of it. And because I tell you the truth, ye believe me not. Which of you convinceth me of sin? And if I say the truth, why do ye not believe me? He that is of God heareth God's words: ye therefore hear them not, because ye are not of God.

"Then answered the Jews, and said unto him, Say we not well that thou art a Samaritan, and hast a devil? Jesus answered, I have not a devil; but I honour my Father, and ye do dishonour me. And I seek not mine own glory: there is one that seeketh and judgeth. Verily, verily, I say unto you, If a man keep my saying, he shall never see death.

"Then said the Jews unto him, Now we know that thou hast a devil. Abraham is dead, and the prophets; and thou sayest, If a man keep my saying, he shall never taste of death. Art thou greater than our father Abraham, which is dead? and the prophets are dead: whom makest thou thyself? Jesus answered, If I honour myself, my honour is nothing: it is my Father that honoureth me; of whom ye say, that he is your God: Yet ye have not known him; but I know him: and if I should say, I know him not, I shall be a liar like unto you: but I know him, and keep his saying. Your father Abraham rejoiced to see my day: and he saw it, and was glad.

"Then said the Jews unto him, Thou art not yet fifty years old, and hast thou seen Abraham? Jesus said unto them, Verily, verily, I say unto you, Before Abraham was, I am.

"Then took they up stones to cast at him: but Jesus hid himself, and went out of the temple, going through the midst of them, and so passed by" (John 8:37-59).

And those who came after me, sought in vain to destroy the memorial of him who was before them.

The resurrection of Jesus and his departure from Israel (see *The Christ of India*) did not end the matter. For two thousand years continuously there have been those desperate to prove either that Jesus was a false prophet or that he never even existed. Either way they intend to destroy his memory. They and their successors never succeed, but they continue doing the work of their father, the devil. The Greek word translated "devil" is *diabolos*, which means "false accuser" and "slanderer." Yet there are many who gladly hear them and adopt their lies for their own.

For the mind of the Most High cannot be anticipated, and his heart is superior to all wisdom.

Only those who have begun to rise in their spiritual evolution can begin to comprehend the ways and plans of God, because his ways and intentions are far beyond those of earthly consciousness. Therefore God counsels us:

"Seek ye the Lord while he may be found, call ye upon him while he is near: Let the wicked forsake his way, and the unrighteous man his thoughts: and let him return unto the Lord, and he will have mercy upon him; and to our God, for he will abundantly pardon.

"For my thoughts are not your thoughts, neither are your ways my ways, saith the Lord. For as the heavens are higher than the earth, so are my ways higher than your ways, and my thoughts than your thoughts.

"For as the rain cometh down, and the snow from heaven, and returneth not thither, but watereth the earth, and maketh it bring forth and bud, that it may give seed to the sower, and bread to the eater: so shall my word be that goeth forth out of my mouth: it shall not return unto me void, but it shall accomplish that which I please, and it shall prosper in the thing whereto I sent it.

"For ye shall go out with joy, and be led forth with peace: the mountains and the hills shall break forth before you into singing, and all the trees of the field shall clap their hands" (Isaiah 55:6-12).

Ode 29

The Lord is my hope, I shall not be confused in him.
For according to his praise he made me, and according to his goodness even so he gave unto me.
And according to his mercies he exalted me, and according to his excellent beauty he lifted me up.
And he brought me up out of the depths of Sheol, and from the mouth of death he drew me.
And I laid my enemies low, and he justified me by his grace.
For I believed in the Lord's Messiah, and it appeared to me that he is the Lord.
And he showed me his sign, and led me in his light,
And he gave me the rod of his power, that I might subdue the thoughts of the Gentiles, and humble the power of the mighty.
To make war by his Word, and to take victory by his power.
And the Lord overthrew my enemy by his Word, and he became like the stubble which the wind carries away.
And I gave praise to the Most High, because he exalted his servant and the son of his handmaid. Alleluia.

The Lord is my hope, I shall not be confused in him. For according to his praise he made me, and according to his goodness even so he gave unto me. And according to his mercies he exalted me, and according to his excellent beauty he lifted me up.

Certainly the most direct means of self-evolution is the practice of yoga meditation, yet there are certain psychological elements that purify and align the intelligence (buddhi) and bring about ascent in consciousness. According to the odist they are:

Praise of God.

This really means two things: the awareness of the praiseworthiness of God and the actual praising of God. If a person will fix his mind on the wondrous actions of God in relation to mankind in general and himself in particular he cannot help but react with wonder and love. Then if he praises God in his heart, either in words or in a movement of consciousness reaching upward though wordlessly toward God, *if it is not an emotion, but an authentic elevation of consciousness*, divine contact will be made to some degree. This is why in the eucharistic liturgies of East and West as one point the priest calls out: "Lift up your hearts!" and the people answer: "We have, unto the Lord!" Ultimately we give glory and praise to God by our life which is so ordered that we will the more quickly attain realization.

Goodness of God.

Realization of the abundant providence of God in our life evokes a response of loving gratitude and awareness of a blessed debt: the obligation to seek God above all else.

Mercy of God.

The mercy of God is the proof of the love of God for us, especially by his aspect as Divine Mother. This produces in us a keen awareness of being a son of God, and inspires us to turn the potential into an actuality.

Exaltation by God.

Certainly anyone with a significant degree of spiritual awakening will be aware that God has been drawing us upward to him through countless births, that he is transmuting us through the process of rebirth. "I looked, and, behold, a door was opened in heaven: and the first voice which I heard was as it were of a trumpet talking with me; which said, Come up hither" (Revelation 4:1).

Beauty of God.

In the Gloria we sing: "We give thanks to thee for thy great glory." All creation and the process of universal evolution is a manifestation of the divine glory. The inner side of things is even more glorious than the outer. Therefore we are stimulated to turn inward and experience that inner glory. This is true "orthodoxy," for the word is derived from *orthodoxia*, which means "right glory." To be orthodox is not to subscribe to formulated verbal dogmas or even pious practices. Rather, orthodoxy is manifesting the glory of God in our lives, a revelation of the truth that "the Lord dwells in the hearts of all beings" (Bhagavad Gita 18:61). Some Eastern Christians translate orthodox as "right praising." This is not literally accurate, but certainly spiritually correct.

All these qualities listed will be inspired and developed in us as the divine image and likeness that is part of our essential being from eternity is evoked by our dedicated search for God: by our immersion in yoga and the yoga life.

And he brought me up out of the depths of Sheol, and from the mouth of death he drew me.

Sheol is a Hebrew word that means grave, pit and the lower or underworld. It is the realm of the dead. Here the odist uses Sheol to represent the realm of spiritual death, the realm of ignorance. "The mouth of death" is the state of being unconscious of both our own spirit and the infinite spirit, God. Unaware of it though we may have been, God has been drawing us up from the pit, from the spiritual grave, from the realm of unconsciousness that is spiritual death, into the realm of consciousness, of life in the dawning light of God's revelation to us.

And I laid my enemies low, and he justified me by his grace.

When life truly manifests in us we become aware of that which darkens us and that which enlightens us. Choosing light over darkness, we then banish from our life and thought all that is inimical to our *theosis* or deification, to our life in Christ as a Christ. "Beloved, now are we the sons of God" (I John 3:2).

For I believed in the Lord's Messiah, and it appeared to me that he is the Lord.

This means that when we have faith in the Messiah, in our Lord Jesus, we will be aware that he spoke the truth when he said: "I and my Father are one" (John 10:30). "He that hath seen me hath seen the Father" (John 14:9). "This is life eternal, that they might know thee the only true God, and Jesus Christ, whom thou hast sent" (John 17:3). "He that believeth on me, believeth not on me, but on him that sent me. And he that seeth me seeth him that sent me." (John 12:44-45).

Those who are one with God are God in an ineffable sense that only they can comprehend. They are not infinite God, but they are finite god. When we see them we see the One of whom they are a part.

And he showed me his sign, and led me in his light, and he gave me the rod of his power, that I might subdue the thoughts of the Gentiles, and humble the power of the mighty. To make war by his Word, and to take victory by his power.

Here we have a picture of the process of spiritual victory every much in the style of the Bhagavad Gita in that it shows the sequence of steps in the process.

He showed me his sign.

In Ode Twenty-Seven we saw that "the expansion of my hands, is his sign." In Ode Forty-Two it is plainer: "I stretched out my hands and approached my Lord, for the stretching out of my hands is his sign. And my expansion is the upright Cross, that was lifted up on the way of the Righteous One." So the sign is both the extension of our minds ("hands") to God and the Cross. The Cross is both the visual form and the gesture of power known as the Sign of the Cross.

And led me in his light.

"When thou saidst, Seek ye my face; my heart said unto thee, Thy face, Lord, will I seek.... For with thee is the fountain of life: in thy light shall we see light" (Psalms 27:8; 36:9). Our eyes are opened and we walk in the inner light that is the Light of Spirit. We live unto and through God.

And he gave me the rod of his power, that I might subdue the thoughts of the Gentiles, and humble the power of the mighty. To make war by his Word, and to take victory by his power.

The Divine Word is the vehicle, the rod of God's power. Those who use it rightly will subdue all foolish, negative and destructive thoughts arising from the unruly part of their nature, "the Gentiles." No matter how powerful our opponents, the Word will vanquish and humble them.

For we must engage in spiritual combat, in spiritual warfare with the Word as our invincible weapon. When by the Word we seize the mastery of all that opposes us and the will of God for us, we shall have taken to ourselves the victory. What is that Word? Soham. (That is why I keep referring you to *Soham Yoga*!)

"In the beginning was the Word, and the Word was with God, and the Word was God. The same was in the beginning with God. All things were made by him; and without him was not any thing made that was made. In him was life; and the life was the light of men" (John 1:1-4).

In the two oldest Upanishads, the Brihadaranyaka and the Isha Upanishad, we find this: "In the beginning this (world) was only the Self [Atman], in the shape of a person [purusha]. Looking around he saw nothing else than the Self. He first said, I am Soham" (Brihadaranyaka Upanisahd 1:4:1). And in the Isha Upanishad, verse sixteen, the Self says: "I am Soham."

Thus, Soham is the "first speaking" of the Absolute Itself: the expression of the knowledge and knowing of the Self. We, too, are Soham. (Again, see *Soham Yoga, the Yoga of the Self.*)

Those who invoke that Word will find that its inmost essence is Life and Light in which they will ascend to infinite Life and Light, to union with God.

And the Lord overthrew my enemy by his Word, and he became like the stubble which the wind carries away.

By putting forth our will in invoking the Word we conquer all that hinders us from ascending in the Light. Yet, since it is the Word and Power that are God, it is really God as the Word who overthrows our enemies, consumes all that is not God and sweeps it away from us. It is through God as Word that we are freed and transformed.

And I gave praise to the Most High, because he exalted his servant and the son of his handmaid.

Therefore we praise God and his manifestation as the Word through which we will have been lifted up and crowned with divine sonship, with Christhood.

ODE 30

Fill ye water for yourselves from the living fountain of the Lord, for it has been opened to you.
And come all ye thirsty and take a drink, and rest by the fountain of the Lord.
For pleasing it is and sparkling, and it gives rest to the soul.
For much sweeter is its water than honey, and the honeycomb of bees is not to be compared with it.
Because it flowed from the lips of the Lord, and it gave a Name from the heart of the Lord.
And it came boundless and invisible, and until it was set in the middle they did not know it.
Blessed are they who have drunk therefrom, and rested thereby. Alleluia.

Fill ye water for yourselves from the living fountain of the Lord, for it has been opened to you. And come all ye thirsty and take a drink, and rest by the fountain of the Lord.

In the Gospel Jesus says: "Whosoever drinketh of the water that I shall give him shall never thirst; but the water that I shall give him shall be in him a well of water springing up into everlasting life" (John 4:14).

The fountain of God is an interior movement proceeding from God who is seated at the core of our being. Each one of us a throne of God. Therefore the call to the fountain is a call to go within and discover the wellsprings of life that are within us. Further, we are to rest in our interior peace.

For pleasing it is and sparkling, and it gives rest to the soul. For much sweeter is its water than honey, and the honeycomb of bees is not to be compared with it. Because it flowed from the lips of the Lord, and it gave a Name from the heart of the Lord.

Here we see that the water is so wondrous and enjoyable because it comes from the mouth of the Lord and bears within it "a Name from the heart of the Lord." This is the Divine Word that is both with God and is God. Therefore nothing could be more necessary to us than that Word. The first step in creation is the vibrating out of the Divine Silence of the Word of Life, the Breath Word which is breathed out in the form of all that exists. And yet it also transcends creation, being essentially divine. It is faithful and true, revealing (witnessing) the Presence within us of God in his fulness as Trinity and Unity. The Word comes from the heart of God and leads us back into that heart.

And it came boundless and invisible, and until it was set in the middle they did not know it.

The Word is infinite and unperceived until it is set in the midst of our consciousness through its invocation and meditation. Those who do so come to know it; others do not.

Blessed are they who have drunk therefrom, and rested thereby.

Those who drink perpetually of that Word of Life, living by its divine power, shall enter into the eternal Sabbath, the Seventh transcendental level of being that is the bosom of the Father (John 1:18), the resting place of the Son and of all sons of God.

ODE 31

The abysses vanished before the Lord, and darkness was destroyed by his appearance.

Error erred and perished on account of him, and contempt received no path, and it was submerged by the truth of the Lord.

He opened his mouth and spoke grace and joy, and he spoke a new song of praise to his Name.

And he lifted up his voice to the Most High, and offered to him those who had become sons through him.

And his face was justified, for thus his Holy Father had given to him.

Come forth ye that have been afflicted, and receive joy.

And inherit your souls by grace, and take to you immortal life,

And they condemned me when I rose up, me who had not been condemned.

And they divided my spoil, though nothing was due to them.

But I endured and held my peace and was silent, that I might not be moved by them.

But I stood unshaken like a firm rock, that is beaten by the waves and endures.

And I bore their bitterness because of humility, that I might redeem my people and instruct it.

And that I might not make void the promises to the Patriarchs, to whom I was promised for the salvation of their seed. Alleluia.

The abysses vanished before the Lord, and darkness was destroyed by his appearance.

"The Lord" spoken of here is Jesus, as will be seen by the context later on. Jesus eliminated all that separated human beings from themselves, one another, the universe and God. He further banished all ignorance and brought the light of perfect knowledge.

Error erred and perished on account of him, and contempt received no path, and it was submerged by the truth of the Lord.

Error was revealed by the light of Christ and melted away at his presence. Disregard and disrespect toward God and his Christ found no place to stand, much less prevail, and only the truth of the Lord, the truth of Spirit, remained for those who believed.

He opened his mouth and spoke grace and joy, and he spoke a new song of praise to his Name.

Jesus told of the love of God for mankind and of his blessings of grace by which sorrow was banished and joy established in the world. Spiritual consciousness was renewed in humanity and new vistas of spiritual understanding were opened by him. Hearts were turned to God in love and praise and away from the world's false premises and promises.

And he lifted up his voice to the Most High, and offered to him those who had become sons through him. And his face was justified, for thus his Holy Father had given to him.

Discipleship became the path to the Father, for through Jesus, the door (John 10:7, 9), they could return to God. And in their own Christhood his disciples became themselves the proof that Jesus was Messiah-Christ.

Come forth ye that have been afflicted, and receive joy. And inherit your souls by grace, and take to you immortal life.

Now Jesus speaks to us, calling us to step out into his light and pass from sorrow and pain into the joy of the Father. Our lost souls will be returned to us through divine grace, and abiding in the consciousness of our eternal spirits we shall dwell in the light and life of immortality.

And they condemned me when I rose up, me who had not been condemned.

At his appearing among us, he who was sinless was condemned as a sinner by sinful men. Those who were laden with transgressions condemned him who was without fault.

And they divided my spoil, though nothing was due to them.

Although Israel was the heritage of Jesus, the leaders of external religion captured and enslaved Israel and its people, even though they had no claim upon them.

But I endured and held my peace and was silent, that I might not be moved by them. But I stood unshaken like a firm rock, that is beaten by the waves and endures.

Jesus refused to enter into controversy and conflict with them, but remained intent on the salvific work for which God had sent him. Therefore they could not deflect him from his purpose in coming among us.

And I bore their bitterness because of humility, that I might redeem my people and instruct it.

For the sake of humanity Jesus endured the scorn and hatred of the wicked, that he might deliver those whom he was destined to save from ignorance and evil and illumine by the light of the truth he would teach them.

And that I might not make void the promises to the Patriarchs, to whom I was promised for the salvation of their seed.

All this was done to fulfill the promises made by God through his prophets to the forefathers of Israel from Abraham onward, that as Moses lead Israel from Egypt, so Jesus the Messiah would lead Israel from this world into the divine kingdom.

Ode 32

> To the blessed the joy is from their heart, and light from him
>   that dwells in them.
> And the Word from the Truth Who is from himself.
> For he hath been strengthened by the Holy Power of the Most
>   High, and he is unshaken for ever and ever. Alleluia.

This is hardly the picture of a Christian that is prevalent today. Here we find that the original Christians had joy arising from their heart and their minds were illumined with the light proceeding from God who was dwelling in them. Furthermore, they knew the Word which came to them from the Self-existent God. "Strengthened by the Holy Power of the Most High, and unshaken for ever and ever."

Alleluia, indeed!

ODE 33

Grace again ran and left the Corruptor, and came down upon him to bring him to naught.

And he made utter destruction from before him, and devastated all his array.

And he stood on a lofty summit and cried aloud, from one end of the earth to the other.

And he drew to him all those who obeyed him, and he did not appear as the Evil One.

But the Perfect Virgin stood, Who was proclaiming and summoning and saying:

O ye sons of men return ye, and ye their daughters come.

And leave the ways of that Corruptor, and draw near unto me.

And I will enter into you, and bring you forth from destruction, and I will make you wise in the ways of truth.

Be not corrupted, nor perish.

Hear ye me and be saved, for the grace of God I am proclaiming in you.

And by my means you shall be redeemed and become blessed: I am your judge.

And they who have put me on shall not be falsely accused, but they shall possess incorruption in the new world.

My chosen ones have walked in me, and my ways I will make known to them that seek me, and I will promise them my Name. Alleluia.

Grace again ran and left the Corruptor, and came down upon him to bring him to naught.

Considering the subsequent self-destruction of the Corruptor, obviously Grace blinded him and led him to his doom, much as do the witches in *Macbeth*. There is a force of righteousness in the universe that is not vengeful but which causes the truth of things to be revealed and darkness to be dispelled, often by its own actions.

And he made utter destruction from before him, and devastated all his array.

The Corruptor, engaged in reflexive destruction, destroyed all of his own supports, sources of power and followers, just as addictive substances eventually destroy those so enamored of and enslaved to them.

And he stood on a lofty summit and cried aloud, from one end of the earth to the other. And he drew to him all those who obeyed him, and he did not appear as the Evil One.

The Corruptor drew to himself all those who had an affinity with him. To many, if not most, "he did not appear as the Evil One." But as Saint Paul wrote: "And no marvel; for Satan himself is transformed into an angel of light. Therefore it is no great thing if his ministers also be transformed as the ministers of righteousness; whose end shall be according to their works" (II Corinthians 11:14-15).

But the Perfect Virgin stood, Who was proclaiming and summoning and saying: O ye sons of men return ye, and ye their daughters come. And leave the ways of that Corruptor, and draw near unto me. And I will enter into you, and bring you forth from destruction, and I will make you wise in the ways of truth.

The power of incorruption, the Perfect Virgin, the Cosmic Orderer, the Holy Spirit, ever calls to us in the depths of our being as well as outside us, urging all humanity to come to her Light, leaving behind the darkness of the Corruptor, and draw near to her. In Ecclesiasticus 24:26 she also calls: "Come over to me."

Those who heed the call shall be "filled with the Holy Spirit" and led by her out of the darkness of spiritual destruction. She shall open the eyes of their spirit and make them "wise in the ways of truth," for she is the Spirit of Truth (John 14:17).

Be not corrupted, nor perish. Hear ye me and be saved, for the grace of God I am proclaiming in you. And by my means you shall be redeemed and become blessed: I am your judge. And they who have put me on shall not be falsely accused, but they shall possess incorruption in the new world.

The teaching and illumination of the Holy Spirit is a profoundly internal matter, and her way alone is the way of blessedness. Yet she is also judge and conveys to us her judgment regarding our ways. But she also empowers us to conform ourselves to *her* ways. Then they shall in truth "walk in newness of life" (Romans 6:4) and incorruption, in the eternal kingdom.

My chosen ones have walked in me, and my ways I will make known to them that seek me, and I will promise them my Name.

This alone is the path of life: living in God, knowing the ways of God and knowing God through his Word.

ODE 34

There is no hard way where there is a simple heart, nor any
    barrier where the thoughts are upright.
Nor is there any whirlwind in the depth of the illuminated thought.
Where one is surrounded on every side by pleasing country,
    there is nothing divided in him.
The likeness of that which is below is that which is above.
For everything is above, and below there is nothing, but it is
    believed to be by those in whom there is no knowledge.
Grace has been revealed for your salvation, believe and live and
    be saved. Alleluia.

There is no hard way where there is a simple heart, nor any barrier where the thoughts are upright.

"Come unto me, all ye that labour and are heavy laden, and I will give you rest. Take my yoke upon you, and learn of me; for I am meek and lowly in heart: and ye shall find rest unto your souls. For my yoke is easy, and my burden is light" (Matthew 11:28-30).

Whining and complaining about the disciplines or other difficulties of spiritual life is a sign of one who is either not able or willing to bear the easy yoke and the light burden of the yoga life. Why? Because of desires and attitudes that are in conflict with authentic spiritual endeavor, the condition which Saint James calls being "double minded" (James 4:8), wanting both materiality and spirituality, the sacred and the profane, the pure and the defiled. The Greek word used by Saint James is *dipsuchos*, which means wavering, uncertain, doubting and divided in interest (especially this latter). It can also mean to have two souls, to be a spiritual schizophrenic. (The word used by Saint James is *dipsuchos*, "two-spirited.") Such a person suffers, pulling themselves apart. Even if they are hypocritical they are also in pain because they have no real aspiration whatsoever, just a desire to make an impression on others. Such people should not be despised, but their dilemma should be understood. To try to hang on to them and cajole them into prolonging the agony is neither righteous nor merciful. They should be allowed to quietly exit and end their conflict. When the heart is "simple" in the sense of being direct and united in its perspective, then the way will not be hard.

When the mind is pure, the thoughts are "upright" in the sense of being true and oriented toward higher things, literally moving up the evolutionary path with joy, happily meeting the conditions and requirements to pursue enlightenment and liberation of the spirit. For such there are no barriers; nothing can stop them from reaching their goal.

Actually, barriers do arise, but the seekers' will and aspiration so easily carry them over all obstacles it is as if they did not exist. Most of the things that impede the spiritual seeker are mirages, illusions and delusions appearing only in their minds. The seeker must decide whether or not to let them have any influence or effect. This spells the difference between failure or success. Saint Paul tells us that Jesus, "for the joy that was set before him endured the cross, despising the shame, and is set down at the right hand of the throne of God" (Hebrews 12:2). This is why the cross is the symbol of Christianity: it is the door to joy and freedom, the path to enthronement at the right hand of God. "No price is too high" is the motto of those destined to win the prize, who "press toward the mark for the prize of the high calling of God in Christ Jesus" (Philippians 3:14).

Nor is there any whirlwind in the depth of the illuminated thought.

There is no confusion, distraction or deflection for those who remain centered and immersed in "the illumined thought" of an illumined mind. The most effective and therefore sure means to do this is to ever be engaged in the continual mental repetition of Soham in time with our breath. It is the supreme illumined thought.

Where one is surrounded on every side by pleasing country, there is nothing divided in him.

In the mind which is happy and at peace there is no conflict. Here, again, it is a matter of the fundamental character of the individual. Further, this verse shows us that successful spiritual practice demands a total environment of the highest elements. We must surround ourselves with divine remembrance and those things that inspire us to press on toward the goal of self-realization. The outer and inner life must be consistent and of a single, positive quality. Then everything goes well. Otherwise things go backward, not forward. We must create the inner and outer environment that guarantees success in spiritual life and keep it consistent and complete. "Jesus said unto him, No man, having put his hand to the plough, and looking back, is fit for the kingdom of God" (Luke 9:62).

The likeness of that which is below is that which is above.

This is the classical hermetic statement: As Above, So Below. The higher worlds are reflected in the lower worlds, so we can learn about them by study of the lower realms. The same is true of the individual person: whatever is going on in the higher bodies is being reflected in the lower bodies. So when we see someone taking up (authentic) meditation we know that a great awakening is beginning in his higher levels. When an aspirant begins purifying his life, especially in the areas of diet, conduct and personal environment, we know that purification has begun in his higher bodies. If we do not see these things in his life, then we know that whatever a person might say or claim, nothing of any real spiritual nature is occurring in him at all.

Finally, this principle tells us that in essence the lower and the higher are really one, are actually the same thing. If we carefully examine all the implications of this we will be enabled to live our life much more truly as aspirants to the Divine.

For everything is above, and below there is nothing, but it is believed to be by those in whom there is no knowledge.

Here again the hermetic principle is presented. That which is above is the root of everything. That which is below is nothing in the sense that it is only a reflection, it is not self-existent. Furthermore, because of the distortion that has taken place during the successive emanations of the various worlds (lokas), it is fundamentally illusory, just as the reflection of an object in agitated water does not show what it really is like. In fact, it is not an object at all and has no substance of its own. The seeming reality of this and all relative worlds is collectively known as Maya. "Maya" means "the Measurer," as it is based on the two delusive "measures," Time and Space. Interestingly enough, Western philosophy considers time and space to be the fundamental realities of existence. But the mystics of all viable spiritual traditions know better. Only those without true knowledge (jnana) born of direct spiritual experience believe in the illusion, like children believing in the magic of a stage magician.

Grace has been revealed for your salvation, believe and live and be saved.

To enumerate the means of grace revealed in the many spiritual traditions of the world, including the Way of Christ, would require a tremendous amount of exposition. If you will allow, I would like to speak of only one, yet that which is the crest jewel of all traditions: Truth. In the first chapter of Saint John's Gospel we are told regarding Jesus: "The Word was made flesh, and dwelt among us,… full of grace and truth.… For the law was given by Moses, but grace and truth came by Jesus Christ" (John 1:14, 17).

Grace and Truth. Truth, or Jnana, is the way to know God, to become one with God as a son of God. Therefore the Sanskrit texts of India speak ever of Brahmajnana, the knowing of God. This is not an intellectual knowing, so Krishna tells Arjuna: "To you I shall explain in full this knowledge, *along with realization*, which being known, nothing further remains to be known in this world" (Bhagavad Gita 7:2). This is "most secret knowledge combined with realization, which having known you shall be free from evil. Royal knowledge, royal secret, this the supreme purifier, readily understood, dharmic, pleasant to practice, eternal" (Bhagavad Gita 9:1-2).

Grace is the "power to become the sons of God" (John 1:12). The word translated "power" is *exousia*, which means privilege, capacity, competency, mastery, authority, power and strength. They all apply here as sadhana shakti, the power to successfully practice yoga and become one with the Eternal.

Although the Odes of Solomon are written in Aramaic, it is worthwhile looking at the Greek word *Charis* used in the translations of the Odes. Charis means "that which affords joy, pleasure, delight and sweetness," the ananda of Satchidananda, the Absolute Divinity.

Those who live in grace and truth and become embodiments of grace and truth shall in truth be "saved" by attaining perfect liberation (moksha) in God.

ODE 35

The fine rain of the Lord overshadowed me in quietness, and it caused a cloud of peace to rise over my head;
That it might guard me at all times; and it became salvation to me.
Everybody was shaken and affrighted, and there came forth from them smoke and judgement.
But I was keeping quiet in the ranks of the Lord; more than shade was he to me, and more than foundation.
And I was carried like a child by its mother, and he gave me milk, the dew of the Lord.
And I grew strong in his gift, and I rested in his perfection.
And I spread out my hands in the ascent of my soul, and I directed myself towards the Most High, and I was redeemed with him. Alleluia.

The fine rain of the Lord overshadowed me in quietness, and it caused a cloud of peace to rise over my head; that it might guard me at all times; and it became salvation to me.

In the Bible rain is often symbol of the blessing and presence of God. "His favor is as a cloud of the latter [*malqoshe*: spring] rain" (Proverbs 16:15). "He shall come down like rain upon the mown grass: as showers that water the earth" (Psalms 72:6). "He shall come unto us as the rain, as the latter and former rain unto the earth" (Hosea 6:3).

The presence of God is as fine rain, refreshing and gentle, not flood rain. It is still, yet it moves in the sense of bringing about transformation.

Peace and rest are its hallmarks. It is also the beginning of life as in the spring. It protects until the goal is reached and then it is revealed as salvation (moksha: liberation)

Everybody was shaken and affrighted, and there came forth from them smoke and judgement.

"Everybody" designates all the alien elements, the barnacles of ignorance accumulated through lifetimes. They are are dislodged, and though they try to avoid the Light and Power that is the "face" of God, the fire of the Holy Spirit reduces them to smoke, not just ashes, and reveals them for the mirages they really are.

But I was keeping quiet in the ranks of the Lord; more than shade was he to me, and more than foundation.

All the while this is going on, the blessed soul is in quietness, at rest among the angels and saints of Christ who have become its constant companions. The spiritual quest begins in peace, proceeds in peace, and ends in Peace. This is an important point for us to keep in mind, because there are supposed spiritual paths that lead into nothing but struggle, conflict and eventual defeat. But the path to God is blessed from the very beginning. God is not just a protector, fosterer and strengthener; he is revealed to us as the very basis of our existence, the Soul of our soul, the Spirit of our spirit, inseparable from us as the Life of our life.

And I was carried like a child by its mother, and he gave me milk the dew of the Lord.

The aspirant comes to realize that he lives and moves in God, in the Holy Spirit, who like a mother feeds him the living water of Divinity, for he himself is essentially divine.

And I grew strong in his gift, and I rested in his perfection. And I spread out my hands in the ascent of my soul, and I directed myself towards the Most High, and I was redeemed with him.

Although all is done by the power of God given freely to us, it is we who bring about our salvation. Our perfection is his, but we assimilate it and become ourselves perfect. Looking only upward and aspiring upward we ascend in consciousness, intent on God Alone. Finally, uniting with God we are free, redeemed from the bondage of birth and death and ignorance. The spiritual path is itself the self-ransom by which we are liberated into Infinite Spirit.

ODE 36

I rested on the Spirit of the Lord, and She raised me on high.
And She made me to stand on my feet in the high place of the Lord, before his perfection and his glory, while I was praising (him) by the composition of his odes.
She gave birth to me before the face of the Lord. And although I was a son of man, I was named a luminary, a son of God.
Because I was glorified among the glorious ones, and great among the great ones.
For according to the greatness of the Most High so She made me, and like his newness he renewed me.
And he anointed me from his own perfection, and I became one of his near ones.
And my mouth was opened like a cloud of dew, and my heart gushed out a gush of righteousness.
And my approach was in peace, and I was established in the Spirit of Providence. Alleluia.

I rested on the Spirit of the Lord, and She raised me on high.
How does someone rest on the Spirit of the Lord? In deep meditation, meditation on the breath, since it is a manifestation of the Holy Spirit (the *Agia Pneuma*, the Holy Breath that pervades all beings), and the sound-form of the Holy Spirit Breath in the cosmos and in us: Soham. The subtle part of the breath in each human being is the life force known as prana in the yogic texts. Inner mental intonations of Soham cause the pranas in the body to become refined and automatically rise

into the head, the thousand-petalled lotus of the sahasrara chakra where enlightenment can begin to be experienced. (See *Soham Yoga, the Yoga of the Self*.)

And She made me to stand on my feet in the high place of the Lord, before his perfection and his glory, while I was praising (him) by the composition of his odes.

Take note that the Holy Spirit did not cause the odist to fall on his face in fear or to grovel before God, lamenting that he was a sinner and unclean. She stood him on his feet, upright and facing God not as a servant or a slave but as a revealed son of God. And he was inspired to sing the praises of his Father in the forms of these sacred odes in which the mysteries of Christ, the transmutation of humanity into Christhood, are made clear.

She gave birth to me before the face of the Lord. And although I was a son of man, I was named a luminary, a son of God. Because I was glorified among the glorious ones, and great among the great ones.

Through the Mother the sons of God receive birth. It is the Holy Spirit who presents God with his sons. But she only does so "before the face of the Lord." Only those who dwell in the remembrance and the invocation of Divine Consciousness and Power will become dwija, the twice-born: first born of earth and then born of the Holy Breath. Although human, each aspiring one becoming a yogi thus becomes "a luminary, a son of God," himself "Light from Light; true God from true God; begotten not made; of one substance with the Father," as the Nicene Creed says about Jesus Christ and all those who become Christs through him.

For according to the greatness of the Most High so She made me, and like his newness he renewed me.

The Mother of All does not make her sons the sons of the Father, because they are that from eternity. Rather, She takes away the darkness and ignorance that blinds them to the truth of their eternal being: God. They are gods, and she enables them to know and demonstrate that.

And he anointed me from his own perfection, and I became one of his near ones.

Jesus prayed: "O Father, glorify thou me with thine own self with the glory which I had with thee before the world was" (John 17:5). That prayer was heard and fulfilled, and the same will be fulfilled for and in us if we make that prayer aright and always.

And my mouth was opened like a cloud of dew, and my heart gushed out a gush of righteousness.

"He that believeth on me, as the scripture hath said, out of his inmost being shall flow rivers of living water" (John 7:38). The same thing is to happen to us if we seek and find (regain) our eternal Christhood.

And my approach was in peace, and I was established in the Spirit of Providence.

"Peace I leave with you, my peace I give unto you: not as the world giveth, give I unto you. Let not your heart be troubled, neither let it be afraid" (John 14:27). Further: "As many as are led by the Spirit of God, they are the sons of God" (Romans 8:14). Divine Providence, supplying all the needs of the awakened spirit, leads it on. As Saint Paul wrote: "We all, with open face beholding as in a glass the glory of the Lord, are changed into the same image from glory to glory, even as by the Spirit of the Lord" (II Corinthians 3:18). And the work of the Mother is completed, is perfected.

ODE 37

> I stretched out my hands to the Lord, and to the Most High I lifted my voice.
> And I spoke with the lips of my heart, and he heard me when my voice reached him.
> His Word came to me, that which gave me the fruits of my labors;
> And gave me rest by the grace of the Lord. Alleluia.

I stretched out my hands to the Lord, and to the Most High I lifted my voice.

There are two positions that may be referred to here. One is simply lifting the hands on high with the palms facing the supplicant, signifying that he is empty-handed and totally dependent upon the Lord. The other is the thymus gesture already described earlier. Both emphasize their emptiness and their hope of receiving from the hand of God that which is desired. Again, total dependency is being indicated as well as humility. It is also a gesture of waiting upon the pleasure and will of God. "I wait for the Lord, my soul doth wait, and in his word do I hope" (Psalms 130:5). "Therefore I will look unto the Lord; I will wait for the God of my salvation: my God will hear me" (Micah 7:7).

And I spoke with the lips of my heart, and he heard me when my voice reached him.

Many years ago I heard a minister tell of a spiritual experience she had read about. Someone sitting in church was "caught up," as Saint Paul put it, during the singing of a hymn. She seemed to be in a realm of pure Light, but she could hear the hymn being sung down below.

However, she only heard the voices of children and of two or three adults. The voices of the others did not reach the high world in which she found herself. Then suddenly she was back down on earth hearing many people singing. But she knew from then on that in the heaven world only a few voices were reaching there and being heard.

When the odist spoke to God with the lips of his heart, his spirit-soul, then his voice reached God. Since the lips of our heart are inside us, not outside, it was an inward speaking and an inward hearing, because God is within us. To communicate with the Divine we must live in the spirit as Saint Paul also said. Spiritual life certainly manifests in our entire life, including our external life, but it is essentially an interior life.

His Word came to me, that which gave me the fruits of my labors.

Communion with God is the ultimate fruit of all spiritual endeavor. If we do not seek and attain this, we are missing the point and the goal altogether.

And gave me rest by the grace of the Lord.

Speaking of spiritual attainment, Saint Paul wrote: "There remaineth therefore a rest to the people of God. For he that is entered into his rest, he also hath ceased from his own works, as God did from his. Let us labour therefore to enter into that rest," (Hebrews 4:9-11). This is the transcendental state outside all lesser conditions.

As mentioned before, the word translated rest is *sabbatismos*, Sabbath, which means literally: "the seventh day." This is a symbol of the seventh level of consciousness, of mystical union with God. It is the cessation of all duality, of all subject-object consciousness, and the state of pure Being beyond all relativity and conditioning. Therefore Saint John wrote: "When he had opened the seventh seal, there was silence in heaven" (Revelation 8:1).

ODE 38

I went up into the Light of Truth as into a chariot, and the Truth led me and caused me to come.

And it carried me across hollows and gulfs, and from the cliffs and gullies it preserved me.

And it became to me a Haven of Salvation, and set me on the step of deathless life.

And he went with me and made me rest and suffered me not to err, because he was and is the Truth.

And there was no danger for me because I walked with him, and I made no error in anything because I obeyed him.

For Error fled away from him, and would not meet him.

But Truth was proceeding in the right way, and whatever I did not know he made clear to me:

All the drugs of Error, and the torments of death which are considered sweetness.

And the corrupting of the Corruptor, I saw when the Bride who was corrupting was adorned, and the Bridegroom who corrupts and is corrupted.

And I asked the Truth: Who are these? and he said to me: This is the Deceiver and the Error:

And they imitate the Beloved and his Bride, and they lead astray the world and corrupt it.

And they invite many to the Banquet, and give them to drink of the wine of their intoxication.

And they make them vomit up their wisdom and intelligence, and they make them mindless.

And then they leave them, and so these go about like madmen and corrupt.

For they are without heart, and do not seek it.

And I was made wise so as not to fall into the hands of the Deceiver, and I congratulated myself that the Truth had gone with me.

And I was established and lived and was redeemed, and my foundations were laid on account of the Lord's hand, for he planted me.

For he set the root, and watered it and endowed it and blessed it, and its fruits will be for ever.

It struck deep and sprang up and spread wide, and it was full and was enlarged.

And the Lord alone was glorified, in his planting and in his cultivation;

In his care and in the blessing of his lips, in the beautiful planting of his right hand;

And in the splendor of his planting, and in the understanding of his mind. Alleluia.

I went up into the Light of Truth as into a chariot, and the Truth led me and caused me to come.

The consciousness, the mind, of the odist is referred to here as ascending into the Light of Truth. What is that Light? In the first chapter of *Autobiography of a Yogi*, Paramhansa Yogananda relays the following experience from his early childhood.

"Sitting on my bed one morning, I fell into a deep reverie.

"'What is behind the darkness of closed eyes?' This probing thought came powerfully into my mind. An immense flash of light at once manifested to my inward gaze. Divine shapes of saints, sitting in meditation posture in mountain caves, formed like miniature cinema pictures on the large screen of radiance within my forehead.

"'Who are you?' I spoke aloud.

"'We are the himalayan yogis.' The celestial response is difficult to describe; my heart was thrilled.

"'Ah, I long to go to the himalayas and become like you!' The vision vanished, but the silvery beams expanded in ever-widening circles to infinity.

"'What is this wondrous glow?'

"'I am Ishwara. I am Light.' The voice was as murmuring clouds.

"'I want to be one with Thee!'

"Out of the slow dwindling of my divine ecstasy, I salvaged a permanent legacy of inspiration to seek God. This memory persisted long after the day of rapture."

God is the ultimate Reality, seen by the yogi as Light. Yogananda often told his students that the subtle light they saw in meditation was God. The implication of this verse is that meditation is the way of ascent, which it certainly is. When the mind is purified and elevated by meditation, then God leads us onward into divine experience. It is not a physical movement, but a transformation of consciousness, which is the essential being of the meditator since pure consciousness and pure spirit are the same thing.

The final clause, "and the Truth led me and caused me to come," sounds peculiar, though it is the literal meaning of the Aramaic text. It means that the odist was caused to move by the Light Itself. The Gayatri Mantra of India, the ancient prayer for enlightenment, says: "We meditate upon that Effulgent Being… may It impel us toward That." The odist found his consciousness also impelled toward the Supreme Consciousness, the Supreme Light in which he ascended.

And it carried me across hollows and gulfs, and from the cliffs and gullies it preserved me.

The ever-changing nature of relative existence, including the mind itself, is a bane to anyone trying to accomplish something, and it is especially so for the yogi-mystic. This verse indicates that the Light of Truth (God) elevated the consciousness of the odist above the ups and downs that plague human beings. One of the traits necessary for enlightenment is steadiness of mind free from all fluctuation. This the odist attained in the Light of Truth.

And it became to me a Haven of Salvation, and set me on the step of deathless life.

The Light of Spirit is itself the haven of salvation, its peaceful abode. It is itself the goal, yet it also takes us to the goal, to itself. As Emily Dickinson said: "Instead of getting to heaven, at last–I'm going, all along." The Light delivered the odist to the step, the threshold, of immortality itself.

And he went with me and made me rest and suffered me not to err, because he was and is the Truth.

Entering into immortal life, the odist was established there. Being in union with God, the Truth, the odist was preserved from all misperceptions, errors or wrong conclusions.

And there was no danger for me because I walked with him, and I made no error in anything because I obeyed him.

The condition of the odist was not merely passive, but he avoided the danger of illusion and delusion by actively aligning himself with God, "walking" with him and obeying that which God was revealing to his illumined intellect. So the odist was actively gaining wisdom and insight by his cooperation with the Light of Truth.

For Error fled away from him, and would not meet him.

Light dispels all darkness, and all error is dispelled by the ascent of our consciousness into the Light and dwelling there. That is why in the Bhagavad Gita (6:46) Krishna the teacher tells Arjuna the student to become a yogi.

But Truth was proceeding in the right way, and whatever I did not know he made clear to me:

True spiritual experience is an active unfolding and expansion of the seeker's consciousness. A hymn of the Saint Thomas Christians says: "By thy light we see the Light: Thou, True Light, dost give the light to thy creatures all. Lighten us with thy glad light, thou the Light divine."

All the drugs of Error, and the torments of death which are considered sweetness,…

The seventy-first section of the Tao Teh King says: "Who[ever] recognizes sick-mindedness [delusion] as sick-mindedness is not sick-minded." He who knows what is delusion is himself undeluded. Therefore the Light of truth revealed to the odist "all the drugs of Error, and the torments of death which are considered sweetness."

We must face the truth: most human beings are drugged by the delusions of the corrupted world, hopelessly addicted to them. Even worse, they consider that the torments of spiritual death are really sweet and desirable; and they become addicted to those drugs, too. In the opera *Aida*, the heroine sings at one point: *Amore, amore, gaudio tormento*: "Love, love, joyful torment!" Love has also been called "the finest frailty of the human mind." Anyone with clear sight can see that such statements are symptoms of addiction, not blessedness. Deluded by such things, the addicts avidly seek for them, believing that without them there is no real life or living. Only the Divine Light shows us their real nature and enables us to know them for what they are: the gates of death and hell.

And the corrupting of the Corruptor, I saw when the Bride who was corrupting was adorned, and the Bridegroom who corrupts and is corrupted.

What is known as bridal mysticism, the concept of the devout soul as the bride and God as the bridegroom, is found in various religious traditions. Although there is a passage about "the voice of the bridegroom, and the voice of the bride" in Jeremiah (33:11), all the other references in the Bible are in the book of Revelation. There the groom is Christ and the bride the Church, the disciples of Christ. A mystical vision of the Church of Christ is found in the twenty-first chapter: "There came unto me one of the seven angels… and talked with me, saying, Come hither, I will shew thee the bride, the Lamb's wife. And he carried me away in the spirit… and shewed me that great city, the holy Jerusalem, descending out of heaven from God, having the glory of God: and her light was like unto a stone most precious, even like a jasper stone, clear as crystal" (Revelation 21:9-11). In the next chapter the seer is told: "The Spirit and the bride say, Come.… And let him that is athirst come. And whosoever will, let him take the water of life freely" (Revelation 22:17).

The idea is that Christ and his Church are the sources of spiritual life, that they call questing souls and impart "the water of life freely."

But there is a false bride and bridegroom created by the Corrupter, the force of cosmic delusion also called Satan, to deceive humanity. Just as the true bride and groom call human beings to light, wisdom and immortality (including freedom from rebirth), so the false bride and groom entice human beings into darkness, delusion and death, including continual earthly rebirth–though they claim it is light, wisdom and immortality.

It is important to notice that these false ones are said to both corrupt and be themselves corrupted. This is because God is the source of all things, therefore all things are good. Evil as the opposite of good does not exist. Rather, evil is a distortion, a misuse or corruption of good. Therefore evil is good which has become twisted and deformed, and the more it twists and deforms, the more it itself becomes twisted and deformed. Nevertheless, since at the core all thing are good because they arise from God, even the evil and false can eventually become restored to the state of good and truth. Just as there is no eternal damnation, so there is no eternal state of evil.

The false bride and groom take on many forms, including false religion, and that is the primary subject of this ode.

And I asked the Truth: Who are these? and he said to me: This is the Deceiver and the Error.

They are the Liar and the Lie. Satan and Deception.

And they imitate the Beloved and his Bride, and they lead astray the world and corrupt it.

Evil's best disguise is to appear as that which is good. "For such are false apostles, deceitful workers, transforming themselves into the apostles of Christ. And no marvel; for Satan himself is transformed into an angel of light. Therefore it is no great thing if his ministers also be transformed as the ministers of righteousness; whose end shall be according to their works" (II Corinthians 11:13-15). Unfortunately, the worlds on the level of this one in which we are now living are far more susceptible and responsive to the false and destructive than to the true and salvific. That is why when a disciple asked Jesus: "Lord, are there few that be saved?" (Luke 13:23), he answered: "Enter ye in at the strait gate: for wide is the gate, and broad is the way, that leadeth to destruction, and many there be which go in thereat: Because strait is the gate, and narrow is the way, which leadeth unto life, and few there be that find it" (Matthew 7:13-14).

And they invite many to the Banquet, and give them to drink of the wine of their intoxication.

In the seventeenth and eighteenth chapters of Revelation the false bride is called Babylon, and the revelator speaks of her making men drunk with the wine of her deception. Foolish people love alcohol because it makes them feel "happy" and "good," even though it is destroying their brains and vital organs. Loving spiritual intoxication, addicted to self-mutilation and self-deception, the religious and metaphysical dupes rush to the latest false teachings and teachers. And then after a while they find another source of spiritual drunkenness and stumble there. "Seminar junkies" are prime examples of what I am talking about. And the religious and spiritual versions of the false bride and groom are but drops in the cesspool of earthly delusiveness.

And they make them vomit up their wisdom and intelligence, and they make them mindless. And then they leave them, and so these go about like madmen and corrupt.

Yes, this is how it all ends. Having gladly cast aside all truth and good sense (for they have cooperated with the false teachers in their deception and destruction), the dupes have no longer any intelligence, but only a devastated mind and personality. Then the false philosophies, meditation methods and teachers leave them: usually incapable of recovering and finding a real spiritual path. Many are permanently damaged psychologically. Often discovery of the dishonesty and immorality of the organizations and teachers so traumatize them that they denounce all spiritual teaching and teachers for the rest of their lives. And that was the intent of the false bride and groom all along. Yet "the Guru" and "the Shakti" are still sought-after commodities in the marketplace of the world.

For they are without heart, and do not seek it.

"Heart" here means the very core of the person, the eternal spirit that is one with God. This does not mean that the victims of the false bride and groom truly do not have a spirit-self, but that they are so out of touch with it (and often incapable of ever touching it in this present life) that they will never wish or try to seek it. For them this incarnation is over, practically speaking, and only a weary passing through time until their death remains for them. The way of life is really always open to them, but they cannot see it or even desire it. They are dead-alive.

Please do not think I am condemning these people. They should not be censured but prayed for, since there may be some way they can live again in spirit. If you know any of them, I hope that you will not just pray for them in this life, but will continue to pray for them after their physical death. Certainly some time in the future they will be healed and restored. Until then they should be given our care and prayers. But I do not know of anyone having been able to reach them in this life.

And I was made wise so as not to fall into the hands of the Deceiver, and I congratulated myself that the Truth had gone with me.

The odist is thankful and appreciative that the Light of Truth preserved him from falling into the clutches of the Deceiver, Satan. He realizes that he was not preserved by his own capacity, but by the grace and gift of God, a grace and gift that the deceived also could have received, but they had no interest in it and so followed their folly.

And I was established and lived and was redeemed, and my foundations were laid on account of the Lord's hand, for he planted me.

"Whosoever heareth these sayings of mine, and doeth them, I will liken him unto a wise man, which built his house upon a rock: And the rain descended, and the floods came, and the winds blew, and beat upon that house; and it fell not: for it was founded upon a rock. And every one that heareth these sayings of mine, and doeth them not, shall be likened unto a foolish man, which built his house upon the sand: And the rain descended, and the floods came, and the winds blew, and beat upon that house; and it fell: and great was the fall of it" (Matthew 7:24-27).

"By faith Abraham, when he was called to go out into a place which he should after receive for an inheritance, obeyed; and he went out, not knowing whither he went. By faith he sojourned in the land of promise, as in a strange country, dwelling in tabernacles with Isaac and Jacob, the heirs with him of the same promise: *For he looked for a city which hath foundations, whose builder and maker is God*" (Hebrews 11:8-10).

Those who are established in the divine unity and not scattered in the diversity of delusion have sure foundations, for their foundations are the very being of God who has guided and guarded them.

For he set the root, and watered it and endowed it and blessed it, and its fruits will be for ever.

The wise person knows that "By grace are ye saved through faith; and that not of yourselves: it is the gift of God: For we are his workmanship" (Ephesians 2:8, 10). And this is possible because we have existed in God eternally, and our nature is his nature that shall be revealed in all of us.

It struck deep and sprang up and spread wide, and it was full and was enlarged.

The consciousness of the persevering devotee-yogi truly does grow deep, high and wide. As Paramhansa Yogananda said, the little cup of the yogi's consciousness becomes expanded to infinity by the advent of God into his entire being.

And the Lord alone was glorified, in his planting and in his cultivation.

Such a perfected one lives for the glory of God alone, for he has *become* God's glory. That is why in the holy rite of the Mass we sing: "We give thanks to thee for thy great glory" in which we live and grow "till we all come in the unity… unto a perfect man, unto the measure of the stature of the fulness of Christ" (Ephesians 4:13).

In his care and in the blessing of his lips, in the beautiful planting of his right hand. And in the splendor of his planting, and in the understanding of his mind.

How so? Because "we have the mind of Christ" (I Corinthians 2:16) as a holy seed that shall in time grow and become the mind, the consciousness, of God.

Ode 39

Mighty rivers are the power of the Lord, which carry headlong those that despise him.
And entangle their paths, and destroy their fords:
And seize their bodies, and corrupt their souls.
For they are more swift than lightning, and more rapid.
But those who cross them in faith shall not be moved.
And those who walk on them without blemish shall not be afraid.
For the sign in them is the Lord, and the sign is the way of those who cross in the Name of the Lord.
Put on therefore the Name of the Most High and know him, and you shall cross without danger, because the rivers shall be subject to you.
The Lord has bridged them by his word, and he walked and crossed them on foot.
And his footsteps stand (firm) on the waters and were not erased; they are as a beam that is firmly fixed.
And the waves were lifted up on this side and on that, but the footsteps of our Lord Messiah stand (firm).
And they are not obliterated, nor are they destroyed.
And a way has been appointed for those who cross after him, and for those who adhere to the course of his faith, and worship his Name. Alleluia.

Shakespeare wrote:

> There is a tide in the affairs of men.
> Which, taken at the flood, leads on to fortune;
> Omitted, all the voyage of their life
> Is bound in shallows and in miseries.
> On such a full sea are we now afloat,
> And we must take the current when it serves,
> Or lose our ventures.

But over one and a half millennia before that the odist wrote more fully about the same with a perspective Shakespeare never dreamed of in *his* philosophy.

Mighty rivers are the power of the Lord, which carry headlong those that despise him.

There are currents or tides in the very substance of this world and all creation, for it is a living entity. The various currents of energy are the life-blood of the universe and the bases of astrology and divination. Some of these rivers are the forces of evolution and some of them are the currents that carry away from evolution whenever the law inherent in the very fabric of the universe is defied or resisted. Sentient beings are either developing or disintegrating, according to the character of the rivers in which they swim.

Before looking at these further it must be clearly understood that the rivers being considered in this ode are not forces of punishment or rejection by God. Duality is an essential for relative existence, so there must be powers moving upward to higher levels of evolution and powers that move downward to degradation and loss of evolution. Whichever stream a human being is vibrating in sympathy with is the one in which he will find himself. It is a matter of like attracting like, the revealing of the character of the individual's will. We may not like the stream in which we find ourselves, but we alone have brought ourselves into it. Everyone in their long path to perfection switches back and forth between the upward and downward streams until becoming evolved enough to remain in the upward-flowing ones.

And entangle their paths, and destroy their fords.

Confusion is the character of all paths of devolution. Stumbling and falling is the fate of those walking there. And even worse, access to the means ("fords") by which they can change over to an upward stream become extremely difficult, almost impossible, for them to gain.

And seize their bodies, and corrupt their souls.

Body and mind become seized by merciless forces and distorted from their intended condition and form. The Bhagavad Gita puts it this way: "Evil-doers, the lowest of men, bereft of knowledge by maya, do not seek me, being attached to (existing within) a demonic mode of existence" (7:15). But I really like Swami Prabhavananda's more poetic and interpretive translation: "The evil-doers turn not toward me: these are deluded, sunk low among mortals. Their judgment is lost in the maze of Maya, until the heart is human no longer: changed within to the heart of a devil." Again, this is not the action of God but solely of the individual.

When I was a child I loved a comic strip called *The Katzenjammer Kids*. The "kids" Hans and Fritz almost always ended up getting spanked in the last frame while off to the side a little girl named Lena would be standing licking a lollipop and saying: "They brought it on themselves." That is always the case.

For they are more swift than lightning, and more rapid.

This is one of the horrors of downward evolution: it came come like a lightning strike and drag a person down to a level of spiritual devastation far more than could have been imagined. The smallest thing can hurl someone downward, requiring lifetimes to regain the level from which they fell. I have seen people seized and swept away in a moment, not even realizing what was happening to them. A kind of psychic amnesia often prevails and what they have lost is unrealized or unknown. "I used to be…," is one of the saddest refrains that can be heard from these people. I have known people that denied they ever aspired to higher consciousness. One friend of mind was a serious yogi leading an exemplary life. Then he began to drift, mostly through reading anti-spiritual philosophy. Suddenly he was gone. Literally. Another friend who had been introduced to yoga by him finally found that he had moved hundreds of miles away and went to see him. She found him totally addicted to alcohol, drugs and sex. All he did was sneer at her for having kept to the spiritual path, and spew out obscenities until she left. His former friends truly grieved over his spiritual death, but there was nothing they could do. As C. S. Lewis wrote, there are two kinds of people in this world: those who say to God, "Thy will be done," and those to whom *God* says, "*Thy* will be done."

But those who cross them in faith shall not be moved.

This is very significant. We are all going to encounter those rivers of destruction and death. That, too, is part of our evolution. In the ninety-fourth chapter of the Aquarian Gospel, Jesus tells his disciples to pray: "Shield us from the tempter's snares that are too great for us to bear; and when they come, give us the strength to overcome." They are going to come to us because we must choose whether we will cross over them or fall into them. As Jesus said, as recorded in India by Akhbar the Great: "This world is a bridge; cross over it, do not build a house on it." Saint Paul told King Herod Agrippa: "I was not disobedient unto the heavenly vision" (Acts 26:19). So if we do not lose that vision but act upon it, we too shall cross over unmoved by the tides of evil.

And those who walk on them without blemish shall not be afraid.

We have to learn how to walk on those dangerous waters fearlessly, and not sink as did Peter (Matthew 14:22-32). The secret is to be totally oriented toward the higher life and to be living according to spiritual principles without compromise or omission.

For the sign in them is the Lord, and the sign is the way of those who cross in the Name of the Lord.

The Bhagavad Gita tells us: "The Lord dwells in the hearts of all beings" (18:61). It is this divine indwelling that ultimately is the salvation of all, for all shall in time come to conscious union with the Highest. Those who unite their consciousness with God shall cross over the ocean of samsara.

Put on therefore the Name of the Most High and know him, and you shall cross without danger, because the rivers shall be subject to you.

Literally we must clothe ourselves in the consciousness of God. God himself is the "wedding garment" Jesus spoke about in a parable

(Matthew 22:1-14). Illumined consciousness is both the sign of union with God and the means to union with God. When we are perfectly one with divine consciousness, then we can cross the rivers of darkness without danger because we shall subjugate them.

The Lord has bridged them by his word, and he walked and crossed them on foot. And his footsteps stand (firm) on the waters and were not erased; they are as a beam that is firmly fixed. If we follow the path of Christ, then we shall do exactly as he did, for he is the example and the proof of the way to eternal life in liberation of the spirit.

And the waves were lifted up on this side and on that, but the footsteps of our Lord Messiah stand (firm).

Just as in his incarnation as Moses the Lord Jesus stretched forth his hand and the waters of the Red Sea were parted so the Hebrews could pass through to freedom, so by the constant practice of yoga meditation we shall find our way being opened to us so we, too, may pass over into Life.

And they are not obliterated, nor are they destroyed.

Jesus' incarnation and life were not temporal but eternal events. They are ever vibrating in the very fabric of this world and are living fountains of spiritual power which we can access and become as transfigured as was he.

And a way has been appointed for those who cross after him, and for those who adhere to the course of his faith, and worship his Name.

The way is to be found in the sacred scriptures which Jesus studied in India, namely the Upanishads, Bhagavad Gita and Yoga Sutras. So we can go to the source through them and ourselves tread the Way of Christ to our own Christhood.

(See *The Upanishads For Awakening, The Bhagavad Gita For Awakening* and *Yoga: Science of the Absolute*.)

ODE 40

As honey drips from the comb of bees, and the milk flows from the woman that loves her children, so also is my hope on Thee, O my God.

As a fountain gushes forth its water, so my heart gushes out the praise of the Lord, and my lips utter praises to him.

And my tongue is sweet in his intimate converse, and my members are anointed by his Odes.

And my face rejoices in his exultation, and my spirit exults in his love, and my soul shines in him.

And he who is afraid shall trust in him, and redemption shall in him be assured.

And his gain is immortal life, and those who receive it are incorruptible. Alleluia.

As honey drips from the comb of bees, and the milk flows from the woman that loves her children, so also is my hope on Thee, O my God.

The second clause of this sentence refers to a very common belief in India that when a mother looks with love on her infant child, milk will spontaneously flow from her breasts. The idea of both symbols, the honey and the milk, is that those who nature has been purified and restored to its true character will naturally, spontaneously fix their hope on God as the source and center of their life, that he will fill their minds and be understood to be the sole reality of all things, including them.

As a fountain gushes forth its water, so my heart gushes out the praise of the Lord, and my lips utter praises to him.

As in the foregoing, the purified and illumined heart will not look upon God as a mere object, however wondrous and awesome, but will stream forth loving glorification of God, because such loving praise is innate in the spirit of every sentient being.

And my tongue is sweet in his intimate converse, and my members are anointed by his Odes.

Margery Kempe in her autobiography (the first in the English language) continually speaks of having such communication with Jesus every day. The speaking of the soul with God can be verbal and it can be only movements of the heart and mind. Indicating this intimate interchange, Solomon wrote: "my beloved is mine, and I am his" (Song of Solomon 2:16). The odes spoken of in this verse are not those of the manuscript, but of the inspiration behind the odes that are expressed by the speaker.

And my face rejoices in his exultation, and my spirit exults in his love, and my soul shines in him.

This should be understood very literally. It is of course a description of a mystical state, but a state that can be described. Often I have had non-esoterics attempt to assure themselves that what I was saying or doing was symbolic and "not meant to be literal or real." But when I assured them that it was real they retreated into themselves and had no more to say. For example when a "contemplative" Christian monk insisted that I was not worshipping an image, but only what the image represented, he was displeased when I told him: "No. I am worshipping the image because God is everything, including that image. Certainly it represents Something, and What it represents is, as the Bible says, 'All in all,' embracing all existence." Such is the way when East and West meet and pass by each other.

And he who is afraid shall trust in him, and redemption shall in him be assured.

Images in Indian religion often have the deity making a gesture called abhaya–Fear Not. Those who take refuge in God shall find all fear erased from their hearts, and the true salvation, the spiritual liberation which they seek, shall be both assured and found in God

And his gain is immortal life, and those who receive it are incorruptible.

The "gain" of the seeker is God. "The word of the Lord came unto Abram in a vision, saying, Fear not, Abram: I am thy shield, and thy exceeding great reward" (Genesis 15:1). The immortality and incorruptibility gained is the immortal and incorruptible Life that is God. "For in him we live, and move, and have our being,… *For we are also his offspring*" (Acts 17:28). The word translated "offspring" is *genos*, which means kind or kindred, the idea being that we are of the same being as God: divine by nature. But God is infinite and we are finite, gods within God.

Ode 41

Let all the Lord's infants praise him, and let them receive the truth of his faith.
And his children shall be acknowledged by him; therefore let us sing in his love.
We live in the Lord by his grace, and life we receive in his Messiah.
For a great day has shined upon us and wondrous is he who hath given us of his glory.
Let us therefore all of us unite together in the Name of the Lord, and let us honor him with its goodness.
And our faces will shine in his light, and our hearts will meditate in his love, by night and by day.
Let us exult with the exultation of the Lord.
All those that see me will be astonished, for from another race am I.
For the Father of Truth remembered me, he who possessed me from the beginning.
For his riches gave birth to me, and the thought of his heart.
And his Word is with us in all our way, the Savior who makes alive and does not reject our souls.
The Man who humbled himself, and was exalted by his own righteousness.
The Son of the Most High appeared, in the perfection of his Father.
And light dawned from the Word, that was of old in him.

The Messiah in truth is one; and he was known before the foundations of the world, that he might enliven souls for ever by the truth of his Name:
A new song to the Lord from them that love him. Alleluia.

Let all the Lord's infants praise him, and let them receive the truth of his faith.

"Except ye be converted, and become as little children, ye shall not enter into the kingdom of heaven" (Matthew 18:3). "Whosoever shall not receive the kingdom of God as a little child, he shall not enter therein" (Mark 10:15). "Jesus said, I thank thee, O Father, Lord of heaven and earth, because thou hast hid these things from the wise and prudent, and hast revealed them unto babes" (Matthew 11:25). "Jesus saith unto them, Yea; have ye never read, Out of the mouth of babes and sucklings thou hast perfected praise?" (Matthew 21:16).

We must become renewed and truly new-born. In Taoism a great deal is said about the "divine embryo" that is "conceived" within those who awaken and begin the search for enlightenment. This is the kind of "infancy" the odist is speaking about. For only such as they can perceive and receive "the truth of his faith."

And his children shall be acknowledged by him; therefore let us sing in his love.

"I will declare the decree: the Lord hath said unto me, Thou art my Son; this day have I begotten thee" (Psalms 2:7). God acknowledges us by lifting us into higher consciousness for which we have prepared ourselves, otherwise it is impossible. Being in God who is love (I John 4:8), our song can only be in and about his love.

We live in the Lord by his grace and life we receive in his Messiah.

God the Father transcends all relative existence. But through the Christ, the Only-Begotten of the Father who is known in India as Ishwara we live in the grace and life of God. In the Odes "Messiah" means either Jesus who was *a* Christ or Ishwara who is *the* Christ. The confusion of Jesus with Christ (Ishwara) is the fundamental reason that exoteric Christianity has developed into such a destructive mess. Ishwara-Christ is a Person, though beyond anything like personality, and is absolutely personal. Every single atom of creation and every single sentient being has his total attention. Grace, a manifestation of love, is the sole motive of his interaction with us. And he communicates with us through that love and leads us to the Father, enabling us to evolve beyond relative existence and re-enter the Bosom of the Father, our eternal home.

For a great day has shined upon us and wondrous is he Who hath given us of his glory.

The new day of new life dawns when the individual spirit has become developed enough to perceive the divine glory as it manifests even in this world. The glory of God is the living presence of God, which is why in the ancient hymn known as the Gloria even the first Christians sang: "We give thanks to thee for thy great glory" of which we are actually a part, for we are a part of God.

Let us therefore all of us unite together in the Name of the Lord, and let us honor him with its goodness.

In both the Old and New Testaments "name" means actual name, but also reputation, fame and remembrance (of). It also implies knowledge of the one named. *Strong's Concordance* says: "The name is used for everything which the name covers, everything the thought or feeling of which is aroused in the mind by mentioning, hearing, remembering, the name, i.e. for one's rank, authority, interests, pleasure, command, excellences, deeds etc.." So all these aspects should be kept in mind.

And our faces will shine in his light, and our hearts will meditate in his love, by night and by day. Let us exult with the exultation of the Lord.

The yogis of India, among whom Jesus was numbered in the Nath Yogi Order, say that God is bliss (ananda), and we are part of that bliss, destined to be blissful with the bliss of God (Brahmananda).

All those that see me will be astonished, for from another race am I.

From earliest time the expression "Christian race" was common within Eastern Christianity, for: "If any man be in Christ, he is a new creature: old things are passed away; behold, all things are become new. And all things are of God" (II Corinthians 5:17-18). Those who see the true sons of God are aware that they are of another species altogether. I have seen this many times in India and America, in various religions. I was privileged to meet with two canonized Eastern Orthodox saints: Saint John Maximovitch of San Francisco and Saint Philaret of New York. my beloved friend Archbishop Seraphim of Chicago was also supernatural, as was Father Arkadius Skepuro, the rector of Archbishop Seraphim's cathedral. They certainly astonished and awed me.

For the Father of Truth remembered me, he who possessed me from the beginning.

We are eternal spirits within the Supreme Spirit, co-eternal with God. His awareness is always with us, guiding us to perfection within his perfection.

For his riches gave birth to me, and the thought of his heart.

The very bounteous Being of God is our origin, and his intention for us is our theosis, our deification, by means of which we shall participate consciously in the riches–the omnipotence, omnipresence and omniscience–of God.

And his Word is with us in all our way, the Savior Who makes alive and does not reject our souls.

Ishwara-Christ is the power of evolution that has been with us ever since we left the transcendent and entered into relative existence. "In him we live, and move, and have our being" (Acts 17:28). Therefore, as Patanjali says: "He is Guru even of the Ancients" (Yoga Sutras 1:26) and of us. God is beyond such petty reactions as being pleased or displeased with us. "The Omnipresent takes note of neither demerit nor merit" (Bhagavad Gita 5:15). God is our light. As the Psalmist sang to him: "In thy light shall we see light" (Psalms 36:9). Until that light dawns for us we dream the fever-dream of ignorance and wrongdoing. But God does not dream the ignorance which is a cornerstone of such delusions as everlasting hell and damnation. God cannot reject a single person because that would be rejecting himself. Knowing himself, God knows us and sees the perfection that each one will eventually maintain, that "one day all his sons shall reach the feet of the Father, however far they stray," as an esoteric Creed says. For they shall reach the feet of the Father through Christ the Son. All of this can be said to a degree regarding any Son of God, including Jesus.

The Man who humbled himself, and was exalted by his own righteousness.

Both Christ-God and the man-Christs humble themselves yet are exalted by the manifestation of their own divinity.

The Son of the Most High appeared, in the perfection of his Father.

Christ and the Christs appear to humanity as saviors and perfect reflections of the Absolute, the Father. Ishwara and the sons of God can say with total truth: "He that hath seen me hath seen the Father" (John 14:9).

And light dawned from the Word, that was of old in him.

Christ is the Word of the Father, the Sun of Righteousness (Malachi 4:2), "the true Light, which lighteth every man that cometh into the world" (John 1:9). And so are those who have become one with him, who were "with the Father, and [were] manifested unto us" (I John 1:2).

The Messiah in truth is one; and he was known before the foundations of the world, that he might enliven souls for ever by the truth of his Name: A new song to the Lord from them that love him.

This is about Ishwara-Christ who projected all the worlds and drew the spirits into their evolutionary orbit and set them on the path to union with the Father as well as himself. This he did through his true name which is also the praise of those awakened souls who seek to return to the Father, the new song by which they return from perpetual birth unto the Unborn and themselves become unborn.

ODE 42

I stretched out my hands and approached my Lord, for the stretching out of my hands is his sign.
And my expansion is the upright Cross, that was lifted up on the way of the Righteous One.
And I became of no use to those who knew me (not), for I shall hide Myself from those who did not take hold of me.
But I will be with those who love me.
All my persecutors have died, and they who trusted in me sought me because I am living.
And I rose up and am with them, and I will speak by their mouths.
For they have rejected those who persecute them; and I threw over them the yoke of my love.
Like the arm of the bridegroom over the bride, so is my yoke over those that know me.
And as the couch that is spread in the chambers of the bridegroom and the bride, so is my love over those that believe in me.
I was not rejected though I was considered to be so, and I did not perish though they thought it of me.
Sheol saw me and was shattered, Death cast me up and many along with me.
I have been gall and bitterness to it, and I went down with it to the extreme of its depth.
And the feet and the head it let go, for it was not able to endure my face.

And I made a congregation of living men among his dead, and I spoke with them with living lips, in order that my word may not be void.

And those who had died ran towards me, and they cried out and said Son of God have pity on us.

And do with us according to Thy kindness, and bring us out from the bonds of darkness.

And open to us the door, by which we shall come out to Thee, for we perceive that our death does not touch Thee.

Let us also be saved with Thee, for Thou art our Savior.

Then I heard their voice, and I placed their faith in my heart.

And I set my Name upon their heads, for they are free men and they are Mine. Alleluia.

I stretched out my hands and approached my Lord, for the stretching out of my hands is his sign. And my expansion is the upright Cross, that was lifted up on the way of the Righteous One.

"As Moses lifted up the serpent in the wilderness, even so must the Son of man be lifted up.… When ye have lifted up the Son of man, then shall ye know that I am he,…. And I, if I be lifted up from the earth, will draw all men unto me" (John 3:14; 8:28; 12:32). Paramhansa Yogananda interprets these statements as meaning that being "lifted up" in full conformity with Christ/Jesus results in the expansion of the aspirant's consciousness, that "the son of man" who must be lifted up is the humanity of each one of us, not just that of Jesus. The "way of the Righteous One" is the Way of the Cross upon which all must journey. A hymn I sang as a child says:

> I must needs go home by the way of the cross,
> There's no other way but this;
> I shall ne'er get sight of the gates of light,
> If the way of the cross I miss.
> Then I bid farewell to the way of the world,
> To walk in it nevermore

> For the Lord says, "Come," and I seek my home
> Where He waits at the open door.

Of course I now understand these words in a very different and better way.

Although the subsequent verses of this ode can be applied symbolically to everyone striving for Christhood, they do seem to specifically be the words that Jesus would speak. Therefore there is a strong possibility that this ode was authored by Jesus himself.

And I became of no use to those who knew me (not), for I shall hide Myself from those who did not take hold of me.

This is very important. God and Christ are of no effect or benefit to those who do not truly *know* God and Christ. Without gnosis there is no true religion and no relation to God and Christ except for the usual generic relation that all things have to God as their origin and goal. No wonder the essential message of the Bhagavad is: Become a Yogi (6:46). Those who do not in an experiential manner "lay hold" on God and Christ and come to know them intimately shall find God and Christ hidden from them. The kingdom of God is within, and therefore our finding and knowing God is an interior matter, a mystical attainment, to "lay hold on eternal life" as Saint Paul exhorts us (I Timothy 6:12).

But I will be with those who love me.

God is love (I John 4:8), and those who love are with God, and he with them. When we understand that love is not an emotion but a spiritual force that attracts and brings about union with its object, we realize that this is not mere sentimentality. Rather, love of God is the essence of yoga and true mystical life.

All my persecutors have died, and they who trusted in me sought me because I am living.

Those who seek to suppress the Christ within shall die in the spirit until they turn and seek Christ who is life. Jesus told his disciples: "Because I live, ye shall live also" (John 14:19) through their union with him. Again, this is no snuggy-warmy feeling, but true gnosis. For he further said: "At that day ye shall know that I am in my Father, and ye in me, and I in you" (John 14:20), in mystical union.

And I rose up and am with them, and I will speak by their mouths.

At Easter the Eastern Christians sing: "Christ is risen from the dead, trampling down death by death, and on those in the graves bestowing life." He is not just with us in the ordinary way people are with one another, but as Saint Paul says: "If ye then be risen with Christ, seek those things which are above, where Christ sitteth on the right hand of God. Set your affection on things above, not on things on the earth. For ye are dead, and your life is hid with Christ in God" (Colossians 3:1-3). So those who live with and in Christ are as hidden from the world and worldlings as is he. So united is the mind (the consciousness) of Christ with those who live in perfect union with him, that he speaks through them and is identified with them. "He who receives you receives me, and he who receives me receives Him who sent me" (Matthew 10:40; John 13:20).

For they have rejected those who persecute them; and I threw over them the yoke of my love.

Jesus said to his enemies: "Ye are from beneath; I am from above: ye are of this world; I am not of this world" (John 8:23), and the same is true of his disciples. They reject all that the enemies of truth stand for and even the world in which they live: not the world of God's creation, but the world of their degraded minds. As the Gita says: "Evil-doers, the lowest of men, bereft of knowledge by maya, do not seek me, being attached to (existing within) a demonic mode of existence" (Bhagavad Gita 7:15). It is good to study the entire sixteenth chapter of the Gita, which is entitled "The Yoga of the Division Between the Divine and the Demonic." No matter how powerful the agents of evil may be, the easy yoke of Christ's love (Matthew 11:30) is the protection of his disciples, and "perfect love casteth out fear" (I John 4:18).

Like the arm of the bridegroom over the bride, so is my yoke over those that know me.

So let us dedicate ourselves to the pursuit of "the light of the knowledge of the glory of God in the face of Jesus Christ" (II Corinthians 4:6).

It will then be said to us: "Ye are a chosen generation, a royal priesthood, an holy nation, a peculiar people; that ye should shew forth the praises of him who hath called you out of darkness into his marvellous light" (I Peter 2:9).

And as the couch that is spread in the chambers of the bridegroom and the bride, so is my love over those that believe in me.

Bridal mysticism is an element in every valid religion, for it is true that God and the questing spirit are destined to be joined in eternal union so it may say: "I am my beloved's, And my beloved is mine.... He brought me to the banqueting house, and his banner over me was love" (Song of Solomon 6:3; 2:4).

I was not rejected though I was considered to be so, and I did not perish though they thought it of me.

Only God and the godly are truly real to the devotee. So Jesus was not rejected by those who were real to him, nor did he die, though the inwardly dead thought he could die. And it should be the same with us.

Sheol saw me and was shattered, Death cast me up and many along with me.

The prison house of the dead was despoiled by Jesus and multitudes arose with him both into this world and into Paradise. For "Jesus, when he had cried again with a loud voice, yielded up the ghost. And, behold, the veil of the temple was rent in twain from the top to the bottom; and the earth did quake, and the rocks rent; and the graves were opened; and many bodies of the saints which slept arose, and came out of the graves after his resurrection, and went into the holy city, and appeared unto many" (Matthew 27:50-53).

I have been gall and bitterness to it, and I went down with it to the extreme of its depth. And the feet and the head it let go, for it was not able to endure my face. And I made a congregation of living men among his dead, and I spoke with them with living lips, in order that my word may not be void.

Jesus is the death of death for those who live in him. "Now if we be dead with Christ, we believe that we shall also live with him: knowing that Christ being raised from the dead dieth no more; death hath no more dominion over him. For in that he died, he died unto sin once: but in that he liveth, he liveth unto God. Likewise reckon ye also yourselves to be dead indeed unto sin, but alive unto God through Jesus Christ our Lord" (Romans 6:8-11). If we live always in the presence, the "face" of God, death and hades shall flee from us, too.

And those who had died ran towards me, and they cried out and said Son of God have pity on us. And do with us according to Thy kindness, and bring us out from the bonds of darkness. And open to us the door, by which we shall come out to Thee, for we perceive that our death does not touch Thee. Let us also be saved with Thee, for Thou art our Savior.

This is a perfect outline of what is required to seek and find life eternal. We must not stroll toward God and his Christ, but run, crying out in spiritual yearning and even desperation for the lovingkindness that is intended for us. We must recognize that we are bound, hopeless and helpless, without his liberating Life. Nor do we remain in the darkness of this world, but rather we escape from it, flee from it, and enter into the light of freedom of spirit. Our state of death does not touch God, but his Life does indeed touch us when we seek and enter it. Jesus, too, was saved and made a son of God by his search, and we can experience the same. Jesus is savior of those who will to be saved and who seek and find their own salvation in the Father just as did he.

Then I heard their voice, and I placed their faith in my heart.

"For by grace are ye saved through faith; and that not of yourselves: it is the gift of God.... For we are his workmanship, created in Christ Jesus unto good works, which God hath before ordained that we should walk in them" (Ephesians 2:8, 10). Faith in the very possibility of finding and knowing God is his indication that we shall find and know him.

And I set my Name upon their heads, for they are free men and they are Mine.

The subtle energy system, astral and causal, of the human being is a mechanism intended to produce enlightenment. The highest faculties of each one of us reside with our spirit in the Thousand-petalled Lotus, the Sahasrara Chakra in the head. The Brihadaranyaka Upanishad (1.4.1) tells us that in the beginning there was only the Supreme Self, Ishwara.

Before beginning the creation "he first said, 'I am Soham [*Soham asmi*].'" This ultimate name of God, Soham, both vibrates and shines there as its essence. Through its japa and meditation we come to realize that we are eternal sons of God, free in the Spirit forevermore.

The awakening of Soham in our consciousness, our "foreheads," is the consummation of the process of salvation in Christ. The capstone of the Christian revelation, the Book of Revelation, tells us: "I looked, and, lo, a Lamb stood on the mount Sion, and with him an hundred forty and four thousand, having his Father's name written in their foreheads.... They shall see his face; and his name shall be in their foreheads" (Revelation 14:1; 22:4) forever.

Amen.

DID YOU ENJOY READING THIS BOOK?

Thank you for taking the time to read *The Odes of Solomon for Awakening*. If you enjoyed it, please consider telling your friends or posting a short review at Amazon.com, Goodreads, or the site of your choice.

Word of mouth is an author's best friend and much appreciated.

Get your FREE Meditation Guide

Sign up for the Light of the Spirit Newsletter and get *Learn How to Meditate Effectively.*

Get free updates: newsletters, blog posts, satsangs and podcasts, plus exclusive content from Light of the Spirit Monastery.

Visit: http://ocoy.org/signup

Glossary

Amrita: That which makes one immortal. The nectar of immortality that emerged from the ocean of milk when the gods churned it.

Ananda: Bliss; happiness; joy. A fundamental attribute of Brahman, which is Satchidananda: Existence, Consciousness, Bliss.

Antahkarana: Internal instrument; the subtle bodies; fourfold mind: mind, intellect, ego and subconscious mind.

Atma(n): The individual spirit or Self that is one with Brahman. The true nature or identity.

Avatar(a): A fully liberated spirit (jiva) who is born into a world below Satya Loka to help others attain liberation. Though commonly referred to as a divine incarnation, an avatar actually is totally one with God, and therefore an incarnation of God-Consciousness.

Bhakta: Devotee; votary; a follower of the path of bhakti, divine love; a worshipper of the Personal God.

Bhakti: Devotion; dedication; love (of God).

Bhakti Marga: The path of devotion leading to union with God.

Bhava: Subjective state of being (existence); attitude of mind; mental attitude or feeling; state of realization in the heart or mind.

Brahmachari(n): One who observes continence; a celibate student in the first stage of life (ashrama); a junior monk.

Brahmajnana: Direct, transcendental knowledge of Brahman; Self-realization.

Brahmananda: The bliss of communion with Brahman.

Buddhi: Intellect; intelligence; understanding; reason; the thinking mind; the higher mind, which is the seat of wisdom; the discriminating faculty.

Chakra: Wheel. Plexus; center of psychic energy in the human system, particularly in the spine or head.

Daya: Mercy; compassion; grace; empathy.

Dwesha: Aversion/avoidance for something, implying a dislike for it. This can be emotional (instinctual) or intellectual. It may range from simple non-preference to intense repulsion, antipathy and even hatred. See Raga.

Dwija: "Twice born;" any member of the three upper castes that has received the sacred thread (yajnopavita).

Grihastha: One who is living in the second stage (ashrama) of Hindu social life; married householder's life.

Ishwara: "God" or "Lord" in the sense of the Supreme Power, Ruler, Master, or Controller of the cosmos. "Ishwara" implies the powers of omnipotence, omnipresence, and omniscience.

Japa: Repetition of a mantra.

Jiva: Individual spirit.

Jnana: Knowledge; knowledge of Reality–of Brahman, the Absolute; also denotes the process of reasoning by which the Ultimate Truth is attained. The word is generally used to denote the knowledge by which one is aware of one's identity with Brahman.

Kalpa: A Day of Brahma–4,320,000,000 years. It alternates with a Night of Brahma of the same length. He lives hundred such years. Brahma's life is known as Para, being of a longer duration than the life of any other being, and a half of it is called Parardha. He has now completed the first Parardha and is in the first day of the second Parardha. This day or Kalpa is known as Svetavarahakalpa. In the Day of Brahma creation is manifest and in the Night of Brahma is it resolved into its causal state.

Karma: Karma, derived from the Sanskrit root *kri*, which means to act, do, or make, means any kind of action, including thought and feeling. It also means the effects of action. Karma is both action and reaction, the metaphysical equivalent of the principle: "For every action there is an equal and opposite reaction." "Whatsoever a man soweth, that shall he also reap" (Galatians 6:7). It is karma operating through the law of cause and effect that binds the jiva or the individual soul to the wheel of birth and death. There are three forms of karma: sanchita, agami, and prarabdha. Sanchita karma is the vast store of accumulated actions done in the past, the fruits of which have not yet been reaped. Agami karma is the action that will be done by the individual in the future. Prarabdha karma is the action that has begun to fructify, the fruit of which is being reaped in this life.

Kosha: Sheath; bag; scabbard; a sheath enclosing the soul; body. There are five such concentric sheaths or bodies: the sheaths of bliss, intellect, mind, life-force and the physical body–the anandamaya, jnanamaya, manomaya, pranamaya and annamaya bodies respectively.

Kripa: Grace; mercy; compassion; blessing. There are three kinds of kripa: 1) sadhana kripa, the grace of self-effort; 2) guru kripa, the grace of a teacher, and 3) divya kripa, divine grace.

Loka: World or realm; sphere, level, or plane of existence, whether physical, astral, or causal.

Mahat Tattwa: The Great Principle; the first product from Prakriti in evolution; intellect. The principle of Cosmic Intelligence or Buddhi; universal Christ Consciousness, the "Son of God," the "Only Begotten of the Father," "the firstborn of every creature."

Mahatma: Literally: "a great soul [atma]." Usually a designation for a sannyasi, sage or saint.

Mantra(m): Sacred syllable or word or set of words through the repetition and reflection of which one attains perfection or realization of the Self. Literally, "a transforming thought" (manat trayate). A mantra, then is a sound formula that transforms the consciousness.

Mantra Yoga: The Yoga of the Divine Word; the science of sound; the path to divine union through repetition of a mantra–a sound formula that transforms the consciousness.

Moksha: Release; liberation; the term is particularly applied to the liberation from the bondage of karma and the wheel of birth and death; Absolute Experience.

Nadi: A channel in the subtle (astral) body through which subtle prana (psychic energy) flows; a physical nerve. Yoga treatises say that there are seventy-two thousand nadis in the energy system of the human being.

Nirvana: Liberation; final emancipation; the term is particularly applied to the liberation from the bondage of karma and the wheel of birth and death that comes from knowing Brahman; Absolute Experience. See Moksha.

Paramananda: Supreme (param) bliss (ananda).

Paramatma(n): The Supreme Self, God.

Paramhansa Yogananda: The most influential yogi of the twentieth century in the West, author of *Autobiography of a Yogi* and founder of Self-Realization Fellowship in America.

Prakriti: Causal matter; the fundamental power (shakti) of God from which the entire cosmos is formed; the root base of all elements; undifferentiated matter; the material cause of the world. Also known as Pradhana. Prakriti can also mean the entire range of vibratory existence (energy).

Raga: Blind love; attraction; attachment that binds the soul to the universe. Attachment/affinity for something, implying a desire for it. This can be emotional (instinctual) or intellectual. It may range from simple liking or preference to intense desire and attraction. Greed; passion. See Dwesha.

Raga-dwesha: The continual cycle of attraction and repulsion; like and dislike; love and hatred.

Sadhaka: One who practices spiritual discipline–sadhana– particularly meditation.

Sadhana: Spiritual practice.

Sadhana Shakti: Both the power to successfully engage in sadhana, the the power that accrues within the sadhaka from his practice of sadhana.

Sahasrara: The "thousand-petalled lotus" of the brain. The highest center of consciousness, the point at which the spirit (atma) and the bodies (koshas) are integrated and from which they are disengaged.

Samsara: Life through repeated births and deaths; the wheel of birth and death; the process of earthly life.

Sankhya: One of the six orthodox systems of Hindu philosophy whose originator was the sage Kapila, Sankhya is the original Vedic philosophy, endorsed by Krishna in the Bhagavad Gita (Gita 2:39; 3:3, 5; 18:13, 19), the second chapter of which is entitled "Sankhya Yoga." *A Ramakrishna-Vedanta Wordbook* says: "Sankhya postulates two ultimate realities, Purusha and Prakriti. Declaring that the cause of suffering is man's identification of Purusha with Prakriti and its products, Sankhya teaches that liberation and true knowledge are attained in the supreme consciousness, where such identification ceases and Purusha is realized as existing independently in its transcendental nature." Not surprisingly, then, Yoga is based on the Sankhya philosophy.

Sannyas(a): Renunciation; monastic life. Sannyasa literally means "total throwing away," in the sense of absolute rejection of worldly life, ways and attitudes. True sannyas is based on viveka and vairagya. It is not just a mode of external life, but a profound insight and indifference to the things of the world and the world itself–not the world of God's creation, but the world of human ignorance, illusion, folly and suffering which binds all sentient beings to the wheel of continual birth and death. The sannyasi's one goal is liberation through total purification and enlightenment. His creed is Shankara's renowned Vedanta in Half a Verse: "Brahman is real. The world is illusion. The jiva is none other than Brahman."

Sannyasi(n): A renunciate; a monk.

Satchidananda: Existence-Knowledge-Bliss Absolute; Brahman.

Shakti: Power; energy; force; the Divine Power of becoming; the apparent dynamic aspect of Eternal Being; the Absolute Power or Cosmic Energy; the Divine Feminine.

Sri Yukteswar Giri, Swami: The guru of Paramhansa Yogananda.

Tapasya: Austerity; practical (i.e., result-producing) spiritual discipline; spiritual force. Literally it means the generation of heat or energy, but is always used in a symbolic manner, referring to spiritual practice and its effect, especially the roasting of karmic seeds, the burning up of karma.

Upanishads: Books (of varying lengths) of the philosophical teachings of the ancient sages of India on the knowledge of Absolute Reality. The upanishads contain two major themes: (1) the individual self (atman) and the Supreme Self (Paramatman) are one in essence, and (2) the goal of life is the realization/manifestation of this unity, the realization of God (Brahman). There are eleven principal upanishads: Isha, Kena, Katha, Prashna, Mundaka, Mandukya, Taittiriya, Aitareya, Chandogya, Brihadaranyaka, and Shvetashvatara, all of which were commented on by Shankara, Ramanuja and Madhavacharya, thus setting the seal of authenticity on them.

Vanaprastha: Literally: a forest dweller. The third stage of life (ashrama) in which, leaving home and children, the husband and wife dwell together in seclusion and contemplation as a preparation to taking sannyasa.

Vijnana: The highest knowledge, beyond mere theoretical knowledge (jnana); transcendental knowledge or knowing; experiential knowledge; a high state of spiritual realization–intimate knowledge of God in which all is seen as manifestations of Brahman; knowledge of the Self.

Vikshepa: The projecting power of the mind, causing external involvement; the movement of pushing outward or away; the projecting power of ignorance; mental restlessness resulting from the awareness moving out from the center that is the Self; Distractions; causes of distractions; projection; false projection; the tossing of the mind which obstructs concentration.

Viveka: Discrimination between the Real and the unreal, between the Self and the non-Self, between the permanent and the impermanent; right intuitive discrimination.

Yajnasthala: An open sided, roofed structure in which the fire sacrifice is performed.

Yogananda (Paramhansa): The most influential yogi of the twentieth century in the West, author of *Autobiography of a Yogi* and founder of Self-Realization Fellowship in America.

Yuga: Age or cycle; aeon; world era. Hindus believe that there are four yugas: the Golden Age (Satya or Krita Yuga), the Silver age (Treta Yuga), The Bronze Age (Dwapara Yuga), and the Iron Age (Kali Yuga). Satya Yuga is four times as long as the Kali Yuga; Treta Yuga is three times as long; and Dwapara Yuga is twice as long. In the Satya Yuga the majority of humans use the total potential–four-fourths–of their minds; in the Treta Yuga, three-fourths; in the Dwapara Yuga, one half; and in the Kali Yuga, one fourth. (In each Yuga there are those who are using either more or less of their minds than the general populace.) The Yugas move in a perpetual circle: Ascending Kali Yuga, ascending Dwapara Yuga, ascending Treta Yuga, ascending Satya Yuga, descending Satya Yuga, descending, Treta Yuga, descending Dwapara Yuga, and descending Kali Yuga–over and over. Furthermore, there are yuga cycles within yuga cycles. For example, there are yuga cycles that affect the entire cosmos, and smaller yuga cycles within those greater cycles that affect a solar system. The cosmic yuga cycle takes 8,640,000,000 years, whereas the solar yuga cycle only takes 24,000 years. At the present time our solar system is in the ascending Dwapara Yuga, but the cosmos is in the descending Kali Yuga. Consequently, the more the general mind of humanity develops, the more good can be accomplished by the positive, and the more evil can be accomplished by the negative. Therefore we have more contrasts and polarization in contemporary life than previously before 1900.

About the Author

Swami Nirmalananda Giri (Abbot George Burke) is the founder and director of the Light of the Spirit Monastery (Atma Jyoti Ashram) in Cedar Crest, New Mexico, USA.

In his many pilgrimages to India, he had the opportunity of meeting some of India's greatest spiritual figures, including Swami Sivananda of Rishikesh and Anandamayi Ma. During his first trip to India he was made a member of the ancient Swami Order by Swami Vidyananda Giri, a direct disciple of Paramhansa Yogananda, who had himself been given sannyas by the Shankaracharya of Puri, Jagadguru Bharati Krishna Tirtha.

In the United States he also encountered various Christian saints, including Saint John Maximovich of San Francisco and Saint Philaret Voznesensky of New York.

For many years Swami Nirmalananda has researched the identity of Jesus Christ and his teachings with India and Sanatana Dharma, including Yoga. It is his conclusion that Jesus lived in India for most of his life, and was a yogi and Sanatana Dharma missionary to the West. After his resurrection he returned to India and lived the rest of his life in the Himalayas.

He has written extensively on these and other topics, many of which are posted at OCOY.org.

Atma Jyoti Ashram
(Light of the Spirit Monastery)

Atma Jyoti Ashram (Light of the Spirit Monastery) is a monastic community for those men who seek direct experience of the Spirit through yoga meditation, traditional yogic discipline, Sanatana Dharma and the life of the sannyasi in the tradition of the Order of Shankara. Our lineage is in the Giri branch of the Order.

The public outreach of the monastery is through its website, OCOY.org (Original Christianity and Original Yoga). There you will find many articles on Original Christianity and Original Yoga, including *The Christ of India*. *Foundations of Yoga* and *How to Be a Yogi* are practical guides for anyone seriously interested in living the Yoga Life.

You will also discover many other articles on leading an effective spiritual life, including *Soham Yoga: The Yoga of the Self* and *Spiritual Benefits of a Vegetarian Diet*, as well as the "Dharma for Awakening" series–in-depth commentaries on these spiritual classics: the Bhagavad Gita, the Upanishads, the Dhammapada, the Tao Teh King and more.

You can listen to podcasts by Swami Nirmalananda on meditation, the Yoga Life, and remarkable spiritual people he has met in India and elsewhere, at http://ocoy.org/podcasts/

You can watch over 100 videos on these topics and more, including recordings of online satsangs where Swami Nirmalananda answers various questions on practical aspects of spiritual life.

Visit our Youtube channel here:
Youtube.com/@lightofthespirit

Reading for Awakening

Light of the Spirit Press presents books on spiritual wisdom and Original Christianity and Original Yoga. From our "Dharma for Awakening" series (practical commentaries on the world's scriptures) to books on how to meditate and live a successful spiritual life, you will find books that are informative, helpful, and even entertaining.

Light of the Spirit Press is the publishing house of Light of the Spirit Monastery (Atma Jyoti Ashram) in Cedar Crest, New Mexico, USA. Our books feature the writings of the founder and director of the monastery, Swami Nirmalananda Giri (Abbot George Burke) which are also found on the monastery's website, OCOY.org.

We invite you to explore our publications in the following pages.

Find out more about our publications at
lightofthespiritpress.com

Books on Meditation

Soham Yoga
The Yoga of the Self

A complete and in-depth guide to effective meditation and the life that supports it, this important book explains with clarity and insight what real yoga is, and why and how to practice Soham Yoga meditation.

Discovered centuries ago by the Nath yogis, this simple and classic approach to self-realization has no "secrets," requires no "initiation," and is easily accessible to the serious modern yogi.

Includes helpful, practical advice on leading an effective spiritual life and many Illuminating quotes on Soham from Indian scriptures and great yogis.

"This book is a complete spiritual path." –Arnold Van Wie

Light of Soham
The Life and Teachings of Sri Gajanana Maharaj of Nashik

Gajanan Murlidhar Gupte, later known as Gajanana Maharaj, led an unassuming life, to all appearances a normal unmarried man of contemporary society. Crediting his personal transformation to the practice of the Soham mantra, he freely shared this practice with a small number of disciples, whom he simply called his friends. Strictly avoiding the trap of gurudom, he insisted that his friends be self-reliant and not be dependent on him for their spiritual progress. Yet he was uniquely able to assist them in their inner development.

The Inspired Wisdom of Gajanana Maharaj
A Practical Commentary on Leading an Effectual Spiritual Life

Presents the teachings and sayings of the great twentieth-century Soham yogi Gajanana Maharaj, with a commentary by Swami Nirmalananda.

The author writes: "In reading about Gajanana Maharaj I encountered a holy personality that eclipsed all others for me. In his words I found a unique wisdom that altered my perspective on what yoga, yogis, and gurus should be.

"But I realized that through no fault of their own, many Western readers need a clarification and expansion of Maharaj's meaning to get the right understanding of his words. This commentary is meant to help my friends who, like me have found his words 'a light in the darkness.'"

Inspired Wisdom of Lalla Yogeshwari
A Commentary on the Mystical Poetry of the Great Yogini of Kashmir

Lalla Yogeshwari was a great fourteenth-century yogini and wandering ascetic of Kashmir, whose mystic poetry were the earliest compositions in the Kashmiri language. She was in the tradition of the Nath Yogi Sampradaya whose meditation practice is that of Soham Sadhana: the joining of the mental repetition of Soham Mantra with the natural breath.

Swami Nirmalananda's commentary mines the treasures of Lalleshwari's mystic poems and presents his reflections in an easily intelligible fashion for those wishing to put these priceless teachings on the path of yogic self-transformation into practice.

Dwelling in the Mirror
A Study of Illusions Produced By Delusive Meditation And How to Be Free from Them

Swami Nirmalananda says of this book:

"Over and over people have mistaken trivial and pathological conditions for enlightenment, written books, given seminars and gained a devoted following.

"Most of these unfortunate people were completely unreachable with reason. Yet there are those who can have an experience and realize that it really cannot be real, but a vagary of their mind. Some may not understand that on their own, but can be shown by others the truth about it. For them and those that may one day be in danger of meditation-produced delusions I have written this brief study."

BOOKS ON YOGA & SPIRITUAL LIFE

Satsang with the Abbot
Questions and Answers about Life, Spiritual Liberty, and the Pursuit of Ultimate Happiness

The questions in this book range from the most sublime to the most practical. "How can I attain samadhi?" "I am married with children. How can I lead a spiritual life?" "What is Self-realization?" "How important is belief in karma and reincarnation?"

In Swami Nirmalananda's replies to these questions the reader will discover common sense, helpful information, and a guiding light for their journey through and beyond the forest of cliches, contradictions, and confusion of yoga, Hinduism, Christianity, and metaphysical thought.

Foundations of Yoga
Ten Important Principles Every Meditator Should Know

An introduction to the important foundation principles of Patanjali's Yoga: Yama and Niyama

Yama and Niyama are often called the Ten Commandments of Yoga, but they have nothing to do with the ideas of sin and virtue or good and evil as dictated by some cosmic potentate. Rather they are determined by a thoroughly practical, pragmatic basis: that which strengthens and facilitates our yoga practice should be observed and that which weakens or hinders it should be avoided.

Yoga: Science of the Absolute
A Commentary on the Yoga Sutras of Patanjali

The Yoga Sutras of Patanjali is the most authoritative text on Yoga as a practice. It is also known as the Yoga Darshana because it is the fundamental text of Yoga as a philosophy.

In this commentary, Swami Nirmalananda draws on the age-long tradition regarding this essential text, including the commentaries of Vyasa and Shankara, the most highly regarded writers on Indian philosophy and practice, as well as I. K. Taimni and other authoritative commentators, and adds his own ideas based on half a century of study and practice. Serious students of yoga will find this an essential addition to their spiritual studies.

The Benefits of Brahmacharya
A Collection of Writings About the Spiritual, Mental, and Physical Benefits of Continence

"Brahmacharya is the basis for morality. It is the basis for eternal life. It is a spring flower that exhales immortality from its petals." Swami Sivananda

This collection of articles from a variety of authorities including Mahatma Gandhi, Sri Ramakrishna, Swami Vivekananda, Swamis Sivananda and Chidananda of the Divine Life Society, Swami Nirmalananda, and medical experts, presents many facets of brahmacharya and will prove of immense value to all who wish to grow spiritually.

Living the Yoga Life
Perspectives on Yoga

"Dive deep; otherwise you cannot get the gems at the bottom of the ocean. You cannot pick up the gems if you only float on the surface." Sri Ramakrishna

In *Living the Yoga Life* Swami Nirmalananda shares the gems he has found from a lifetime of "diving deep." This collection of reflections and short essays addresses the key concepts of yoga philosophy that are so easy to take for granted. Never content with the accepted cliches about yoga sadhana, the yoga life, the place of a guru, the nature of Brahman and our unity with It, Swami Nirmalananda's insights on these and other facets of the yoga life will inspire, provoke, enlighten, and even entertain.

Spiritual Benefits of a Vegetarian Diet

The health benefits of a vegetarian diet are well known, as are the ethical aspects. But the spiritual advantages should be studied by anyone involved in meditation, yoga, or any type of spiritual practice.

Diet is a crucial aspect of emotional, intellectual, and spiritual development as well. For diet and consciousness are interrelated, and purity of diet is an effective aid to purity and clarity of consciousness.

The major thing to keep in mind when considering the subject of vegetarianism is its relevancy in relation to our explorations of consciousness. We need only ask: Does it facilitate my spiritual growth–the development and expansion of my consciousness? The answer is Yes.

BOOKS ON THE SACRED SCRIPTURES OF INDIA

The Bhagavad Gita for Awakening
A Practical Commentary for Leading a Successful Spiritual Life

Drawing from the teachings of Sri Ramakrishna, Jesus, Paramhansa Yogananda, Ramana Maharshi, Swami Vivekananda, Swami Sivananda of Rishikesh, Papa Ramdas, and other spiritual masters and teachers, as well as his own experiences, Swami Nirmalananda illustrates the teachings of the Gita with stories which make the teachings of Krishna in the Gita vibrant and living.

From *Publisher's Weekly*: "[The author] enthusiastically explores the story as a means for knowing oneself, the cosmos, and one's calling within it. His plainspoken insights often distill complex lessons with simplicity and sagacity. Those with a deep interest in the Gita will find much wisdom here."

The Upanishads for Awakening
A Practical Commentary on India's Classical Scriptures

The sacred scriptures of India are vast. Yet they are only different ways of seeing the same thing, the One Thing which makes them both valid and ultimately harmonious. That unifying subject is Brahman: God the Absolute, beyond and besides whom there is no "other" whatsoever. The thirteen major Upanishads are the fountainhead of all expositions of Brahman.

Swamiji illumines the Upanishads' value for spiritual seekers from the unique perspective of a lifetime of study and practice of both Eastern and Western spirituality.

The Bhagavad Gita–The Song of God

Often called the "Bible" of Hinduism, the Bhagavad Gita is found in households throughout India and has been translated into every major language of the world. Literally billions of copies have been handwritten or printed.

The clarity of this translation by Swami Nirmalananda makes for easy reading, while the rich content makes this the ideal "study" Gita. As the original Sanskrit language is so rich, often there are several accurate translations for the same word, which are noted in the text, giving the spiritual student the needed understanding of the fullness of the Gita.

All Is One
A Commentary On Sri Vaiyai R. Subramanian's Ellam Ondre

Swami Nirmalananda's insightful commentary brings even further light to Ellam Ondre's refreshing perspective on what Unity signifies, and the path to its realization.

Written in the colorful and well-informed style typical of his other commentaries, it is a timely and important contribution to Advaitic literature that explains Unity as the fruit of yoga sadhana, rather than mere wishful thinking or some vague intellectual gymnastic, as is so commonly taught by the modern "Advaita gurus."

Sanatana Dharma
The Eternal Religion

Sanatana Dharma, commonly called Hinduism, is not just beautiful temples, colorful festivals, gurus and unusual beliefs. It is, simply put, "The Way Things Are" on a cosmic scale. It is the facts of existence and transcendence.

Swami Nirmalananda has edited for the modern reader a book originally printed nearly one hundred years ago in Varanasi, India, for use as a textbook by students of Benares Hindu University. Its original title was *Sanatana Dharma, An Advanced Text Book of Hindu Religion and Ethics*.

A Brief Sanskrit Glossary
A Spiritual Student's Guide to Essential Sanskrit Terms

This Sanskrit glossary contains full translations and explanations of hundreds of the most commonly used spiritual Sanskrit terms, and will help students of the Bhagavad Gita, the Upanishads, the Yoga Sutras of Patanjali, and other Indian scriptures and philosophical works to expand their vocabularies to include the Sanskrit terms contained in these, and gain a fuller understanding in their studies.

BOOKS ON ORIGINAL CHRISTIANITY

The Christ of India
The Story of Original Christianity

"Original Christianity" is the teaching of both Jesus and his Apostle Saint Thomas in India. Although it was new to the Mediterranean world, it was really the classical, traditional teachings of the rishis of India that even today comprise the Eternal Dharma, that goes far beyond religion into realization.

In *The Christ of India* Swami Nirmalananda presents what those ancient teachings are, as well as the growing evidence that Jesus spent much of his "Lost Years" in India and Tibet. This is also the story of how the original teachings of Jesus and Saint Thomas thrived in India for centuries before the coming of the European colonialists.

May a Christian Believe in Reincarnation?

Discover the real and surprising history of reincarnation and Christianity.

A growing number of people are open to the subject of past lives, and the belief in rebirth–reincarnation, metempsychosis, or transmigration–is commonplace. It often thought that belief in reincarnation and Christianity are incompatible. But is this really true? May a Christian believe in reincarnation? The answer may surprise you.

"Those needing evidence that a belief in reincarnation is in accordance with teachings of the Christ need look no further: Plainly laid out and explained in an intelligent manner from one who has spent his life on a Christ-like path of renunciation and prayer/meditation."—Christopher T. Cook

The Unknown Lives of Jesus and Mary
Compiled from Ancient Records and Mystical Revelations

"There are also many other things which Jesus did, the which, if they should be written every one, I suppose that even the world itself could not contain the books that should be written." (Gospel of Saint John, final verse)

You can discover much of those "many other things" in this unique compilation of ancient records and mystical revelations, which includes historical records of the lives of Jesus Christ and his Mother Mary that have been accepted and used by the Church since apostolic times. This treasury of little-known stories of Jesus' life will broaden the reader's understanding of what Christianity really was in its original form.

Robe of Light
An Esoteric Christian Cosmology

In *Robe of Light* Swami Nirmalananda explores the whys and wherefores of the mystery of creation. From the emanation of the worlds from the very Being of God, to the evolution of the souls to their ultimate destiny as perfected Sons of God, the ideal progression of creation is described. Since the rebellion of Lucifer and the fall of Adam and Eve from Paradise flawed the normal plan of evolution, a restoration was necessary. How this came about is the prime subject of this insightful study.

Moreover, what this means to aspirants for spiritual perfection is expounded, with a compelling knowledge of the scriptures and of the mystical traditions of East and West.

The Gospel of Thomas for Awakening
A Commentary on Jesus' Sayings as Recorded by the Apostle Thomas

When the Apostles dispersed to the various area of the world, Thomas travelled to India, where evidence shows Jesus spent his Lost Years, and which had been the source of the wisdom which he had brought to the "West."

The Christ that Saint Thomas quotes in this ancient text is quite different than the Christ presented by popular Christianity. Through his unique experience and study with both Christianity and Indian religion, Swami Nirmalananda clarifies the sometimes enigmatic sayings of Jesus in an informative and inspiring way.

The Odes of Solomon for Awakening
A Commentary on the Mystical Wisdom of the Earliest Christian Hymns and Poems

The Odes of Solomon is the earliest Christian hymn-book, and therefore one of the most important early Christian documents. Since they are mystical and esoteric, they teach and express the classical and universal mystical truths of Christianity, revealing a Christian perspective quite different than that of "Churchianity," and present the path of Christhood that all Christians are called to.

"Fresh and soothing, these 41 poems and hymns are beyond delightful! I deeply appreciate Abbot George Burke's useful and illuminating insight and find myself spiritually re-animated." –John Lawhn

The Aquarian Gospel for Awakening (2 Volumes)
A Practical Commentary on Levi Dowling's Classic Life of Jesus Christ

Written in 1908 by the American mystic Levi Dowling, The Aquarian Gospel of Jesus the Christ answers many questions about Jesus' life that the Bible doesn't address. Dowling presents a universal message found at the heart of all valid religions, a broad vision of love and wisdom that will ring true with Christians who are attracted to Christ but put off by the narrow views of the tradition that has been given his name.

Swami Nirmalananda's commentary is a treasure-house of knowledge and insight that even further expands Dowling's vision of the true Christ and his message.

Wandering With The Cherubim
A Commentary on the Mystical Verse of Angelus Silesius–The Cherubinic Wanderer"

Johannes Scheffler, who wrote under the name Angelus Silesius, was a mystic and a poet. In his most famous book, "The Cherubinic Wanderer," he expressed his mystical vision.

Swami Nirmalananda reveals the timelessness of his mystical teachings and The Cherubinic Wanderer's practical value for spiritual seekers. He does this in an easily intelligible fashion for those wishing to put those priceless teachings into practice.

"Set yourself on the journey of this mystical poetry made accessible through this very beautifully commentated text. It is text that submerges one in the philosophical context of the Advaita notion of Non Duality. Swami Nirmalananda's commentary is indispensable in understanding higher philosophical ideas, for Swami's language, while readily approachable, is rich in deep essence of the teachings."–Savitri

Books on Buddhism & Taoism and More

The Dhammapada for Awakening
A Commentary on Buddha's Practical Wisdom

Swami Nirmalananda's commentary on this classic Buddhist scripture explores the Buddha's answers to the urgent questions, such as "How can I find find lasting peace, happiness and fulfillment that seems so elusive?" and "What can I do to avoid many of the miseries big and small that afflict all of us?" Drawing on his personal experience, the author sheds new light on the Buddha's eternal wisdom.

"Swami Nirmalananda's commentary is well crafted and stacked with anecdotes, humor, literary references and beautiful quotes from the Buddha. I have come to consider it a guide to daily living." –Rev. Gerry Nangle

The Tao Teh King for Awakening
A Practical Commentary on Lao Tzu's Classic Exposition of Taoism

"The Tao does all things, yet our interior disposition determines our success or failure in coming to knowledge of the unknowable Tao."

Lao Tzu's classic writing, the *Tao Teh King*, has fascinated scholars and seekers for centuries. Swami Nirmalananda offers a commentary that makes the treasures of Lao Tzu's teachings accessible and applicable for the sincere seeker.

Bio-Magnetic Therapy
Healing in Your Hands

In *Bio-Magnetic Therapy* Swami Nirmalananda teaches the techniques to strengthen your vitality and improve the body's natural healing ability in yourself and in others with specific methods that anyone can use.

Bio-Magnetic Therapy is a simple and natural way to increase the flow of life-force into the body for general good health and to stimulate the supply and flow of life-force to a troubled area that has become vitality-starved through some obstruction. It does not cure; it simply aids the body to cure itself by supplying it with curative force.

How to Read the Tarot
A Practical Method Using the Rider-Waite Deck

Discover Swami Nirmalananda's unique method of reading the Tarot specifically for use with the Rider-Waite deck, with detailed instructions on how to use the cards to develop your intuition for understanding the meanings of the cards. Illustrated with color plates of each of the cards of the Rider-Waite deck with full explanations of their symbolism.

More Titles
The Four Gospels for Awakening
Light from Eternal Lamps
Vivekachudamani: The Crest Jewel of Discrimination for Awakening

www.ingramcontent.com/pod-product-compliance
Lightning Source LLC
Chambersburg PA
CBHW020352170426
43200CB00005B/141